D1194113

BELGIUM'S RETURN TO NEUTRALITY

BELGIUM'S RETURN TO NEUTRALITY

*An Essay in the Frustrations
of Small Power Diplomacy*

BY

DAVID OWEN KIEFT

CLARENDON PRESS · OXFORD

1972

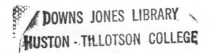

Oxford University Press, Ely House, London W.1

GLASGOW NEW YORK TORONTO MELBOURNE WELLINGTON
CAPE TOWN IBADAN NAIROBI DAR ES SALAAM LUSAKA ADDIS ABABA
DELHI BOMBAY CALCUTTA MADRAS KARACHI LAHORE DACCA
KUALA LUMPUR SINGAPORE HONG KONG TOKYO

MADE AND PRINTED IN GREAT BRITAIN BY
WILLIAM CLOWES & SONS, LIMITED
LONDON, BECCLES AND COLCHESTER

For my parents

PREFACE

WHEN Leopold III became King of the Belgians in 1934, his country was firmly committed to collective security. Belgium was an enthusiastic member of the League of Nations, a grateful participant in the Locarno agreements, and France's military collaborator by virtue of an agreement signed on the morrow of the First World War. Since 1919 Belgium had sought safety through active co-operation with her larger neighbours, and the growing menace of Nazi Germany suggested that she had good reasons to continue doing so. Yet, by early 1937 Belgium had severed her military connection with France, ended her Locarno engagements, and lost her enthusiasm for the League.

Historians and other writers usually treat Belgium's return to neutrality as a postscript to the Rhineland affair. Sympathetic accounts say that Belgium was devoted to collective security until March 1936, that she was the victim of Anglo-French weakness and indecision, and that neutrality or 'independence' (as Belgian statesmen preferred to call it) was the only policy which offered the slightest chance of non-involvement in the coming struggle. Unsympathetic accounts sometimes deplore the influence of King Leopold, who is accused of having led his country to break her 'alliance' with France and thus to be guilty of a serious treaty violation. This interpretation seemed more plausible when Leopold later abdicated in the wake of a constitutional struggle; it seemed especially satisfactory to Frenchmen who were seeking explanations for their own defeat in 1940.

These interpretations, whether or not they give Belgium the benefit of the doubt, contain major misunderstandings and mistakes. Few historians have understood Leopold's relatively unimportant role in shaping Belgian foreign policy during the first four years of his reign or the nature of Belgium's ambiguous and confusing relationship with France. Few have recognized that her return to neutrality was the culmination of a process begun years earlier. But the most common mistake is a failure to discern the close connection between Belgian foreign policy and the structure of Belgian domestic politics. Indeed, the decisive factor in the development of the 'policy of independence' was the political crisis which gripped Belgium in 1936 and which momentarily threatened to divide her bilingual population along ideological as well as national lines.

It is no surprise that historians have neglected a careful examination of these problems. Small power diplomacy has less significance than that of the great powers. However, Belgium merits special attention. The fact that she is the strategic, industrial, and mercantile heart of Western Europe has always rendered her more important than her size would indicate or her people would like. From Philip II and the Armada to William II and the Schlieffen Plan, Belgium was a crucial element in the European balance of power. After the First World War something else was added to her traditional importance: Belgium became an essential link in the French system of alliances and thus was indirectly involved in Eastern European affairs.

It was therefore of some consequence that this little country found its international obligations too heavy. It is also of real interest that the government of a people genuinely devoted to liberal institutions could truthfully say after its return to neutrality and after its inevitable defeat in 1940 that 'never did foreign policy meet with such genuine approval in Belgium'.[1]

[1] Belgium, *The Official Account of What Happened, 1939–1940* (New York, 1942), p. 42.

ACKNOWLEDGEMENTS

THIS monograph is a revised version of a doctoral dissertation completed at the University of California, Berkeley, in 1966. I owe much gratitude to Professor Raymond Sontag, who directed the dissertation and who was my friend and teacher throughout my years in graduate school. Thanks are due also to Professors William Slottman and Paul Seabury, who read the dissertation and made many helpful suggestions. I was lucky to have the advice and encouragement of two Belgian friends, Luc Huyse and Wilfried Martens, with whom I was associated in the Harvard International Seminar. Like many students of modern European history I have benefited from the expert assistance of Mrs. Agnes Peterson of the Hoover War Memorial Library. I am grateful also for a grant from the Graduate School of the University of Minnesota. This made it possible for me to work in the Public Record Office in London, where the British Foreign Office archive for the inter-war period is now located. I was very impressed by the efficient and courteous assistance which the PRO gives to visiting scholars. Thanks are due to Professor Anna Cienciala of the University of Kansas, who read the revised manuscript and who also made some useful suggestions. I am grateful to Linda Mack for her advice in regard to the index.

It goes without saying that any mistakes contained herein are my own.

Saint Paul, Minnesota   DAVID KIEFT

CONTENTS

CONTENTS

LIST OF MAPS

ABBREVIATIONS

Annales	*Annales parlementaires de Belgique*
BPB	*Bulletin périodique de la presse belge*
Contribution	*Contribution à l'étude de la question royale*
DDB	*Documents diplomatiques belges*
DDF	*Documents diplomatiques français*
DGFP	*Documents on German Foreign Policy*
DIA	*Documents on International Affairs*
FO	(British) Foreign Office Archives
FRUS	*Foreign Relations of the United States*
GFMA	German Foreign Ministry Archives (Selected German Foreign Office records microfilmed for the (British) Foreign Office and the (U.S.) State Department German war documents project)
Survey	*Survey of International Affairs*

BELGIAN FOREIGN POLICY
IN THE AGE OF LOCARNO

1. *Paul Hymans*

Paul Hymans was a respected and influential figure in foreign capitals as well as his own. The Belgian Foreign Minister had represented his country at the Paris Peace Conference and was the first President of the General Assembly of the League of Nations. During the 1920s he remained one of those statesmen who embodied European confidence in international cooperation; for Belgians he was the familiar and trusted architect of their postwar foreign policy. A speech by Hymans was always a notable event, and none was so important as that which he delivered to the Chamber of Deputies in March 1931. Many Belgians were asking if international obligations might involve their country unnecessarily in matters having nothing to do with Belgian security. More specifically, they were worried about Belgium's connection with France. Hymans's review of Belgian foreign policy was an attempt to eliminate these misgivings.

Hymans began his speech by describing the system of permanent neutrality which for almost a century had left Belgium in peace. The durability of the system had presupposed a European balance of power, and this had been destroyed by the World War. Not only was obligatory neutrality now incapable of preserving Belgian integrity, but it was also incompatible with the feelings of national dignity and independence which had been intensified by participation in the war. Before the war Belgium had been guaranteed by five of the great powers; after the war she instinctively turned to the two who still honoured their commitment. 'At the end of the war we believed, and we still do, that the *entente* of France and England was the most solid foundation of European peace.'[1]

---

[1] Belgium, Corps législatif, *Annales parlementaires de Belgique* (Chamber), 1930/1931, 4 Mar. 1931, p. 888. (Henceforth this will be cited as *Annales*.)

Hymans explained that it was in anticipation of a similar arrangement with Great Britain that in 1920 Belgium signed a Military Agreement with France. The Franco-Belgian Military Agreement was not an alliance. It dealt with strictly technical matters and assumed only a common response to German aggression in the West. The sovereignty of both countries remained intact. Belgium reserved the right to determine the circumstances in which the Agreement became operative. Hymans emphasized that the Agreement was the natural result of wartime co-operation:

It was 1920. Belgium knew that she lacked the strength to defend herself. France knew the dangers to which she was exposed by a German army wheeling through the North. The soldiers of the two countries had struggled side by side. The war was over. The memory of the war remained in the minds of all. The lessons of the 1914 campaign had not been forgotten. In the hour of danger it was necessary to be ready.[1]

Such was the background of the Military Agreement.

Hymans insisted that Belgian policy was not, nor had it ever been, oriented towards one country only. Collaboration during the war, tradition, and geography led Belgian diplomats to seek an agreement with Great Britain and their efforts nearly succeeded. In 1922 the two governments settled on the text of a treaty in which Britain would guarantee Belgium against a German attack. The treaty was discussed at the inter-allied conference at Cannes, 'but unexpected incidents brought an end to the conference'.[2] The treaty project was temporarily abandoned.

Belgium's desire for a British guarantee made the Locarno agreements a great source of satisfaction. Hymans explained that one of the purposes of Locarno was to replace formally Belgian neutrality with a collection of guarantees. Because an Italian guarantee was added to that of France and Britain, the agreements were all the more advantageous. The great powers had recognized the *status quo* in the West, and they had done so without compromising Belgian sovereignty. Did Locarno render the military agreement with France useless? Hymans did not think so. To be sure, Locarno was 'more precise, more formal,

---

[1] Ibid., p. 890.   [2] Ibid., p. 888.

more solemn than the Franco-Belgian Agreement, which is not a treaty in the strict sense of the word'.[1] The latter simply provided the technical conditions of the co-operation anticipated by Locarno, and, for that matter, by the League Covenant. These arrangements overlapped with and complemented one another. There were no contradictions. Hymans assured his audience that the French shared this interpretation.

In conclusion Hymans stressed Belgium's devotion to collective security. 'Our policy remains one of peace . . . It is inspired by the generous and clairvoyant ideal of European co-operation and agreement whose progressive and slow realization M. Briand seeks with admirable understanding of the practical necessities and moral laws of our times.'[2]

This speech was the fullest public exposition of Belgian foreign policy made between the two World Wars. Until 1936 Belgium's representatives abroad were often instructed to refer foreign governments to it as the official answer to most inquiries about Belgian policy. Likewise, it was the official answer to the questions being raised at home. In most respects, it was a satisfactory answer to those questions.

Hymans knew that the fundamentals of his foreign policy were supported by a large majority of his countrymen. Most agreed that the major task of postwar Belgian diplomacy was to find security without undermining national sovereignty. Because obligatory neutrality had prevented Belgium from carrying on an independent policy in the nineteenth century, her people had cultivated little active interest in international affairs. This relative lack of interest still prevailed after the war, and the government could conduct its diplomacy without much domestic interference.[3] Hymans, Henri Jaspar, and Émile Vandervelde, each of whom represented one of the three major parties[4] and who alternated as Foreign Minister in the 1920s, pursued the same goals. Loyalty to the League and to Locarno was taken for granted. Most Belgians would have endorsed with-

---

[1] Ibid., p. 891.
[2] Ibid., p. 892.
[3] It is remarkable how little attention was given to foreign policy in both the Flemish and Walloon press, even in the 1930s.
[4] They were Liberal, Catholic, and Socialist, respectively.

out reservation these words of Prosper Poullet, a leading Flemish politician and a former Prime Minister:

Belgium aims to be an active agent of international co-operation in Europe. She attaches the greatest importance to fostering relations of peace and confidence in the League of Nations and offers her co-operation in its activities. That policy is stamped with the seal of continuity. It is independent of those political groupings on which our governments are based.[1]

Flemings and Walloons agreed that a return to obligatory neutrality was out of the question: it was reminiscent of the 1914 disaster and offensive to national pride.

But there remained the Franco-Belgian Military Agreement, and on this matter bilingual Belgium was seriously divided. French-speaking Walloons considered the Agreement an essential element in Belgian security, the natural result of a close historical connection with the Republic, and a sensible response to the ever present threat of renewed German aggression. Dutch-speaking Flemings had a different opinion. The Agreement did not enhance Belgium's security; it compromised it by risking Belgian involvement in every Franco-German quarrel. Belgium's historical ties with France were no source of satisfaction to Flemings, who were still struggling to come into their own in their country's political and cultural life. Collaboration with France abroad meant more French influence at home and was therefore an obstacle to the aims of Flemish nationalism. 'Voluntary neutrality' within the framework of the League and Locarno seemed to most Flemings the policy best suited to Belgium's peculiar needs.[2]

Except for Flemish extremists who denounced the Agreement from the outset, Flemish politicians were inclined during the early 1920s to accept government explanations about the technical, non-political nature of the Agreement. But after Locarno it was hard for them to see why Belgium should maintain a special relationship with France; it became still harder after the

---

[1] Quoted in Émile Vandervelde, 'Belgian Foreign Policy and the Nationalities Question', *Foreign Affairs* (New York, 1933), XI, 4, 670.

[2] O. de Raemaeker, *België's Internationaal Belied, 1919–1939* (Brussels, 1945), pp. 122–32; Ludovic Moyersoen, *Prosper Poullet en de Politiek van zijn Tijd* (Bruges, 1946), pp. 453–502; and Arie Wolter Willemsen, *Het Vlaamse-Nationalisme, 1914–1940* (Groningen, 1958), pp. 81–3.

Franco-Belgian occupation of the Rhineland ended in 1930. Because the terms of the Agreement were secret, rumour and suspicion multiplied easily. France had made public the text of her agreements with Poland and Czechoslovakia. Why not the one with Belgium? asked the Flemings.[1] The French press made matters worse by references to the Franco-Belgian 'brotherhood in arms'.[2] Flemings were outraged when in 1927 Marshal Pétain publicly referred to Belgium as the 'advance guard of Latin civilization'.[3] Such a remark seemed more than a rhetorical flourish after the publication of memoirs by Marshal Joffre, who complained about the handicaps imposed on the French military in 1914 by its careful observation of Belgian neutrality.[4] And then there was the embarrassing episode of the 'Utrecht forgery'. In February 1929 there appeared in a Dutch newspaper under the headline *A Remarkable Document, Aggressive Intentions of the Belgian General Staff against Holland. The Franco-Belgian Military Treaty* a document which purported to be the Military Agreement. According to it Belgium was going to violate Dutch territory in the event of war with Germany and was going to assist France, if the latter became involved in war with Italy.[5] Although the forgery was soon exposed, it caused plenty of commotion in the Netherlands and Germany, as well as in Belgium herself.

It is not surprising that by 1930 Belgian Socialists, who had never been enthusiastic about the Military Agreement anyway and who were led by a former Foreign Minister, Vandervelde, should second the Flemish contention that the Agreement was at best useless and, at worst, dangerous.[6] This meant that over half the members of the Chamber of Deputies hoped for its

---

[1] The agreement was not published precisely because it was non-political and technical and had been negotiated by the French and Belgian General Staffs.

[2] Vandervelde, Foreign Affairs (1933) XI, 4, 670.

[3] Corbin to Paul Boncour, 21 Apr. 1933, in France, Ministère des affaires étrangères, *Documents diplomatiques français, 1932–1939*, (Paris, 1967), Ser. I, III, no. 160 (n.2). (Henceforth this will be cited as *DDF*.)

[4] Ibid. See also *The Personal Memoirs of Joffre, Field Marshal of the French Army* (New York, 1932), trans. by Colonel T. Bentley Mott, I, 106, 129–30.

[5] Académie royale de Belgique, Commission royale d'histoire, *Documents diplomatiques belges, 1920–1940* (Brussels, 1964), II, nos. 190–7. (Henceforth this will be cited as *DDB*.) See also Pierre van Zuylen, *Les Mains libres, 1914–1940* (Brussels, 1950), pp. 252–3.

[6] On a visit to Paris in late 1930 Vandervelde offered Briand his opinion that the Agreement was useless. Briand replied that his own thinking on the matter 'was not

abrogation. Because the Agreement had been arranged by the Belgian General Staff and had never been submitted for approval to the Chamber, Flemish and Socialist opposition could be made effective only by holding up legislation on national defence.[1] This was the situation to which Hymans had addressed himself in 1931. This would be the situation in 1936, when the Agreement was eliminated altogether.

2. *The Franco-Belgian Military Agreement*

It is impossible to read the text of the Franco-Belgian Military Agreement of 1920 without concluding that certain misgivings about it were well founded.[2] The problem was not that its authors had Machiavellian intentions, as some liked to think. The problem was that its authors were careless. The Agreement was in some respects remarkably imprecise. Most of its provisions dealt with the occupation of the Rhineland. There were also provisions for a common response to a German mobilization, for French protection of the Belgian coastline, and for the defence of Luxembourg (which, evidently, was not consulted about this). Whether these latter provisions remained operative after the Rhineland occupation was an endless source of controversy between Paris and Brussels. The French insisted that they were operative; the Belgians insisted that they were not. There was a provision for a co-ordinated defence of the French and Belgian frontiers after the occupation ended. But the Foreign Ministry in Brussels would argue later that this was no longer in effect, either. There was no provision for terminating the Agreement. Even its title was vague: 'Military Agreement for the Event of Non-provoked German Aggression.' Aggression against whom?[3] If this meant aggression against both France

far removed' from that of Vandervelde. Gaiffier to Hymans, 28 Dec. 1930, *DDB*, II, no. 224.

[1] Vandervelde, Foreign Affairs (1933), XI, 4, 668 and van Zuylen, *Les Mains libres*, pp. 255-8.

[2] 29 June 1920, *DDB*, I, no. 175. (This document is the text of the Military Agreement.) For a complete description of the negotiation of the Agreement, see Jonathan Helmreich, 'The Negotiation of the Franco-Belgian Military Accord of 1920', in *French Historical Studies* (Raleigh, 1964), III, no. 3, 360–78.

[3] Hymans thought that the vagueness of the Agreement on what constituted the *casus foederus* was an advantage, as it left both parties considerable freedom of choice. Of course, the French did not see things in this way. Hymans to Cartier, 10 Nov. 1930, *DDB*, II, no. 217.

and Belgium, the Agreement failed to indicate Belgian obligations in the event of a German attack against France only. The
provision for a common response to German mobilization was
also confusing. Did this mean a mobilization which threatened
France and Belgium? Or, did it mean as well one that threatened Poland and Czechoslovakia? In general, the Agreement
was sufficiently vague to permit its signatories to read into it
whatever suited their own purposes best.

The French assumed that Belgium was an ally and considered her a very necessary ally. Belgian collaboration was
essential for two reasons. The first was related to France's
ability to aid her Central European allies militarily. A look at
the topography of Western Europe tells the whole story. Paul
Reynaud sums it up this way:

> The German defensive system had a weak point. An offensive
> starting from the French frontier . . . would run into the Rhine, or
> the Harz Mountains, or the Hünsruck and Eifel Mountains. An
> offensive starting from Liège would strike, on the other hand, into
> the Rhine about Cologne, Düsseldorf, and the Ruhr.[1]

Without the co-operation of Belgium a French offensive against
Germany could be launched only through the narrow strip of
territory between the Rhine and Moselle. This would involve
not only topographical problems. It would also expose France
to a possible repetition of the events of 1914: a German attack
through Belgium *à la* Schlieffen would catch the French army, if
it were advancing into Germany between the Rhine and the
Moselle, in a 'revolving door', as it were. This lesson from
recent history and elementary considerations of topography and
geography made the necessity of an alliance with Belgium so
obvious that France needed it to make her entire system of
alliances credible as well as practical.

The other reason for Belgium's strategic importance to France
was still more crucial. Most experts agreed that the best place
to stop another German attack was in Belgium. For the French
General Staff the ideal situation was one in which it could
anticipate a German attack by directing the French armies to
take up a position behind the Meuse River and thus to take

---

[1] Paul Reynaud, *In the Thick of the Fight, 1930–1945* (New York, 1955), trans. by
James Lambert, p. 152.

advantage of Belgium's natural line of defence as well as her fortified places such as Liège. Furthermore, the length and the irregularities of France's own north-eastern frontier—France's frontier with Belgium—made an extension of the Maginot Line from Luxembourg to the English Channel difficult and expensive. Many of France's most valuable industrial assets are located near that frontier. To have converted it into a defensive zone would have served to destroy rather than protect them.[1] So it was that 'Marshal Pétain never ceased to insist . . . that the best way of defending our northern frontier was to move in advance across Belgium'.[2] From 1927, when the possibility of fortifying the north-eastern frontier was first officially discussed, until 1935, when German rearmament gave the French some second thoughts about leaving it completely exposed, it was assumed that the French army would take up a defensive position in Belgium and that it could do so in times of diplomatic tension as well as in times of war.[3]

Given Belgium's vital importance for French military planning, it would have been natural for the French General Staff to undertake elaborate arrangements with its Belgian counterpart. There is no evidence that it ever did so, at least not until 1936.[4] In fact, if Belgian critics of the Military Agreement had known how little it amounted to in practice, some of their misgivings would not have existed. In the late 1920s and early 1930s there were no arrangements at all to facilitate a French

[1] Theodore Draper, *The Six Weeks War. France, May 10–June 25, 1940* (New York, 1944), pp. 3–7; Pierre Cot, *Triumph of Treason*, trans. by Sybille and Milton Crane (Chicago, 1944), pp. 183–4; Général Paul Émile Tournoux, *Haut Commandement. Gouvernement et défense des frontières du nord et de l'est, 1919–1939* (Paris, 1960), pp. 59–67, 80–1; and Alfred David Coox, 'French Military Doctrine, 1919–1939: Concepts of Ground and Aerial Warfare', (unpublished Ph.D. dissertation, Harvard, 1951), pp. 44–53.

[2] Général Gamelin, *Servir* (Paris, 1946), I, 85.

[3] Ibid. Gamelin later said: 'Until 1936 it was understood that the Belgians would call on us in times of political tension . . .' France, *Commission d'enquête sur les événements survenus en France de 1933 à 1945* (Paris, 1947), II, 408.

[4] Of course, it is possible that the French sought to do so and met with a refusal from the Belgian General Staff. The historian must be very cautious with regard to these matters because the available evidence is so scanty. All of the French documents on the Military Agreement seem to have disappeared. The official collection of Belgian documents on the inter-war years does not include General Staff memoranda, and Belgian diplomats themselves were not always up to date on what the military was doing. See, e.g., Vandervelde to Gaiffier, 13 May 1927, *DDB*, II, no. 152. See also *DDF*, Ser. II, I, vii–viii.

offensive on behalf of Poland or Czechoslovakia. This is not surprising. France's strategic doctrine and the very existence of the Maginot Line made active French assistance to these countries a dubious expectation in any case. 'How can one believe that we should again think of an offensive when we have spent milliards in order to construct a fortified barrier?' asked General Maurin in 1935. 'Would we be mad enough to advance beyond this barrier on some unpredictable venture?'[1] In brief, Belgian fears about being dragged along on an excursion launched on behalf of France's central European allies had little foundation in reality. But members of the Belgian parliament had no way of knowing this because of the secrecy surrounding the Military Agreement. And Belgian diplomats had no way of knowing what the French might have planned for the future.

Critics of the Military Agreement would have been startled if they had discovered how little planning there was for a joint-defence against a German attack. In this respect too, the Military Agreement produced few concrete results. There were contacts between the General Staffs via military attachés. They took place in 1926, 1927, and 1928.[2] Information was exchanged, and the technical conditions for a defensive arrangement were established, at least in theory. Those who participated in these discussions valued them highly.[3] But these exchanges were strictly verbal and had little or no impact on actual military planning. Gamelin later wrote that by 1930 there existed plans for the French to move into Belgium, that their 'ally' was agreeable to this, but that the French army's role in Belgium 'was not exactly determined'.[4] Although it is impossible to determine precisely what was transpiring between the French and Belgian General Staffs, it is possible to conclude confidently that very little was transpiring between them. By 1931 France's 'ally' had adopted military plans designed to render unnecessary any French penetration of Belgian territory during periods of diplomatic tension. The Foreign Ministry informed Belgian diplomats abroad that

'our General Staff has established a defensive disposition to be

[1] Quoted in Reynaud, *In the Thick of the Fight*, p. 109.
[2] Foreign Ministry memorandum, 14 Jan. 1931, *DDB*, II, no. 230.
[3] Gaiffier to Vandervelde, 29 Apr. 1927, ibid., no. 151.
[4] Gamelin, *Servir*, II, 25.

realized by our own means and which would extend over the entirety of the eastern frontier, from Dutch Limburg as far as the Grand Duchy of Luxembourg. The French armies thus would not have to penetrate preventively our territory in order to assure the security of their eventual connection with our own forces.'[1]

Two years later the Chief of the Belgian General Staff, Nuyten, revealed to the British military attaché in Brussels that the government was ready to protect Belgian neutrality—against France! If, during a 'precautionary period' prior to mobilization, France did not give Belgium assurances of respecting her neutrality, Belgium would arrange a defensive disposition facing France. The general also noted that relations between the French and Belgian General Staffs were not particularly cordial and that he himself attached no importance to the Military Agreement at all.[2]

Was the Military Agreement serving any useful purpose? As far as most Belgian diplomats were concerned, it was not. Since Locarno it had seemed to them dangerous and out of date. As one diplomat put it, it 'gives the impression of a badly meshed gear'.[3] The most influential and persistent critic of the Military Agreement was the Political Director of the Foreign Ministry, Pierre van Zuylen, who was later described by one of his colleagues as 'the living personification of Belgium's *dossier diplomatique* from 1914 to 1940'.[4] Van Zuylen never wearied of arguing that the Military Agreement should be done away with and that Belgium's greatest benefactor was Britain, not France. It is no wonder that he was thoroughly distrusted by the Quai d'Orsay, which tended to attribute its troubles with Belgium to his influence. French diplomats preferred to work with van Zuylen's immediate superior in the Foreign Ministry, Secretary General Fernand Vanlangenhove, to whom the French attributed more *largeur d'esprit*,[5] because he seemed better disposed to them. If Vanlangenhove was less suspicious of

[1] Foreign Ministry memorandum, 14 Jan. 1931, *DDB*, II, no. 230.
[2] Granville to Vansittart, 4 May 1933, FO, 371/16740/C4041/1788/18. The general did admit also that plans for a defensive disposition against Germany were the only ones he dared to put on paper.
[3] Memorandum by Mélot, Mar. 1928, *DDB*, II, no. 168.
[4] Vicomte Jacques Davignon, *Berlin, 1933–1940. Souvenirs d'une mission* (Brussels, 1951), p. 42.
[5] Laroche to Flandin, 6 Apr. 1936, *DDF*, Ser. II, II, no. 27.

MAP 1: Belgium's principal cities and waterways

French intentions than his associate, his basic position was none the less much the same. It was his opinion that in a Europe divided into satisfied and dissatisfied camps, Belgium would render herself a great service by staying outside both of them.[1] Like their counterparts in other capitals the permanent officials of the Belgian Foreign Ministry represented a consistent point of view which reflected their country's traditional diplomacy. Belgium's traditional international position was one of non-alignment. The fact that non-alignment had been imposed on Belgium in the nineteenth century did not, in their opinion, make unimposed non-alignment any less suitable to Belgian needs in the twentieth century. It therefore followed that the high officials of the Foreign Ministry, like the Chief of the General Staff, regarded the existence of the Military Agreement as contrary to Belgium's vital interests. In 1931 they made their first attempt to eliminate it.

Shortly before Hymans's speech to the Chamber of Deputies, with domestic opposition to the Military Agreement growing louder daily, Marshal Pétain committed the first of two famous verbal *faux pas*. In October 1930 the Marshal informed the Belgian ambassador in Paris that since Belgium was going to be involved necessarily in any Franco-German war, the French army might be compelled to cross into Belgium without consulting the Brussels government first; in fact, it might be forced to do so against that government's will.[2] Shortly thereafter the ambassador reported that such ideas existed in other circles, too: Raymond Poincaré had insisted that Belgium ought to assist France, should the latter go to the aid of Poland.[3] This was precisely what critics of the Military Agreement, both inside and outside the Foreign Ministry, had feared. It is no wonder that Hymans decided that the time had come to clear up the confusion.

Hymans and Vanlangenhove met in January 1931 with French Foreign Minister Briand and Alexis Léger, who was then the Political Director of the Quai d'Orsay. Their discus-

[1] In 1931 Vanlangenhove wrote that 'the first precaution which is imperative is to remain outside the two opposing groups, not to get involved in their quarrels, not to compromise oneself with any one of them, and to avoid the appearance of doing so.' Memorandum by Vanlangenhove, 2 Feb. 1931, *DDB*, II, no. 233.

[2] Gaiffier to Hymans, 17 Oct. 1930, ibid., no. 215 (n.1).

[3] Ibid. See also van Zuylen, *Les Mains libres*, pp. 253–4.

sion was a prototype of many future discussions. The Belgian case was simple. Hymans called attention to the mounting criticism of the Military Agreement and pointed out that the government's military legislation was in danger because of it. Those provisions of the Military Agreement which were still in effect had been absorbed by the Locarno agreements, which had superseded the 'undeniable imperfections' of the Military Agreement. The Belgians proposed an exchange of letters in which the military co-operation would be characterized as being 'regulated exclusively' by Locarno.[1] Léger disliked the use of the word 'exclusively' because it precluded Belgium's obligation to mobilize in the event of German mobilization. This was provided for only in the Military Agreement. Furthermore, said Léger, the Belgian proposal would eliminate the Military Agreement's provision for the defence of the Belgian coastline. Vanlangenhove quickly remarked that such provisions had been inoperative since the Rhineland occupation ended. Léger then presented a French counter-proposal. The two governments would exchange letters limiting their obligations to situations provided for by Locarno and the League Covenant. This was acceptable to the Belgians.[2] What they disliked was that the proposed letters would acknowledge that the Military Agreement 'had never had and never would have any other purpose than to prepare and to assure practically the technical conditions . . . for the eventual exercise of military cooperation between Belgium and France in the event of non-provoked aggression by Germany'.[3] This sounded like a reaffirmation of the Military Agreement. The discussions ended without the problem having been solved.

There followed several weeks of haggling between the two foreign ministries about the wording of the proposed letters. These arguments—there were many more—were very complex. But the fundamental issues were basic and therefore simple. For France it was a matter of maintaining the efficiency of an entire

[1] Memorandum by Vanlangenhove, Mar. 1931, *DDB*, II, no. 236.

[2] This formula was not as generous as the Belgians thought. They would learn later that the French interpretation of the League Covenant and, in particular, article 16 of the Covenant obligated Belgium to grant 'right of passage' to a French army going to the assistance of Poland or Czechoslovakia.

[3] Memorandum by Vanlangenhove, Mar. 1931, *DDB*, II, no. 236. See also van Zuylen, *Les Mains libres*, pp. 258–62.

system of alliances, or at least the appearance of such efficiency.[1] Great powers never easily acquiesce in the dismantlement of arrangements which they deem vital to their own security. For Belgium it was a matter of maintaining sovereign control over her own foreign policy. Small powers never willingly turn over to a great power the right to make decisions affecting their physical survival, unless their survival depends on doing so.[2]

Of course, the Belgians had other, more specific reasons for distrusting Léger's proposal. Political Director van Zuylen argued that the clause concerning the 'technical conditions' for future military co-operation might be interpreted by the French as preserving all the questionable stipulations of the Military Agreement and even be considered by them as a justification for a premature despatch of French troops to Belgian soil à la Pétain.[3] General Émile Galet, who was then Chief of the Belgian General Staff, had his doubts, too. As long as there was any peacetime co-operation between the French and Belgian armies, he said, the Germans would feel compelled to take precautions against Belgium, and these precautions could themselves lead to war between Belgium and Germany.[4] It was Galet's opinion, as was so with many other Belgian military men, that Belgium would have a wider margin of security without the Military Agreement.

These were weighty arguments. But the French had their way. On 20 February 1931, Hymans and the French ambassador in Brussels exchanged letters whose wording was similar to that proposed initially by Léger.[5]

Why did the Belgians give in to the French on a matter of such importance? On at least one occasion the cabinet seriously

[1] When agreement was reached on the wording of the proposed letters, Briand wanted the letters kept secret. He and Léger never said why. It is possible that they felt a revelation of the true state of Franco-Belgian relations would expose the weakness of the Maginot strategy and raise doubts about the value of French promises in Warsaw and Prague. Common sense does suggest that the less they said about relations with their 'ally', the better it would be for them.

[2] President de Gaulle's partial withdrawal from NATO after the Cuba missile crisis bears a suggestive resemblance to Belgium's progressive withdrawal from the French inter-war system of alliances.

[3] Memorandum by Vanlangenhove, Mar. 1931, DDB, II, no. 236.

[4] Ibid.

[5] Ibid. See also van Zuylen, Les Mains libres, pp. 253–64 and Paul Hymans, Mémoires (Brussels, 1958), II, 625–6, 929–30.

considered offering the Chamber of Deputies a unilateral interpretation of the Military Agreement.[1] But this would have been
a real embarrassment for the French, and the Belgians knew it.
Paul Hymans agreed with his associates in the Foreign Ministry
that the agreement was out of date: 'But the denunciation of
the agreement . . . would offend the sentiments of many people,
in France as well as in Belgium. The matter has a very important psychological aspect, and it ought to be treated with in-
finite tact.'[2] Of course, Belgium's 'tact' was not rooted solely in
sentiment and generosity. It was in Belgium's interest to treat
her larger neighbours with respect. But the fact remains that
Hymans, and his successors, tried hard to understand the French
point of view and tried to adjust their policies accordingly.
The French themselves, on the other hand, never made any
such attempt to understand and co-operate with the Belgians.

It is hard to escape the impression that the French did not
take the Belgians seriously, at least not until it was too late. The
possibility that Belgium's national interests might not be identical to those of France did not occur to the Quai d'Orsay and its
representatives in Brussels. The attitude of Ambassador Charles
Corbin, a distinguished diplomat who served in Brussels in 1932
and early 1933, is a good example of French condescension towards Belgium. Whenever the Belgians asked questions about
their obligations to France, Corbin wrote them off as a response
to Flemish agitation and failed to recognize that they reflected
also the genuine misgivings of professional diplomats and
soldiers. 'Even Belgian statesmen whose intellectual development and memories of the war bring them closest to our conceptions and policies rarely have the courage to defend openly
that which they recognize to be their national interest', reported the ambassador.[3] Even when three foreign ministers,
past and present, expressed their doubts, Corbin did not think
they meant what they said. When former Foreign Minister
Henri Jaspar wrote an article criticizing Belgium's connection
with France, Corbin dismissed him as an opportunist adjusting
himself to public opinion: the Quai d'Orsay knew 'how good

[1] Memorandum by Vanlangenhove, Mar. 1931, *DDB*, II, no. 236.
[2] Memorandum by Hymans, 6 Jan. 1931, ibid., no. 227. See also Gaiffier to
Hymans, 27 Dec. 1930, no. 223.
[3] Corbin to Herriot, 23 Oct. 1932, *DDF*, Ser. I, I, no. 269.

M. Jaspar is at scenting the wind . . . .'[1] When former Foreign Minister Vandervelde publicly expressed his misgivings, the ambassador suggested that he was simply fishing for Flemish votes.[2] When incumbent Foreign Minister Hymans requested clarification of a clause of the Locarno agreements, Corbin reported that the Belgian government wanted mostly to 'silence the eternal polemic of the *Flamingants* . . . .'[3] General Galet, who was one of Belgium's most respected soldiers, was not respected in Paris. He had a 'doctrinaire spirit' and a 'high opinion of himself', wrote Corbin: 'The Department [Quai d'Orsay] made up its mind about General Galet long ago.'[4] Evidently, the ambassador had made up his mind about what constituted the best interests of Belgium. Such an attitude was unlikely to lead to goodwill. Indeed, French condescension irritated and humiliated the Belgians. It is not surprising that relations between the two foreign ministries should grow progressively worse.[5]

Despite their dissatisfaction with the letters exchanged in February 1931, the Belgians were relieved that the letters had formally subordinated the unwanted Military Agreement to the League and Locarno. The trouble was that there was uncertainty about the obligations deriving from these. The League Covenant contained the principle of solidarity against aggression, but it had never been determined if this implied obligatory military sanctions. The French thought it did, and they continued to assume that Belgium would be obliged to mobilize on behalf of their Central European allies.[6] Another problem was the provision in the Locarno agreements for an immediate response to a 'flagrant violation' of the Versailles Treaty, i.e., outright aggression against Belgium or France, or abrogation of the treaty clauses relating to the Rhineland demilitarization. Would Belgium be obliged to assist France in the Rhineland, if

---

[1] Corbin to Herriot, 3 Nov. 1932, ibid., no. 293.
[2] Corbin to Paul Boncour, 25 Feb. 1933, ibid., II, no. 346.
[3] Corbin to Paul-Boncour, 10 Mar. 1933, ibid., no. 394.
[4] Corbin to Paul-Boncour, 15 Feb. 1933, ibid., no. 306.
[5] When Paul-Henri Spaak became Foreign Minister in 1936 he was 'astonished' that his advisers in the ministry were so badly disposed towards France. He soon discovered for himself that French diplomats could be 'haughty, disdainful, very sure of themselves'. Paul-Henri Spaak, *Combats inachevés. De l'Indépendance à l'Alliance* (Brussels, 1969), p. 38.
[6] Van Zuylen, *Les Mains libres*, pp. 274–6.

Britain and Italy chose not to do so?[1] If such questions were highly complicated, from the Belgian viewpoint their essence remained very simple: to what extent was Belgium obliged to be the tool of French foreign policy? Marshal Pétain still had his own ideas, and in January 1933 he made his second *faux pas*. Pétain informed the Belgian ambassador in Paris that French troops would cross over into Belgium whether they were invited or not. 'We don't intend to allow the recurrence of an experience which nearly cost the existence of France', he said. The ambassador asked what France would do if Germany attacked Poland, pointing out that Belgium did reserve the right to determine whether military co-operation would take place. 'We will enter your country in any case', said Pétain. 'Even if we should resist?' 'We will resist you!' was the answer.[2] One account of this exchange reports that the ambassador then said: 'In that case we will receive you with cannon fire.'[3] Whether Pétain's words actually represented the thinking of French military planners is doubtful. Generals Weygand and Gamelin hastened to assure the startled Belgians that French troops would not enter Belgium except on the basis of a decision taken in common by the two governments.[4] None the less, Pétain's remarks made those unanswered questions about the League and Locarno seem all the more pressing. Once again, Hymans decided that the time had come to clear up the muddle.

In March 1933 Hymans spelled out for Ambassador Corbin Belgium's interpretation of Locarno: France's guarantee of Belgium could not be imposed unilaterally.[5] In other words, if Germany 'flagrantly violated' Belgian integrity or the demilitarized zone of the Rhineland, France could not send troops into Belgium without the prior agreement of the Belgian government. Corbin made no objections and requested only that the

---

[1] Ibid., pp. 280–1.

[2] Général van Overstraeten, *Albert I. Léopold III. Vingt ans de politique militaire belge. 1920–1940* (Bruges, 1949), pp. 99–100. See also Gaiffier to Hymans, 5 Jan. 1933, *DDB*, III, no. 4.

[3] Van Zuylen, *Les Mains libres*, p. 276.

[4] Gaiffier to Hymans, 13 Jan. 1933, *DDB*, III, no. 5 and Hymans to Gaiffier, 17 Feb. 1933, no. 6. See also Tournoux, *Haut Commandement*, pp. 80–1, 161. Tournoux, whose book is the best study of French inter-war military planning, writes that the French generals knew that a Belgian invitation was necessary before their armies could cross into Belgium.

[5] Memorandum by Hymans, 10 Mar. 1933, *DDB*, III, no. 15.

Belgians make no public declarations on the matter.[1] And for months there was no more discussion of it.[2] It was therefore with considerable surprise that in December 1933 the Belgians received from the hands of Corbin's successor, Paul Claudel, a Quai d'Orsay memorandum which said the following: (1) under the Locarno agreements French military assistance to Belgium could not be imposed without Belgian consent, but (2) under the Versailles Treaty Belgium did have the obligation to open her territory to French troops, should the Rhineland provisions of that treaty be flagrantly disregarded.[3] Because any German violation of the Locarno agreements necessarily entailed a violation of the Versailles Treaty, the Belgians concluded that the French had simply returned to their earlier position by using a more circuitous route. In February 1934 Hymans handed to Claudel a memorandum elaborating further Belgium's interpretation of Locarno and Versailles and asking for more discussions.[4] This time the French apparently decided that the safest course would be to ignore the problem altogether.[5] This was Belgium's last formal attempt to clarify her connection with France until early 1936.

While the Quai d'Orsay was neglecting the requests and questions of its worried 'ally', an entirely different issue suddenly made the growing dispute public. The Belgians were very eager for the success of the Disarmament Conference, and they agreed with the British that German demands for the removal of the disarmament clauses of the Versailles Treaty were reasonable. Brussels felt that there was hope for some form of disarmament and that the rigid French position was both unrealistic and inopportune.[6] This was the background of the

[1] Ibid.

[2] There was another exchange concerning the Military Agreement. In May the Belgians learned that Eduard Daladier, who had just become French Minister of War, had told a committee of the French Senate that 'save for certain modifications' the most important clauses of the Military Agreement were still in force. Hymans quickly presented his objections to Daladier. There is no record of the latter's response, if there was one. Gaiffier to Hymans, 6 May 1933, ibid., no. 28 and Hymans to Gaiffier, 16 May 1933, no. 30.

[3] Claudel to Hymans, 2 Dec. 1933, ibid., no. 86. See also van Zuylen, *Les Mains libres*, pp. 282–3.

[4] Hymans to Claudel, 8 Feb. 1934, *DDB*, III, no. 114.

[5] Van Zuylen, *Les Mains libres*, pp. 283–5.

[6] Comte de Broqueville, 'Pourquoi j'ai parlé en Mars 1934,' in *La Revue générale* (Brussels, 1939), CXXII, 289–98; and Hymans, *Mémoires*, II, 663–83.

unexpected statement by Prime Minister de Broqueville in March 1934, in which he dissociated Belgium from the French position. De Broqueville told the Belgian Senate that the Versailles Treaty was wrong in attempting 'to maintain a great power in a state of disarmament for an indefinite period of time' and that it was necessary to 'put aside our sterile regrets as well as our vain hopes'.[1] Actually, the Franco-Belgian difference of opinion on the disarmament question was of little significance in the long run. But it did serve to make clear to the public in both countries that France could no longer assume Belgian partnership in all circumstances.

Given Belgium's growing list of grievances against France, one wonders again why the Belgians did not unilaterally sever their special connection with France—the Military Agreement of 1920. Most knowledgeable Belgians thought it was a liability. It had resulted in little real military co-operation between the two countries. It had produced nothing but anger and suspicion. Strictly speaking, Belgium was not an ally of France. She could have denounced the agreement without violating any solemn engagements. 'We considered many times the elimination of this nuisance', writes van Zuylen, 'but we drew back from Offending our friends ....'[2] What was true in 1931 was true in 1934 and 1935. Belgium had better reasons than ever to fear the consequences of offending France. Nazi Germany's rearmament, her withdrawal from the League of Nations, and her disrespect for the Versailles Treaty indicated that this was no time for Belgium to lay down the law to her stronger friends. Segments of the Belgian press were talking about the danger of war and calling for closer co-operation with France. The Flemish and Socialist representatives in the parliament temporarily halted their campaign against the Military Agreement.[3] Many Belgians were having second thoughts. Many of them did not know what to think.

[1] *Annales* (Senate), 1933/1934, 6 Mar. 1934, p. 562.
[2] Van Zuylen, *Les Mains libres*, p. 332.
[3] *Annales* (Chamber), 1933/1934, 29 and 30 Nov. 1933, pp. 133–5, 175–7; Jane K. Miller, *Belgian Foreign Policy Between Two Wars, 1919–1940* (New York, 1951), pp. 198–202; and Lerchenfeld to Neurath, 25 Feb. 1933, in United States, Department of State, *Documents of German Foreign Policy* (Washington, 1957), Ser C, I, no. 39. (Henceforth this will be cited as *DGFP*.)

On the one hand, Belgium's need for French friendship was more obvious than ever because of the growing German menace. On the other hand, Belgium's chances of becoming involved in a Franco-German quarrel having nothing to do with herself were increasing every year. Belgium wanted French protection, but she was reluctant to pay the French price. Paul Hymans, who was always a great friend of France, was very aware of the ambiguity and delicacy of Belgium's position. During one of his meetings with Louis Barthou and Sir John Simon, the energetic French Foreign Minister suddenly said: 'Hymans has a legitimate wife, France, and a mistress, England.' The Belgian replied: 'Why not say that I have two mistresses!'[1]

3. Belgium and Great Britain

Anthony Eden's account of Barthou's remarks about Belgian fidelity notes that he added: '. . . Belgium pays more attention to the mistress than to the wife'.[2] It must have seemed to the French that their little neighbour was far more zealous in currying favour with the British than with them. The importance of British friendship and protection was a matter on which Fleming and Walloon, Catholic and Socialist, politician and diplomat were in complete harmony. Belgian diplomats often repeated the theme that 'this state constitutes our supreme safeguard'.[3] Their confidence in Britain was not mere wishful thinking. It reflected four hundred years of history. British policy towards Belgium, said a Foreign Ministry memorandum, was 'determined by the fundamental and consistent interest which the protection of our independence has had for Great Britain'.[4]

Belgium had been a vital security interest of Britain since the age of power politics began. From the sixteenth to the eighteenth centuries Britain sought to keep Belgium in friendly hands and, preferably, weak hands. Louis XIV's ambitions in Belgium were twice an immediate cause for British intervention in a continental war. Revolutionary France's activities there provided another occasion for British intervention. Bonaparte

---

[1] Hymans, *Mémoires*, II, 968–9.
[2] Anthony Eden, Earl of Avon, *Facing the Dictators* (Boston, 1962), p. 104.
[3] Foreign Ministry memorandum, 14 Jan. 1931, *DDB*, II, no. 230.
[4] Ibid.

attributed Britain's unyielding hostility towards his empire to a desire to free the great Belgian seaport, Antwerp. He was exaggerating, but he had a good point anyway. Belgium's location at or near the mouths of the great western European rivers made her the most valuable piece of real estate in Europe, for commercial and strategic reasons. Britain naturally remained as concerned about Belgium in the nineteenth and twentieth centuries as she had been earlier. Her guarantee was the most reliable pillar of newly independent Belgium's security until 1914. Belgians themselves were convinced that their noninvolvement in the Franco-Prussian War was the result of British warnings to the two belligerents.[1] It was no secret that one thing on which the British cabinet had been in accord in August 1914 was the need to defend Belgium. Respect for Belgium's independence and integrity was, in Churchill's words, 'a public law, not an act of expediency'. Great Britain's permanent interest in Belgium had become 'a wonderful, unconscious tradition'.[2]

When the British reaffirmed their ancient policy and renewed their guarantee to Belgium in the Locarno agreements, the Belgians were delighted, especially after the failure of the Anglo-Belgian treaty project of 1922. None the less, the Belgian Foreign Ministry was not quite satisfied because Locarno was effective only in the event of aggression in the West. When the Belgians became fully aware of the interpretation which the French might give the Military Agreement and realized that it could involve them willy-nilly in a conflict beginning in Central Europe, they decided to ask for another guarantee from the British. 'It was the best way for us to avoid a battle precipitated by France and—more important still—to increase our security against Germany.'[3] It was with this in mind that Hymans and van Zuylen travelled to London in May 1934 for talks with Sir John Simon and other members of the British cabinet.

---

[1] For a description of Britain's interests in Belgium during the nineteenth century and her policy before the Franco-Prussian War in particular, see Richard Millman, *British Foreign Policy and the Coming of the Franco-Prussian War* (Oxford, 1965), pp. 114–144, 198–207; and Alfred Pribram, *England and the International Policy of the European Great Powers, 1871–1914* (London, 1966), pp. 3–4.

[2] Winston Churchill, *The Gathering Storm* (Boston, 1948), p. 208.

[3] Van Zuylen, *Les Mains libres*, p. 295.

The Belgians proposed an arrangement closely resembling the one almost signed in 1922: the British would give an unambiguous promise to aid Belgium in the event of non-provoked aggression. Simon wondered what this would add to the existing arrangements. The Belgians replied that Locarno was subject to so many conditions that the Germans might doubt British intentions. 1870 had demonstrated the value of a forthright British commitment. 1914 had demonstrated the need for one. A British guarantee should be 'so precise, so obvious and so automatic' that any potential adversary would back down. Hymans granted that Locarno would function in the event of war. What he wanted was something which would prevent Locarno from having to function. Belgium wanted a 'preventive' guarantee, not just a 'repressive' one. Hymans expressed the fear that some German violation of the demilitarized zone would cause the French to request the use of Belgian territory. A British guarantee would enable Belgium to say 'no' to France, and it would serve as a warning to Germany. Van Zuylen pointed out that an 'inviolable barrier' across one of the 'nerve centres' of Western Europe would contribute to the security of all.[1]

London seemed impressed with the Belgian arguments, but nothing was settled. As the weeks passed it became clear that Simon was unwilling to sign a treaty which would be interpreted as directed against Germany. It is possible, too, that Simon disliked the Belgian proposal because an Anglo-Belgian treaty would give the French ideas of their own: '... we don't want the French to ask for the same thing ...' he had told Hymans.[2] The Foreign Secretary soon revealed that he thought the most sensible step for the Belgians would be to sign a non-aggression pact with the Germans.[3] This did not seem so sensible to the Belgians. The state of public opinion, reluctance to weaken existing arrangements, and a fear of antagonizing France caused

[1] Foreign Ministry memorandum, 23 May 1934, *DDB*, III, no. 130; Simon to Ovey, 17 May 1934, FO, 432/1/247/C3097/4; van Zuylen, *Les Mains libres*, pp. 298–310; and Hymans, *Mémoires*, II, 680–3.

[2] Foreign Ministry memorandum, 23 May 1934, *DDB*, III, no. 130.

[3] Simon to Ovey, 31 May 1934, FO, 432/1/3279/C3449/4; and Memorandum by Hymans, 31 May 1934, *DDB*, III, no. 132.

them to reject a proposal which, from their point of view, would add little to Locarno.[1]

So ended the Belgians' last effort before 1936 to pin down an unambiguous British commitment. The effort was not a complete failure. Although it produced no treaty, it did induce Prime Minister Baldwin to make this declaration in the House of Commons in July:

Let us never forget this; since the days of the air, the old frontiers are gone. When you think of the defence of England you no longer think of the chalk cliffs of Dover; you think of the Rhine. That is where our frontier lies.[2]

Such words were certain to get a warm welcome in Belgium. For the government they were as useful as they were reassuring: they could be used to convince the always sceptical Chamber of Deputies that Belgium need not depend on the distrusted French alone. The trouble was that they were only words.

Henri Jaspar, who succeeded Hymans as Foreign Minister and who remained in that office only a few months, informed British Ambassador Ovey that he would welcome a chance to discuss with Simon the military aspect of Anglo-Belgian relations. Ovey reported to London that Jaspar was pleased with the British attitude, 'but he wants more'.[3] Simon soon let Jaspar know that Belgium was not going to get more. When the latter reluctantly agreed that further discussion would thus be useless, Simon informed him that this was 'a very wise attitude'.[4]

The Belgians tried a different channel. In January 1935 Defence Minister Albert Devèze told the British military attaché in Brussels that some understanding between the British and Belgian General Staffs was necessary. Devèze thought it would be especially worthwhile for Britain to have a timely warning of the approach of German planes. All arrangements would be

---

[1] Memorandum by Hymans, 31 May 1934, *DDB*, III, no. 132; Köpke to Adelmann, 12 June 1934, *DGFP*, Ser. C, II, no. 497; and van Zuylen, *Les Mains libres*, pp. 311–12.

[2] Great Britain, *Parliamentary Debates* (Commons), 292, 30 July 1934, 2339. Simon made a similar statement in the House of Commons two weeks earlier. Ibid., 13 July 1934, 697–8.

[3] Ovey to Simon, 31 Aug., 1934, FO, 432/1/C5962/3279/4.

[4] Simon to Ovey, 15 Sept. 1934, ibid., C6224/3279/4. See also Memorandum by Jaspar, 14 Sept. 1934, *DDB*, III, no. 140.

hypothetical. Britain would be committed to nothing.[1] The British were not interested. In October 1935, during an unofficial visit to the War Office in London, Devèze tried again. He suggested that the Belgian Chief of Staff pay a visit to London. The British did not want this, either, and their military attaché in Brussels was instructed to see that the proposed visit did not take place.[2] In December the Belgians made a more oblique approach. An air force general, in London ostensibly for the purpose of negotiating the purchase of aircraft, suggested that contacts between the Belgian Air Force and the British Air Ministry could be useful. The Belgians were concerned about their shortage of fighter aircraft; the British might want to hear about the excellent condition of Belgium's ground observation service.[3] The British were no more responsive than before, and the matter was dropped. Why were they reluctant to follow up Belgian suggestions? A brief note by Anthony Eden, who had just become Foreign Secretary, probably provides the best explanation. It was necessary to proceed with caution in these matters, said Eden, because the Germans might be looking for an excuse to violate the Rhineland.[4]

So, for the time being, the Belgians had to settle for words.

4. *Belgium and Germany*

After the war German-Belgian relations were, at best, correct. Contacts between Berlin and Brussels could never be as confident and as cordial as they had been earlier. For Belgians there was the memory of an invasion and occupation during which the Germans had worked for Belgian disunity by encouraging Flemish separatism. This memory was still vivid when Hitler became German Chancellor in 1933. Belgian fears, however, now stemmed from more than just unpleasant recollections. There were several good reasons for the Belgians to consider the Nazis dangerous.

One of them was Nazi contempt for the Locarno agreements. Belgium's ambassador in Berlin during the early 1930s, Count

---

[1] Report by Fraser, 18 Jan. 1935, FO, 371/18789/ C516/516/4. The military attaché notes that Devèze was reverting to an 'old thesis'. Evidently there had been earlier approaches.

[2] Sargent to Wigram, 25 Oct. 1935, ibid., C7274/516/4.

[3] Memorandum by Wigram, 31 Dec. 1935, FO, 371/19850/C270/270/4.

[4] Minute by Eden, ibid.

André Kerchove de Denterghem, had no illusions about this. He reminded his superiors that before Hitler came to power, he had declared *urbi et orbi* that his regime would not recognize any of the treaties subscribed to by the German government since 1919.[1] The German Foreign Office assured the ambassador that Germany had no intention of violating the Locarno agreements.[2] But, as Kerchove noted, Hitler always avoided reaffirming those agreements in public.[3] And protestations of goodwill from this government meant little: they were 'like the sunshine before the storm, and, in this country, tornadoes come as abruptly and unexpectedly as they do below the equator'.[4]

To make matters worse, Belgium had been the postwar recipient of a prosperous piece of German territory—the cantons of Eupen and Malmédy—and the Nazis were not likely to forget it. Belgians themselves had always disagreed about the value of the cantons; many felt that it was unequal to the trouble they caused. The residents of Eupen and Malmédy were also of a divided opinion. Some remained loyal to Germany; others welcomed Belgian sovereignty as a means of escaping a Socialist and, later, a Nazi government in Berlin.[5] Most of them probably felt, in the depths of their hearts, that they had the best of both worlds. During the day they could enjoy the prosperous German city Aachen, which was just a tram-car ride away from Eupen; during the night they could sleep peacefully, knowing that they enjoyed also the civil liberties guaranteed to citizens of Belgium.[6] In any event, the German government never doubted for a moment its rightful ownership of the cantons, and it had constantly sought their return. Shortly after Locarno the Germans nearly succeeded in repossessing them in return for a cash payment. Opposition in the Belgian cabinet and British fears of a precedent-setting territorial change compelled Foreign Mini-

---

[1] Kerchove to Hymans, 14 Feb. 1934, *DDB*, III, no. 116.

[2] Kerchove to Hymans, 17 Nov. 1933, ibid., no. 82 and Kerchove to Hymans, 29 Dec. 1933, no. 102.

[3] Kerchove to Hymans, 14 Feb. 1934, ibid., no. 116.

[4] Kerchove to Hymans, 28 May 1934, ibid., no. 131.

[5] Louis de Lichtervelde,'Les cantons de l'est', in *La Revue générale* (Brussels, 1937), LXX, 129–47.

[6] This was the observation of the British Consul in Liège. 'We Germans here in Belgium are in a land of plenty', he was told. Clive to Eden, 5 Oct. 1937, FO, 432/3/C6907/6645/4.

ster Vandervelde to turn down the German offer.[1] It is unfortunate that he did so. Although by the 1930s the cantons
were fully integrated administratively into the Belgian community, it did nothing to slow a growing pro-German movement. Eupen and Malmédy were an easy target for Nazi subversion, and after 1933 there was one incident after another.
The *Heimattreue Front*, the largest German political organization
in the cantons, was soon winning over half the votes in both
national and provincial elections.[2] Hitler himself made it clear
to the Belgians that his renunciation of Alsace and Lorraine
did not apply to Eupen and Malmédy, and he insisted that it
would be best not to speak of the problem at all.[3]

Much more important to Germany than Eupen and Malmédy was Belgium's special connection with France. 'In her
struggle with Germany', General von Seeckt had written,
'France can count upon different states. The first of these states is
Belgium.'[4] The Germans wanted the elimination of the Franco-
Belgian Military Agreement, and this was so before the advent
of Hitler. After Hymans' speech to the Chamber of Deputies in
1931 the Wilhelmstrasse indicated its partial satisfaction. It
hoped that Hymans's clarification of the Agreement was just a
'first step' towards another, namely, its denunciation.[5] Because
the dismantlement of the French alliance system was a goal of
Hitler's early foreign policy, it followed that Berlin would respond with interest when Sir John Simon suggested a special

[1] Hymans, *Mémoires*, I, 467–78; van Zuylen, *Les Mains libres*, pp. 225–7; and
Miller, *Belgian Foreign Policy Between Two Wars*, pp. 94–102.

[2] Louis de Jong, *The German Fifth Column in the Second World War* (Chicago, 1965),
trans. by C. M. Geyl, p. 197.

[3] Meissner to Neurath, 25 Oct. 1935, *DGFP*, Ser. C, IV, no. 381 and Neurath to
Hoesch, 20 Dec. 1935, no. 471. It should be noted that on one occasion Hitler did
say to Ambassador Kerchove that 'that which goes for Alsace goes for your
country too'. But there is no reason to think that this was more than a momentary
aberration. Kerchove to Hymans, 28 May 1934, *DDB*, III, no. 131.

[4] Quoted in Georges Castellan, *Le Réarmament clandestine du Reich* (Paris, 1954),
pp. 459–60. The existence of this assumption was one of the things which the Belgians feared most. In 1933 Ambassador Kerchove suggested to Hymans a further
clarification of the military agreement, so that 'the German Government would
thus be obliged to stop including Belgium among the powers which, automatically,
are hostile to Germany and determined to attack her ...'. Hymans thought that
the earlier clarification was sufficient and did not follow up the suggestion. Kerchove to Hymans, 25 July 1933, *DDB*, III, no. 41 and Hymans to Kerchove, 8
Aug. 1933, no. 44.

[5] Everts to Hymans, 10 Mar. 1931, ibid., II, no. 239.

German–Belgian non-aggression pact. Simon's proposal was made shortly after de Broqueville's statement before the Belgian Senate on disarmament, and the Germans apparently thought that there was real prospect of a shift in Belgian foreign policy. They made an unofficial approach. The Belgians gave it a lukewarm reception. And the matter was forgotten.[1] But not for long. Joachim von Ribbentrop thought that Belgium could be lured away from France, and he believed that a solemn disavowal of Eupen and Malmédy would be a sufficient German *quid pro quo* for Belgian non-alignment. In September 1935 Ribbentrop travelled secretly to Brussels, where his suggestion met with a flat refusal.[2]

After their talks with Ribbentrop the Belgians never ceased to assure Berlin of their interest in better relations, but the Germans were given no solid reason to anticipate a significant change. Their embassy in Brussels reported to the Wilhelmstrasse that 'in view of the mood of her population and in view of her international position, Belgium could not afford to conclude a non-aggression pact with Germany and would still have to exercise a certain caution as regards emphasizing her friendly relations with Germany'.[3] Émile Vandervelde put it more succinctly when he remarked that the Belgian government did not want 'to furnish . . . M. von Ribbentrop with a pretext for making another visit here'.[4]

5. *Belgium, Italy, and the League of Nations*
Although the Belgians considered Locarno their most reliable guarantee, they placed high hopes in another: the League Covenant. Since the League's founding, Belgium had been one

[1] The Belgians might have been better disposed towards a treaty with the Germans if they could have obtained one from the British. Phipps to Simon, 21 June 1934, *Documents on British Foreign Policy* (London, 1957), ed. by E. L. Woodward and Rohan Butler, Ser. II, VI, no. 466. See also Minute by Vansittart, 24 May 1934, no. 431 and Simon to Phipps, 26 May 1934, no. 432; Hoesch to Neurath, 27 May 1934, *DGFP*, Ser. C, II, no. 467; and Memorandum by Hymans, 31 May 1934, *DDB*, III, no. 132.

[2] Erich Kordt, *Nicht aus der Akten* (Stuttgart, 1950), pp. 119–22. It is impossible to determine the exact nature of Ribbentrop's proposal, if he actually made a concrete proposal. He was not negotiating under Foreign Office auspices, and the only known record of these conversations is the rather sketchy one in the book by Kordt, who accompanied Ribbentrop on his trip to Brussels.

[3] Memorandum by Bräuer, 28 Dec. 1935, *DGFP*, Ser. C, IV, no. 477.

[4] Laroche to Flandin, 1 Feb. 1936, *DDF*, Ser. II, I, no. 123.

of its most enthusiastic participants. Hymans's election as President of the first General Assembly was a source of great pride. Throughout the 1920s the Belgian representatives at Geneva had worked hard to enlarge the role played by small states in League activities and had supported all attempts to strengthen the League's peace-keeping apparatus. Loyalty to the League was taken for granted by almost all Belgian politicians, with the familiar exception of the Flemish Nationalists.[1] It is thus ironic that fulfilment of League obligations during Italy's invasion of Ethiopia should give Belgians their first serious qualms about collective security.

Belgians valued Italian friendship highly. Both countries were Catholic, and they had close dynastic ties. 'Italy was one of our best customers', complained a liberal newspaper after the Ethiopian crisis began.[2] Economic sanctions did mean a heavy loss for Belgian exporters. But the worst aspect of Belgium's dilemma—essentially the same dilemma facing France and Britain—was that Italy was a guarantor of the Locarno agreements and therefore a guarantor of Belgium's boundaries. 'We will strictly oppose all violation of these arrangements', Mussolini had told the Belgians.[3] Belgians had warmly welcomed the birth of the short-lived Stresa Front, especially since Britain and Italy had on that occasion reaffirmed their loyalty to Locarno.[4] Would not sanctions against Mussolini's enterprise in Africa undermine the value of Italy's guarantee of the *status quo* in Western Europe? It is no wonder that sanctions were regarded in Belgium with mixed emotions. Only the Socialists supported them without hesitation. Many others were openly hostile. Some members of parliament felt that the safest course would be to remain neutral altogether.[5]

Mixed emotions notwithstanding, Belgium had little choice but to follow the French and British lead and to participate in sanctions. The same contradictions and indecisiveness which discredited the diplomacy of the two great powers was reflected

[1] Miller, *Belgian Foreign Policy between Two Wars*, pp. 209–12.
[2] France, Ministère des affaires étrangères, *Bulletin périodique de la presse belge*, no. 121, 7 Feb. 1936, p. 2. (Henceforth this will be cited as *BPB*.)
[3] Memorandum by Broqueville, 23 Sept. 1933, *DDB*, III, no. 49.
[4] Van Zeeland to Ovey, 4 May 1935, ibid., no. 152.
[5] *Le Peuple*, 4 Oct. 1935, p. 1; *L'Indépendance belge* 9 Oct. 1935, p. 3; and *BPB*, no. 120, 12 Nov. 1935, p. 7 and no. 121, 7 Feb. 1936, p. 2.

in the attitude of their little partner. 'Our country is simultaneously faithful and realistic', said the Belgian delegate at Geneva.[1] While Belgium faithfully fulfilled her obligations, her realistic Foreign Ministry assured the Italian government that Belgium meant nothing 'inimical' towards Italy.[2] It was the Belgian representative on the sanctions co-ordinating committee who proposed that France and Britain be delegated the responsibility of working out a compromise with Italy.[3] When this proposal led directly to the ill-starred Hoare-Laval plan, Brussels went on hoping for a compromise. The events of early 1936 would make one seem all the more urgent.

'In this unfortunate affair the Belgian Government did nothing of which to be ashamed', Pierre van Zuylen later wrote.[4] Belgium was, in fact, generally successful in not offending anybody, which was all a small power could hope for in such circumstances.

6. *Conclusion*

By the time sanctions against Italy ended in the summer of 1936, the problem of combining respect for solemn obligations with national self-interest, faith with realism, had assumed more formidable proportions. But the ingredients of Belgium's dilemma had existed for years. She had a special connection with France, which she did not want. She did want one with Great Britain, but she could not get it. She could have had a non-aggression pact with Germany, but she did not want one. She wanted cordial relations with Italy, but Mussolini's friendship was worthless. Such was Belgium's situation before 1936. Most politicians and voters had no idea how unsatisfactory their country's international position was. As usual, they were preoccupied with domestic events.

But the Foreign Ministry had few illusions. Belgium's most distinguished diplomat, Paul Hymans, put it this way to young

---

[1] *BPB*, no. 120, 12 Nov. 1935, p. 7.

[2] Ibid., no. 121, 7 Feb. 1936, pp. 4–5.

[3] Arnold J. Toynbee, *Survey of International Affairs, 1935* (London, 1936), II, 286–7 (Hereafter this will be cited as *Survey*); and Viscount Templewood, *Nine Troubled Years* (London, 1954), p. 173. The available evidence does not reveal whether the Belgian representative did this on his own initiative or at the behest of the French and the British.

[4] Van Zuylen, *Les Mains libres*, p. 321.

King Leopold shortly after his accession to the throne in 1934: If she [Belgium] follows France, she can, step by step, find herself in a war against Germany with France and her allies in central Europe without the support of England. She would risk material destruction and the rending of her national unity. For a defensive war, in which she was fighting for her independence, her territory, her honour, Belgium would find her way again as in 1914. But the risk of a political war, at the side of France alone, would be rejected by a large part of the country.[1]

In 1936 events both at home and abroad would dramatize these considerations for both the government and the people. Belgium would first sever her special connection with France, and then she would abandon collective security altogether.

[1] Report by Hymans to the Council of Ministers meeting under the presidency of the King, 24 Apr. 1934, *DDB*, III, no. 127.

II

POLITICS AND MILITARY REFORM

1. *The Depression*

Belgian political life in the early 1930s was dominated by the
Depression, which had had catastrophic consequences in a
country so heavily industrialized and so dependent on foreign
trade. One cabinet after another applied standard deflationary
measures without getting the expected results. By the end of
1934 the country was threatened with bankruptcy. Unemployment, an alarming gold outflow, shrinking internal trade, and a
growing government deficit indicated that Belgium was on the
brink of a major disaster. The futility of the government's
deflationary policy was all the more striking when viewed
against the background of reviving world trade. World prices
were far below Belgium's prices, and her industries were unable
to compete. Belgian business was approaching a 'state of suspended animation'.[1]

In retrospect, devaluation of the currency seems the obvious
solution to the predicament. In 1935, however, it was not
obvious to the Belgian public, which associated devaluation
with unpleasant memories of the inflationary process experienced in the 1920s. Nor was it obvious to the leaders of the
Catholic-Liberal coalition which had kept the upper hand in
Belgian politics since the end of the First World War. Most
Belgian politicians were economic conservatives. Keynesian
ideas about government involvement in the nation's economic
life seemed extravagant and dangerous to the bankers and
financiers who dominated the outgoing cabinet in March 1935.
Even when devaluation became inevitable, a majority of the
representatives in the Chamber of Deputies still supported the
defunct policies of the fallen government. Devaluation was

---

[1] *The Times* (London), 20 May, 1936, p. 17. See also Fernand Baudhuin,
Histoire économique de la Belgique (Brussels, 1946), I, 320–8.

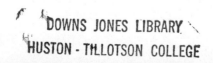

generally deplored, but no one seemed to have any better ideas.[1]

In order to understand how serious this crisis was, one must reflect on the complicated and delicate political structure of Belgium. Since the introduction of universal equal suffrage in 1919[2] no party had commanded a majority in national elections. Postwar reconstruction, inflation, and then the Depression were confronted by ordinarily short-lived coalition cabinets which were sometimes constructed on the basis of sheer political expediency and last-minute bargaining. The individual parties often imposed their vetoes on constructive approaches to Belgium's overwhelming problems. Cabinets were in the habit of resigning before a vote of 'no confidence'. Parliamentary efficiency was undermined by absenteeism and indecorous behaviour. In fact, the public's respect for the Senate and Chamber of Deputies was dwindling fast. The parliament seemed incapable of solving certain major problems. It was clearly incapable of coping with the Depression, just as it had been unable to prevent the fall of the franc in 1926. It was now customary to grant an incoming cabinet 'special powers'. Government 'technicians' were more trusted than the politicians. Many Belgians were wondering if the constitution of 1831 or, for that matter, parliamentary government in general were suited to the needs of the twentieth century.[3]

The failure of the political parties to work together constructively was only part of the story. Within the parties themselves there was just as much dissension. The Liberals could boast

[1] Frans van Kalken, *Entre deux guerres. Esquisse de la vie politique en Belgique de 1918 à 1940* (Brussels, 1945), p. 72; Carl-Henrik Höjer, *Le régime parlementaire belge de 1918 à 1940* (Uppsala, 1946), p. 236; Henry L. Shepherd, *The Monetary Experience of Belgium, 1914–1936* (Princeton, 1936), pp. 199–204; and Hymans, *Mémoires*, II, 737.

[2] Universal suffrage existed before the war, but its effects had been watered down by 'plural voting'. Some citizens, e.g., property owners, had more than one vote.

[3] Frans van Kalken, 'De Jaren van Crisis in België', in *Algemene Geschiedenis der Nederlanden* (Gouda, 1958), XII, 219–20 and John Bartier, 'La politique intérieur', in Henri Pirenne, *Histoire de Belgique des origines à nos jours* (Brussels, 1948), IV, 440. The most useful handbook of modern Belgian political history is Theo Luykx, *Politieke Geschiedenis van België van 1789 tot heden* (Brussels, 1964). An interesting, concise description of Belgian party politics from the early nineteenth century to the present is Val R. Lorwin's 'Belgium: Religion, Class, and Language in National Politics' in Robert A. Dahl, ed., *Political Oppositions in Western Democracies* (New Haven, 1966).

more internal harmony than the Socialists and the Catholics, but even among them the strain was evident. The myriad of fads, movements, and quarrels which pervaded the Belgian parties in the early 1930s does not lend itself easily to descriptive generalization. Perhaps the most which can be said of all the major parties is that they were experiencing a conflict of generations: 'The young of all parties had in common a greater faith than their elders in state intervention in economic, financial, and social questions.'[1]

This does not mean that there was a working consensus among the young, because the Belgian political spectrum contained elements of every ideological tendency then existing in western Europe. Most of those elements were present in the Catholic party, or 'Catholic Union', alone. Inside this loosely organized collection of interest-groups opinion ran the gamut from profound conservatism to a position approaching that of the Socialists. One segment of the party joined conservative Liberals in defending *laissez-faire* economic doctrines. Many young intellectuals flirted with the ideas of Charles Maurras and cast aspersions on Belgium's constitutional monarchy; others admired Pius XI's famous encyclical, *Quadragessimo Anno*, and demanded justice for the working classes. Although the Catholic Union was the largest party, differences between conservatives and 'Christian Democrats', not to mention those between Flemings and Walloons, rendered it far less effective than its numbers would indicate.[2]

Although they were better organized than the Catholics, the Socialists, or 'Belgian Labour Party', were in the throes of their own ideological struggle. Since the war the Socialists had almost equalled the Catholics in electoral strength, had sat in several cabinets, and had become an accepted and familiar part of Belgian political life. This was done under the leadership of Émile Vandervelde, who was a former President of the Second International. The old guard of Belgian socialism continued to profess its Marxist faith, and it paid lip-service to the notion of a final revolution. But one suspects that only Belgium's handful of Communists took these ideas seriously. Be that as it may, the

---

[1] Höjer, *Le Régime parlementaire belge de 1918 à 1940.* p. 237.

[2] Bartier in Pirenne, *Histoire de Belgique des origines à nos jours*, p. 438n and Chanoine A. Simon, *Le Parti catholique belge* (Brussels, 1958), pp. 111–15, 125–6.

ideological unity of the Socialists was challenged by the writings of Henri de Man, a Flemish intellectual whose influence in Belgium was analogous to that of Eduard Bernstein in Germany several decades earlier. De Man advocated the transformation rather than the overthrow of capitalism and argued that a peaceful change in the control of industry and the banking system would serve the interests of society better than a class conflict. He argued also, in Keynesian fashion, that the traditional methods of fighting economic depression were outmoded and that the policy of deflation should be replaced by one of active government participation in the nation's economy. De Man hoped that a Socialist programme revised along these lines would attract the support of the lower-middle-class, which, he feared, would stumble into fascism if it were not offered a promising alternative. De Man's ideas received a lukewarm reception from the old guard, but they appealed greatly to most Socialist voters and to young intellectuals. By late 1933 de Man's celebrated *Plan du Travail*, his blueprint for a 'new deal', had been accepted as part of the official Socialist platform. His most ardent and influential convert was a gifted young firebrand who until his encounter with de Man had been one of the party's most radical leaders and the editor of a semi-Trotskyite newspaper (as well as a one-time Davis Cup tennis player)—Paul-Henri Spaak.[1]

A representative system of government which gave expression to every shade of opinion from fascism on the right to communism on the left would have made Belgian politics hectic enough. However, every ideological and factional dispute was compounded by the ceaseless tension between Flemings and Walloons. One marvels that the government functioned as well as it did.

The struggle of the Flemings to achieve equality in the political, social, and cultural life of their country had begun in the mid-nineteenth century. It was a struggle unlike that of other oppressed nationalities, because the Flemings constituted the

[1] Baudhuin, *Histoire économique de la Belgique*, I, 337–41; Mieke Claeys-van Haegendoren, *25 Jaar Belgisch Socialisme. Evoluties van de Verhouding van de Belgische Werkliedenpartij tot de parlementaire democratie in België van 1914 tot 1940* (Antwerp, 1967), pp. 311–39; Peter Dodge, *Beyond Marxism: the Faith and Works of Hendrik de Man* (The Hague, 1966), pp. 129–63; and J. H. Huizinga, *Mr. Europe. A Political Biography of Paul-Henri Spaak* (London, 1961), pp. 56–60.

majority of the Belgian population.[1] Until the First World War Flemish leaders sought only modest linguistic reforms within the existing constitutional framework. The experience of the war itself, which greatly intensified Flemish national consciousness and the postwar advent of universal equal suffrage accelerated achievement of the Flemings's 'minimalist' programme: by the early 1930s their language had achieved at least legal equality in every dimension of Belgian life. The vast majority of Flemings were loyal Belgians, and during the war most had remained impervious to the charms of separatism held out by the Germans during the long occupation[2] 'We Flemings do not care to be either French *sans culottes,* or Prussian

MAP 2: Belgium's linguistic frontier

[1] Approximately 61 per cent versus 39 per cent. Probably the closest parallel to Flemish nationalism is Irish nationalism. The Catholic priesthood played an important and similar role in both movements. Likewise, both involved class conflict, although in Belgium this aspect of the movement was more subtle and complex.

[2] The best recent accounts of Flemish separatism during the First World War are found in the study by Willemsen, *Het Vlaamse-Nationalisme 1914–1940,* and in the memoir by J. Wullus-Rudiger, *En la marge de la politique belge, 1914–1956* (Brussels, 1957).

slaves, or Dutch heretics', ran the nineteenth century saying.[1] This remained the prevailing sentiment in Flanders.

Unfortunately, the First World War gave birth to the most disruptive new element in Belgian politics. A few Flemings, known as 'Activists', had co-operated with the German invader and sought to detach Flanders from Wallonia. The result was a legacy of distrust and suspicion between the two linguistic groups. After the war some discontented veterans joined ranks with the Activists and founded a small but flamboyant party of extremists who did more than anyone to envenom parliamentary life. The Flemish Nationalists—sometimes called 'Frontists' because many had served in the trenches during the war— became a bigger problem after 1933, when they reorganized themselves in the *Vlaams Nationaal Verbond* (Flemish National Union). The *VNV* and its *Leider* (Leader), Staf de Clerq, admired the Nazis, talked about building a corporative state, and advocated the division of Belgium. In at least a few Flemish hearts there always lurked a desire for the union of Flanders with the Netherlands. It was hoped that passage of the new language legislation would immunize Flemings to this kind of extremism. However, the half-hearted application of the new laws caused more and more Flemings to wonder whether some form of federalization might be their only road to national fulfilment.[2] Because many Belgians were already dubious about the future of parliamentary government, the programme of the *VNV* was all the more attractive and thus all the more dangerous. The *VNV* was winning members, and its ideas were making headway among Flemish Catholics.[3]

By early 1935 the Belgian public was disillusioned and dissatisfied with its leaders. A small minority would have welcomed a basic change in the structure of the Belgian state. A majority agreed that a basic change in the composition of the government was now essential. It was clear that any new cabinet

[1] Quoted in Vandervelde, *Foreign Affairs* (1933), XI, 4, 667.
[2] The best history of Flemish nationalism after the First World War is Willemsen, *Het Vlaamse-Nationalisme 1914–1940*. See also Shephard B. Clough, 'The Flemish Movement', in Jan-Albert Goris ed., *Belgium* (Berkeley, 1946), pp. 108–26; Lorwin in Dahl, ed. *Political Oppositions in Western Democracies*, pp. 158–64; and Bartier in Pirenne, *Histoire de Belgique des origines à nos jours*, pp. 439–40.
[3] Willemsen, *Het Vlaamse-Nationalisme 1914–1940*, pp. 257–8

would need the support of a broad coalition, a union of the three major parties. Such a coalition would be the only one capable of generating the confidence and parliamentary votes needed to execute drastic economic measures. Therefore, great enthusiasm greeted the news that King Leopold III had invited Paul van Zeeland to head a government of national union in order 'to accomplish the economic renovation of the country'.[1] It was enthusiasm mixed with desperation. As van Zeeland himself later wrote: 'Joints were cracking in the whole national community.'[2]

2. Paul van Zeeland

Van Zeeland was the youngest man ever to become Belgian Prime Minister, and he had had little experience in politics. Six months as a minister-without-portfolio was the sum of it. He was the only Prime Minister since the 1880s without a formal connection with a political party. Van Zeeland had made his reputation as an economist. He was a professor at Louvain, a vice-governor of the National Bank of Belgium, and the spokesman for a group of economists who thought that deflationary measures were leading their country to ruin.[3]

Van Zeeland's personality and interests were unconventional for a Belgian politician. He was soft-spoken and courtly, and he did not comfortably fit into the Chamber of Deputies, which was the scene of perpetual commotion. The new Prime Minister was not a spellbinder, and sometimes he could not even make himself heard. However, in the cabinet or in other small groups where he could exercise quietly his extraordinary powers of persuasion, van Zeeland worked very effectively. He was intensely intellectual and elegantly educated, holding doctorates in law and Thomistic theology from Louvain as well as a degree in economics from Princeton University. 'If there is one thing I fear', he said, 'if there is one stage in the development of ideas which I detest, it is confusion.'[4] His devotion to cool rationality

[1] Quoted in Höjer, *Le Régime parlementaire belge de 1918 à 1940*, p. 239.
[2] ***, *The Van Zeeland Experiment* (New York, 1943), trans. by Helene van Gelder, p. 5.
[3] Baudhuin, *Histoire économique de la Belgique*, I, 335–7.
[4] Quoted in Jean Duchesne, *1934–1940. Un tournant dans l'histoire de Belgique* (Brussels, 1967), p. 74. For descriptions of van Zeeland's background and personality, see Jean Albert Noville, *Paul van Zeeland au service de son temps* (Brussels,

and order was, in one respect, a handicap. He was never completely at home in Belgian political life, which was always disorderly and which became more disorderly than ever during
his two-and-a-half years as Prime Minister. Van Zeeland was
accustomed to success and unaccustomed to criticism. This was
also a handicap in a profession in which no one enjoys perpetual
success and in a country where no politician can do more than
keep all the parties and factions in a state of mild dissatisfaction.
In Belgium, if one group was completely happy, some other
group was completely unhappy. There was no ultimate, perfect
solution to Belgium's problems, although van Zeeland tried very
hard to find one.

The new Prime Minister was more at home in the world of
diplomacy. He also assumed the post of Foreign Minister, a
position for which his patrician tastes and extensive education
suited him well. Like his good friend and contemporary,
Anthony Eden, whom he closely resembled, van Zeeland became a well-known and respected figure in international politics. Unfortunately, there was no perfect solution to Belgium's
international problems either.

Van Zeeland's youth and relative unfamiliarity to most
Belgians account for the instant enthusiasm of a public which
knew the old leaders only too well. Most members of van Zeeland's fifteen-man cabinet were young. Five were in office for the
first time; four others had held office for only the briefest periods.
Vandervelde and Hymans represented the older generation,
but they were ministers-without-portfolio. Another conspicu-
ous feature of the new government was that it was very radical,
at least by Belgian standards. Ten ministers were clearly progressive or 'democratic'.[1] The coming to office of Henri de Man
and Paul-Henri Spaak suggested the beginning of a new political era, especially to a public which had experienced fifteen
years of honest but unimaginative government. Spaak, the
'Benjamin of the outfit', was only thirty-six years old.[2]

Van Zeeland's plans were very ambitious. To renovate the

1954), pp. 11–12; Verax, 'M. Paul van Zeeland', in *Revue des deux mondes* (Paris,
1936), XXXII, 520–32; and Spaak, *Combats inachevés*, pp. 30–3.

[1] Höjer, *Le Régime parlementaire belge de 1918 à 1940*, pp. 240–1.

[2] *The Van Zeeland Experiment*, p. 38. De Man was Minister of Public Works, and
Spaak was Minister of Transport.

economy was only part of his programme. He wanted also to reform Belgium's political institutions and to render her government more efficient. He intended to initiate extensive social reforms and to improve the quality of Belgian life in general. But the economy came first: 'When a ship hits the rocks and is in danger of sinking, the first step is to stop the leaks, and try to limit the damage.'[1] The most important aspects of his first programme were devaluation of the currency, a lowering of taxes and interest rates, increased government control of banks, and extensive public works projects. In other words, Belgium received a 'new deal'. The 'experiment' produced dramatic results within months. Unemployment declined, gold returned to the country, internal trade revived, and the standard of living rose. The economy was climbing from the doldrums to what seemed like a new 'boom'. Van Zeeland's sharpest critics conceded that his accomplishments were impressive. The Chamber of Deputies, which had only grudgingly given him a vote of confidence in March 1935, awarded him an ovation one year later. The Prime Minister commanded more prestige and confidence than any of his postwar predecessors.[2] Most important, van Zeeland had given Belgians hope. Many pessimists now allowed that perhaps there was a middle way, that the fabric of Belgian society might be preserved, and that parliamentary government could have a future in Belgium.

The story, alas, does not end here. The great paradox of van Zeeland's short political career was that the more successful his economic policies became, the more dispensable their author became. The restoration of economic health eliminated the primary reason for the government coalition's existence and thus threatened to open again the Pandora's box of discord still present in Belgian politics. *Laissez-faire* Liberals who were frankly impressed with van Zeeland's skill as a manipulator of the economy were not so impressed when they later got

[1] Ibid. This book, whose author is anonymous, is the most thorough description of van Zeeland's domestic programme and accomplishments. More concise descriptions are Shepherd, *The Monetary Experience of Belgium*, pp. 207–230; Baudhuin, *Histoire économique de la Belgique*, I, 342–52; and van Kalken, *Entre deux guerres*, pp. 74–5.

[2] At the end of his long career Spaak wrote 'I have rarely, I believe that I can write that I have never seen a Prime Minister enjoy as much prestige in the country and exercise as much influence over the parliament.' Spaak, *Combats inachevés*, p. 31.

acquainted with his plans for social reforms. Socialists who were likewise awed by his skill as an economist were less awed by his other plans, which, in their opinion, did not go far enough or move fast enough.[1] As long as van Zeeland concentrated on strictly economic problems, he was the undisputed master; as soon as he turned to other matters, his support would waver. It was already wavering in one section of the population. Lower-middle-class creditors and *rentiers* were not enjoying the 'devaluation honeymoon'. They were more discouraged by their own short-term losses than they were enthusiastic about their country's reviving economy.[2] For whom would these people vote in the general election of 1936?

Such considerations notwithstanding, in late 1935 most Belgians looked forward confidently to the coming year. Van Zeeland's popularity was immense, and it was assumed that his tripartite coalition would continue. The three main topics of domestic discussion were that the Prime Minister's special powers would soon end, that an election was impending and that the parliament was about to discuss the important question of military reform.[3]

3. Albert Devèze and his Military Reform Project

Among the matters which were a perennial source of trouble for Belgian politicians, none was so important and potentially so disruptive as national defence. It was natural that a country which had been neutral for almost a century should have little pride in a military tradition. But it was unnatural that a country so exposed geographically should be so reluctant to make the sacrifices necessary for effective defence. The fact is that in the early 1930s the Belgian army was under-manned and under-equipped; its fortifications were weak; its morale was low.

The most formidable obstacle to the Belgian defence effort after the war was the anti-militarism of the Socialists and the left-wing Catholics, the Christian Democrats, most of whom were Flemish. The anti-militarism of both groups had traditional roots. Socialist internationalism, Christian pacifism, a reluctance to compel large families to bear the heavy burden of

---

[1] Luykx, *Politieke Geschiedenis van België van 1789 tot heden*, p. 364 and *The Van Zeeland Experiment*, p. 123.

[2] Ibid., pp. 112–7.   [3] *Le Peuple*, 31 Jan. 1936, pp. 1–2.

conscription, and the desire to use available funds for other purposes were part of Flemish and Socialist thinking. Such thinking was reinforced by simple war-weariness and the disillusionment which followed the occupation of the Ruhr in 1923. The presence of Socialists and 'Christian Democrats' in the German government during the 1920s helped to create a false sense of security, as did the so-called 'spirit of Locarno'. What little concern for national defence remained was weakened further by the Depression. As the government deficit grew, the ordinary expenditures for defence were constantly reduced.[1]

Another factor which aggravated and confused the military question was the existence of two schools of thought on how Belgian defences should be structured. Some military men, 'the school of General Maglinse', argued that the army should defend Belgium at her frontiers. Maglinse, who was Chief of Staff from 1919 to 1926 and who signed the Military Agreement with France, thought, as did most French generals, that the First World War had demonstrated the weakness of isolated fortifications and the impregnability of a continuous frontier equipped with all the resources of modern technology. His followers wanted extensive border fortifications and a large number of men under arms. These were the essentials of a system which would make the Belgian army the natural extension of the French army. 'Integral defence of the frontier' found its warmest political support in the Walloon-dominated Liberal Party because geography had fated Wallonia to undergo the first impact of an invasion from the East.[2]

The 'school of General Galet' was more popular in Flanders. Galet was King Albert's aide-de-camp during the war, was head of the *École militaire* after the war, and finally became Chief of Staff in 1929. Among his most devoted admirers was Colonel Robert van Overstraeten, who was King Leopold's aide-de-camp and who later was considered by the French to be

---

[1] *BPB*, no. 121, 12 Feb., 1936, p. 23; J. Wullus-Rudiger, *La Défense de la Belgique en 1940* (Villeneuve-sur-Lot, 1940), pp. 106–8; and Colonel B. E. M. Gilbert, *L'Armée dans la nation* (Brussels, 1941), pp. 30–45. For the attitude of the Socialists on military questions, see Claeys-van Haegendoren, *25 Jaar Belgisch Socialisme*, pp. 423–4.

[2] Van Overstraeten, *Albert I. Léopold III. Vingt ans de politique militaire belge*, pp. 41–2 and Oberkommando des Heeres, General Stab des Heeres, *Denkschrift über die belgische Landesbefestigung* (Berlin, 1941), pp. 27–9.

the 'evil genius' behind the King's actions in 1940. Galet and his disciples were very dubious about the value of the military agreement with France. They were dubious also about the value of assistance from a French army which was, in their opinion, insufficiently trained, insufficiently mobile, and wedded to a mistaken concept of war.[1] As opposed to the Maglinse school, they argued that Belgium should rely on her great rivers and fortresses like Liège and Antwerp and that she would be better served by a smaller but better equipped, very mobile professional army which, if necessary, could retreat to a position behind the Scheldt River and with British assistance hold out indefinitely.[2] Because this plan was less expensive and required fewer conscripts, it appealed to many members of parliament. Unfortunately, the area west of the Scheldt was entirely Flemish. Furthermore, the concept 'defence in depth' implied the immediate abandonment of a Walloon province, Luxembourg. It is no wonder that the ideas of General Galet were not as well received in Wallonia as they were elsewhere.[3]

Because the Socialists and Christian Democrats were either lukewarm or hostile in the matter of national defence, it was left to the Liberals and conservative Catholics to defend the interests of the army and to provide Belgium's ministers of defence. There was no more able and controversial advocate of a strong army than Albert Devèze, who was President of the Liberal Party and who became Minister of Defence in 1932 and remained in that position for four years. Devèze was energetic, intelligent, and formidable in debate; he was at home in both the French and Flemish languages. His ability and expert knowledge of military affairs were conceded by everybody. However,

[1] Van Overstraeten, *Albert I. Léopold III. Vingt ans de politique militaire belge*, pp. 47–55.

[2] The theories of Galet and van Overstraeten resemble those of Charles de Gaulle. De Gaulle was, in fact, among the first Frenchmen to anticipate Belgium's defection from the French system and among the few to sympathize at all with Belgium's 'policy of independence.' Charles de Gaulle, *Vers l'armée de métier* (Paris, 1944), pp. 28–9 and 'Le problème belge', in *Revue des questions de défense nationale* (Paris, 1945), New Series, I, 1–5. See also Lieutenant-General Galet, *Albert. King of the Belgians in the Great War* (London, 1931), trans. by Major-General Sir Ernest Swinton, pp. 8–10, 69–70 and Capitaine-Commandant R. van Overstraeten, *Des principes de la guerre à travers les ages*, I, i–iv.

[3] Wullus-Rudiger, *La Défense de la Belgique en 1940*, pp. 166–70; Général van Overstraeten, *Au service de la Belgique. Dans l'étau* (Paris, 1960), pp. 20–3; *Denkschrift*, pp. 27–9; and van Kalken, *Entre deux guerres*, p. 69.

because he was a Liberal, he was distrusted by the Socialists. Because he was an ardent *francophone*, he was detested by the *flamingants*.[1] Because he was the most articulate exponent of the Maglinse school, he was the *bête noire* of the Galet school and therefore no favourite at the Royal Palace. Both Albert and Leopold were firm supporters of General Galet and his disciple, General Nuyten, who succeeded Galet as Chief of Staff in 1932 and whom Devèze eventually forced out of office.[2]

The debate about military strategy had very unfortunate consequences. First of all, it politicized and thus over-dramatized issues which should have been left to experts. Devèze himself was partly to blame for this. He thoroughly enjoyed being Minister of Defence.[3] And he liked to talk. The more he talked, the more popular and the more hated he became.[4] When a non-party technician replaced Devèze in 1936, the atmosphere improved immediately. By then, however, most of the damage was done. Secondly, the existence of two schools of thought on strategy worried the French unnecessarily. They wondered whether the Belgian army, led by its ill-advised King, would retire without a fight to its Flemish redoubt and throw open to the Germans a convenient doorway to France. This nightmare haunted the French, and their suspicions about Leopold and his advisers took firm root long before the catastrophe of 1940. The fact is that the Belgians never seriously contemplated retiring without a fight to a position behind the Scheldt, and French suspicions and inquiries served only to insult Belgian pride and to render relations between the two countries still worse.[5] Finally, the tension between the King and the General Staff, on the one hand, and the Ministry of Defence, on the other, was extremely awkward.[6] The King was Commander-in-Chief of

[1] *Francophone* and *flamingant* were the words used to denote advocates of the Walloon and Flemish causes.

[2] British ambassador Ovey noted apropos Nuyten's dismissal and the public's approval of it that 'integral defence of the frontier' was a 'creed which tolerates no heresies'. Ovey to Simon, 16 Oct. 1934, FO, 432/1/C6868/12/4.

[3] He was even credited with 'Napoleonic aspirations', a distinction achieved by few Belgians. Memorandum by Ovey, 2 Jan. 1935, ibid., C16/16/4.

[4] 'He plays to the gallery and talks far too much', reported Ambassador Ovey. Ovey to Wigram, 23 June 1936, ibid., 371/19849/C4574/202/4.

[5] The Foreign Ministry in Brussels began receiving these inquiries in 1936.

[6] The French were fully aware of the situation, and their military attaché acted accordingly. He did his business with the Ministry of Defence instead of the General Staff. Granville to Vansittart, 4 May 1933, FO, 371/16740/C4041/1788/18.

the army in times of war; the Minister of Defence was responsible for the army to parliament in times of peace. An open
quarrel between them would have served no one's purposes.
It was hard enough getting military legislation through the
parliament even in the best circumstances. Furthermore, the
argument between the Royal Palace and the Defence Ministry
concerned means, not ends.[1] A compromise was both necessary
and possible. Devèze discovered that Belgium's meagre resources
would not permit him to fortify substantially the entire frontier,
and he adjusted his plans accordingly.[2] Leopold and his advisers admitted that Devèze's ambitious programme for fortifying the frontier would contribute something to Belgium's
security.[3] And they gave the Defence Minister their grudging
support.

It is easy to see why the concept 'integral defence of the
frontier' was so appealing in the 1930s, even if the events of
1940 did vindicate its critics. Permanent frontier defences
seemed most desirable at a time when military thinkers were re-
evaluating the potential of offensive warfare. The increased
mobility of an attacking army might deprive Belgium of the
time necessary to mobilize her reserves, while an air attack
could incapacitate her railroads. Moreover, the fact that the
Maginot Line did not cover the Franco-Belgian frontier made a
German invasion of France through Belgium all the more
probable.[4] While considerations like these had troubled the
experts for years, events in Germany were disposing the Belgian
public to think more seriously about their country's lagging
defences. Devèze was therefore given a careful hearing when he
began his campaign to convince Belgians that the country
needed a permanent screen behind which the reserves could
mobilize and which would give the French and British ample

[1] Some observers thought that the whole quarrel was much exaggerated. Ovey to
Wigram, 23 June 1936, FO, 371/19849/C4574/202/4 and minute by Rumbold, 9
June, 1936, ibid., 19850/C4189/270/4.
[2] He discovered that there were insufficient resources for the heavy fortification
of Belgian Luxembourg. Instead, he placed there only shelters for machine gunners
which were quickly dubbed 'political pill boxes'. It was assumed that their primary
function was to help Devèze save face before his Walloon constituency. Ibid.
[3] Van Overstraeten, Dans l'étau, p. 45.
[4] The Belgian government deeply regretted that the French had not extended the
Maginot Line from Longwy to the Channel coast. Gaiffier to Hymans, 5 Jan.,
1933, DDB, III, no. 4 and Gaiffier to Hymans, 6 Nov. 1933, no. 78.

time to come to Belgium's rescue.[1] Although the ordinary budget was being compromised by the government's deflationary measures, Devèze squeezed from parliament extraordinary credits for improving equipment, motorizing certain divisions, and strengthening fortifications.[2] None the less, as late as December 1935 an essential part of his programme was unrealized. In fact, it had not yet been introduced to parliament.

The Belgian army was badly handicapped by the brevity of the period of compulsory military service. The wave of optimism and anti-militarism in the 1920s had caused its reduction to eight months. This meant that the maximum number of troops could be kept at the frontier from April through October only, which was assumed to be the most dangerous time of the year. Because the incoming and outgoing classes did not overlap, the army was under-garrisoned from November until March. 'The system of defence (couverture) ought to be permanent', said Devèze; 'the danger is permanent.'[3] In December it was revealed that the Defence Minister would request a revision of the law which determined the length of military service. By February 1936, when Devèze laid before parliament a bill providing for an eighteen-month period of service, a full-scale debate was already under way.

The Socialists never tired of insisting that they wanted Belgium to have adequate defences and that they were committed to no particular strategic school of thought. However, if the number of troops was sufficient one year earlier, why was such a drastic reform needed now? Some Socialists suspected that Devèze had concealed his intentions in order to guarantee their participation in the van Zeeland government and that they had been tricked.[4] Their leadership was divided. The General Council of the party first instructed the Socialist members of the cabinet to support the proposed reform. But there was so much popular dislike of the eighteen-month period of

[1] Lt. Colonel C. Requette, 'Serions nous prêts', in La revue belge (Brussels, 1936), II, no. 1, 221–33; Richard Whittier, 'Belgium emphasizes Security', in Contemporary Review (London, 1937), CLI, no. 853, 29–37; and Documents parlementaires (Chamber), 1935/1936, no. 96, p. 2.

[2] BPB, no. 121, 12 Feb. 1936, p. 23 and Wullus-Rudiger, La Défense de la Belgique en 1940, pp. 167–8.

[3] BPB, no. 121, 12 Feb. 1936, p. 23.

[4] Le Peuple, 2 Feb. 1936, pp. 1–2; 5 Feb. 1936, p. 1; and 6 Feb. 1936, p. 1.

service that a special congress of the party was convened to consider the whole matter. Almost every speaker attacked the proposal and expressed distrust of Devèze. The upshot was a nearly unanimous resolution asking that the military question be submitted to a commission of inquiry and offering a formula which Socialists could support without reservation—'a minimum of sacrifice with a maximum of return'.[1] No one could object to that formula.

The reaction of the Flemish Catholics paralleled that of the Socialists. They objected to the abrupt fashion in which the Devèze plan had been introduced. Although few denied the possibility of a military reform, they all wanted more precise information and, like the Socialists, they hoped that the question would be submitted to a commission for further examination.[2] The criticism of certain Flemish newspapers was less cautious. It was noted that a national election was imminent. Devèze and the Liberal Party were accused of political opportunism. The most influential Flemish organ, De Standaard, put it this way: 'the Liberal Party needs an electoral platform and an aura of patriotism, the country is suddenly in danger and our national defences are inadequate . . .'[3]

Devèze must have known that his project would exacerbate all the old suspicions surrounding the Franco-Belgian Military Agreement. His critics immediately pointed out that 'integral defence of the frontier' bore a striking resemblance to 'extension of the Maginot Line'. Émile Vandervelde remarked privately that the proposed reform could be explained only if Devèze intended to make the Belgian army the left wing of the French army.[4] The organ of the Socialist party, Le Peuple, argued that Belgium should be prepared to defend herself, while taking care not to become entangled in an alliance system like the one which caused the World War. The Agreement with France should be made public, or it should be denounced.[5] In mid-February the Flemish Catholics of both the Chamber of Deputies and Senate endorsed a statement saying that the Agreement

[1] Ibid., 24 Feb. 1936, p. 1. See also ibid., 23 Feb. 1936, pp. 1, 3; L'Indépendance belge, 7 Feb. 1936, pp. 1, 3; and The Times, 25 Feb. 1936, p. 13.
[2] Le Peuple, 5 Feb. 1936, p. 3 and L'Indépendance belge, 26 Feb. 1936, p. 3.
[3] BPB, no. 121, 12 Feb. 1936, p. 21.
[4] Laroche to Flandin, 5 Feb. 1936, DDF, Ser. II, I, no. 137.
[5] Le Peuple, 26 Feb. 1936, p. 1 and BPB, no. 122, 23 May 1936, p. 10.

with France had always troubled the Flemish population, that 'certain ministerial declarations have added a new element to this distrust'[1] and that the 'moral forces of the country have been weakened' by the Agreement.[2] One observer noted that Flemish orators were convincing their audiences that Belgium was no more than a *département* of the French Republic.[3]

Devèze was not the man to leave criticism unanswered. He insisted that his plan was strictly defensive and Belgian in its orientation and that it had no connection with the Franco-Belgian Military Agreement.[4] When the Socialists asked why no fundamental change had been necessary a year earlier, Devèze pointed to the worsening international situation. He argued also that the only way the eastern and northern frontiers could be adequately protected without lengthening the period of service was to remove troops from the south and west; this would satisfy no one.[5] He summed up his argument this way: 'This project is not mine, it is that of the General Staff of the army, it is that of the best qualified technicians. They have studied every angle of the problem long and carefully. It is absolutely wrong that there are any hidden political motives.'[6]

Although his critics remained unconvinced, Devèze could take comfort in the knowledge that most Belgian politicians now agreed that some sort of military reform was necessary. The trouble was that everyone wanted it on his own terms. The need for stronger fortifications and better equipment was generally conceded. But eighteen months of compulsory military service was a different matter. The only party which gave Devèze

---

[1] This was a reference to some badly timed and tactless remarks about the Military Agreement made by Devèze and the Liberal Minister of Public Instruction, Bovesse, who said publicly that it would be 'mad' and 'criminal' to abandon the Military Agreement. Ovey to Eden, 7 Feb. 1936, FO, 432/2/C778/270/4.

[2] *L'Indépendance belge*, 19 Feb. 1936, pp. 1, 3.

[3] Ibid., 14 Feb. 1936, p. 1.

[4] The available evidence suggest that this was indeed the case. In fact, the French military was unenthusiastic about that aspect of Devèze's programme which concerned the fortification of the frontier itself. The French generals would have preferred that the Belgians concentrate on strengthening their natural lines of defence like the one along the Meuse River. Van Overstraeten, *Albert I. Léopold III*, pp. 146–7, 162–4. See also Paget to Wigram, 3 Mar. 1936, FO, 371/19850/C1356/270/4.

[5] Many Belgian soldiers served in units stationed near their homes.

[6] *L'Indépendance belge*, 25 Feb. 1936, p. 1.

wholehearted support was his own Liberal Party. When in late February his proposal was put to a preliminary vote in the Chamber of Deputies, almost all the Socialists and Flemish Catholics combined with the Flemish Nationalists and the Communists to defeat it by a substantial margin.[1]

This was a bad setback for Paul van Zeeland and his government of national union, and its timing could not have been worse. Military questions did not fall within the special powers which had been granted to him in March 1935 and which were now about to run out. The most successful coalition in years had been looking forward confidently to the coming election. Now there was an issue which threatened to leave it in a shambles. Van Zeeland himself indicated privately that his government would resign if the essence of Devèze's reform was not accepted soon.[2] But even the members of his cabinet were now arguing among themselves about 'defence in depth' à la Galet and 'integral defence of the frontier' à la Maglinse.[3] It is not surprising that the government took the line of least resistance and accepted the Socialist and Flemish suggestion that the whole matter be submitted to a mixed commission of inquiry.[4]

Parliamentary investigation and government procrastination might postpone a crisis. There was some hope that the experts would find an acceptable compromise. None the less, van Zeeland and his associates knew that this issue was dangerous. No other issue touched simultaneously so many sensitive nerves in Belgian politics. No other touched so directly that most sensitive nerve in Belgian foreign policy—the Military Agreement with France. In order to induce Belgians to shoulder their military obligations, the van Zeeland government would have to convince them, once and for all, that their army was strictly national and served Belgian interests alone.

---

[1] Ibid., 28 Feb. 1936, p. 3.

[2] Ovey to Eden, 6 Mar. 1936, FO, 371/19850/C1456/270/4.

[3] Henri de Man, *Après coup* (Brussels, 1941), pp. 260–2. De Man was one of those who argued on behalf of a small, mobile professional army. See also Laroche to Flandin, Feb. 1936, *DDF*, Ser. II, I, no. 136 and van Overstraeten, *Albert I. Léopold III*, pp. 194–200.

[4] *Documents parlementaires* (Senate), 1935/1936, no. 202, p. 2 and Ovey to Eden, 31 Mar. 1936, FO, 371/19850/C2562/270/4. The commission was formally constituted in late March and included army men as well as members of the parliament.

4. The End of the Franco-Belgian Military Agreement

The great debate about military reform caught the attention of the Belgian public at a time when popular dissatisfaction with France was more intense than at any time since the war. The sudden incursion of the military question was bound to make matters worse. What made these months unique was that for the first time Flemish complaints about France were being echoed by many Walloons.

There were a number of reasons for France's unpopularity, and two of them could have been eliminated if an alert French government had realized the intensity of Belgian feelings. First, of all, there were the barriers which hindered the flow of Belgian goods to French markets. For years Belgian exporters had felt that they were being treated unfairly by the French. When the Depression induced the Paris government to impose import quotas on top of its high protective tariff, the Belgians were more handicapped and more annoyed than ever. No effective method of adjusting commercial relations between the two countries was found until mid-1936, and by then the damage to France's reputation was done.[1] No less irritating and much more publicized was French treatment of the thousands of Walloon labourers who crossed the border daily to work in French factories. The Belgians were discriminated against in the matter of salaries, and the French government had placed a quota on the number of Belgians permitted to work in France. Paris indicated a willingness to satisfy Belgian demands, but in early 1936 this problem, too, remained outstanding.[2] Belgians had always resented French condescension, real or imagined, towards *les petits belges*, and now they resented it more than ever. A stage revue then playing in Brussels had the following exchange 'As for you, *les petits belges*, our hearts are wide open to you', a Frenchman was made to say. 'Yes', was the Belgian reply, 'but your frontiers are closed.'[3]

[1] *The Times*, 18 Oct. 1935, p. 13; *BPB*, no. 121, 12 Feb. 1936, pp. 6–9; and Miller, *Belgian Foreign Policy Between Two Wars*, pp. 196–8. In May 1936 the two governments agreed to hold biannual meetings for the purpose of adjusting commercial relations and dealing with commercial problems as they arose.

[2] *Documents parlementaires* (Senate), 1935/1936, no. 27, pp. 6–8; *BPB*, no. 121, 12 Feb. 1936, p. 6; and *The Times*, 29 Jan. 1936, p. 9.

[3] Quoted ibid., 20 May 1936, p. 17.

Problems like import quotas and the salaries of *frontaliers* were negotiable and would have had less significance if they had arisen at another time. Far more momentous were the questions raised by the conclusion of the Franco-Soviet Pact in May 1935. Belgians were apprehensive about the implications of this treaty, and government assurances that Belgium was unaffected by it did little to allay their misgivings. Belgium had been among the last European countries to recognize the Soviet Union, and she had done so in 1935 only because the Socialists had made recognition a prerequisite for their participation in the van Zeeland government. Diplomatic relations with Moscow did lead to some advantageous commercial arrangements, but these could never compensate for the profound suspicion of the Soviet Union felt by Catholic and middle-class Belgians.[1] Furthermore, the actual ratification of the Franco-Soviet. Pact in February 1936 took place at a time when Belgians were giving more than their usual attention to French foreign policy. A War Ministry memorandum described the situation concisely: 'The ratification of the treaty and, all the more, a Franco-Soviet military agreement, would risk unfortunate consequences for us in Belgium at the moment . . . when the Franco-Belgian Military Agreement is being violently attacked.'[2]

If France went to the aid of her new ally, might not Belgium be dragged along? This question inevitably connected the Military Agreement with the Franco-Soviet Pact at the very moment when the debate about national defence was reaching a climax. To be sure, Belgian feelings about this were varied and complex, and they are difficult to summarize. The Socialists considered the Franco-Soviet Pact a great contribution to European stability, while they regarded the Military Agreement as useless. The Liberals had the opposite viewpoint: France's connection with the Soviet Union was dangerous, but the maintenance of the Military Agreement was essential. Of course, the Military Agreement seemed more dangerous than ever to Flemish Catholics and Nationalists, whose leading newspaper, *De Standard*, characterized the Franco-Soviet Pact as 'the

[1] Miller, *Belgian Foreign Policy Between Two Wars*, pp. 216–20.
[2] War Ministry memorandum, 27 Jan. 1936, *DDF*, Ser. II, I, no. 106.

triumphal march of Bolshevism'.[1] Whatever the shade of their opinion most Belgians would have accepted this description of their dilemma in the influential Walloon paper, *Le Libre Belgique*:

The problem, alas, is not so simple. If one segment of our opinion— which does not include Flemings only—desires the denunciation of the agreement of 1920, it is without doubt because the international situation appears singularly more troubled than fifteen years ago; it is because the policy of eastern alliances pursued by France and especially the Franco-Soviet Pact threaten to involve our southern neighbour in perilous military adventures; and, in the last analysis, [it is because] many Belgians fear seeing our country herself entangled in the wake of France in the dreadful cog-wheels of a war from which we ought to remain far removed.[2]

Never had so many Belgians, both Fleming and Walloon, been so sceptical and worried about their country's connection with France.

The French were inclined to interpret the agitation against the Military Agreement as evidence of widespread 'neutralism'.[3] They were mistaken. The only group represented in the parliament which was, strictly speaking 'neutralist' was the Flemish Nationalists, whose influence was then negligible. The overwhelming majority of Belgians did not want the denunciation of the Locarno agreements or the obligations involved in League membership. When van Zeeland informed the French ambassador that he remained a resolute partisan of collective security, his attitude reflected that of his cabinet as well as that of most members of parliament.[4] In fact, there appears to have been little dispute within the government about the value of maintaining staff contacts with the French. The only thing at stake was the secret agreement of 1920, which, it was feared, con-

---

[1] *BPB*, no. 122, 23 May 1936, p. 11. See also ibid., pp. 9–11; ibid., no. 121, 12 Feb. 1936, pp. 9–10; *L'Indépendance belge*, 27 Feb. 1936, p. 3. For an elaborate argument on behalf of preserving the Military Agreement, see Auguste Melot, 'Des conversations Barnardiston à l'accord militaire franco-belge', in *Le Flambeau* (Brussels, 1936), XIX, no. 3, 257–71.

[2] *BPB*, no. 122, 23 May 1936, p. 9.

[3] War Ministry memorandum, 27 Jan. 1936, *DDF*, Ser. II, I, no. 106 and Laroche to Flandin, 5 Mar. 1936, no. 282; and Kerchove to van Zeeland, 26 Feb. 1936, *DDB*, III, no. 169.

[4] Laroche to Flandin, 5 Mar. 1936, *DDF*, Ser. II, I, no. 282 and van Zuylen, *Les Mains libres*, p. 337.

tained political obligations (and which, according to the French
interpretation, did contain such obligations). It had been a
source of discord in Belgian politics for fifteen years. Now that
the military reform project was in trouble and now that the
French were more unpopular and suspect than ever, the denunciation of the Military Agreement was a foregone conclusion. It was 'the prerequisite for strengthening our army'.[1]

The first official recommendation that the Military Agreement be denounced came from the Committee of National
Security, three cabinet members who had been studying defence
questions since the previous autumn.[2] Defence Minister Devèze
was himself a member of this committee. Even this most ardent
francophile now considered the Military Agreement expend-
able.[3] The French embassy in Brussels seemed amenable. The
councillor of the embassy intimated that there was no reason for
preserving the Agreement; the military attaché admitted that
France would sacrifice little by the elimination of an agreement
which caused so much distrust. Both conceded that most of its
stipulations were out of date and that only the one concerning
staff talks had any real meaning.[4]

Talks began in January 1936. The Belgians quickly discovered that the Quai d'Orsay and the French General Staff
had ideas of their own, regardless of what their representatives
in Brussels were saying.[5] As far as the Belgians were concerned,
this was not the time for a prolonged discussion. The preliminary vote on Devèze's reform bill was only weeks away, and it
was already obvious that the project might be defeated. Van
Zeeland therefore hurried to Paris, where on 15 February he
met with Foreign Minister Flandin.[6]

---

[1] Ibid., p. 333.

[2] Le Peuple, 9 Feb. 1936, p. 3, and de Man, Après coup, p. 260. De Man, de
Schrijver, and Devèze, who represented the three major parties, were the members
of the committee.

[3] Devèze informed van Zeeland that the mistaken significance attributed to the
Military Agreement was 'the major obstacle to my military project'. Devèze to
van Zeeland, 24 Jan. 1936, DDB, III, no. 160.

[4] Devèze to van Zeeland, 17 Jan. 1936, ibid., no. 159; van Zuylen, Les Mains
libres, pp. 333-4; and van Overstraeten, Albert I. Léopold III, p. 200.

[5] Devèze to van Zeeland, 24 Jan. 1936, DDB, III, no. 160 and Memorandum by
Vanlangenhove, 27 Jan. 1936, no. 161.

[6] Distrust of France was so intense by now that some considered this trip as
another piece of evidence that Belgium was a French satellite. De Standaard called

Flandin came straight to the point. The denunciation of the Agreement would be disastrous. It would encourage the spirit of revenge in Germany. Even if the Agreement were maintained, any modification of its text would be interpreted as a shift in the direction of Belgian policy. Van Zeeland replied that he would gladly maintain the *status quo*, but political circumstances would not permit him to do so. The Agreement was out of date. Staff talks could continue within the framework of Locarno. Van Zeeland emphasized that Flemish opinion was hostile to the Agreement. In other countries, notably Germany, there were suspicions that the Agreement provided for a joint offensive action. Distrust of the Agreement was greater than ever. If it were not denounced, the Belgian government would be in a delicate situation. Its plans for military reform might be defeated. Van Zeeland called attention to a proposed street demonstration soon to take place in Brussels in order to provoke the denunciation of the Agreement.[1]

Flandin did not give in. He thought it would be better for the two governments to agree on the text of a declaration which did not denounce the Military Agreement, but which made its meaning more precise. He recommended that the Belgian Foreign Ministry draw up such a declaration.[2] This was similar to the procedure which Hymans had reluctantly accepted in 1931.

A few days after van Zeeland's return to Brussels the Foreign Ministry sent to Paris the rough draft of declaration. It stated that the political purposes of the Military Agreement had been absorbed by Locarno, that its military provisions had been effective only during the Rhineland occupation, and that it had therefore lost its *raison d'être*.[3] Four days later, on 25 February, the French replied. In their opinion the only provisions of the Military Agreement which had lapsed were those which dealt with the Rhineland occupation itself; the others, they said, remained effective.[4] In other words, despite all the efforts to

---

van Zeeland's trip 'the greatest blunder of Belgian foreign policy since 1918.' Ovey to Eden, 18 Feb. 1936, FO, 432/2/C1018/202/4.

[1] Foreign Ministry record of conversation held in Paris, 15 Feb. 1936, *DDB*, III, no. 163.

[2] Ibid.

[3] Kerchove to Flandin, 21 Feb. 1936, ibid., no. 165.

[4] Kerchove to van Zeeland, 25 Feb. 1936, ibid, no. 167. The French General

clarify the meaning of the Agreement, the French position had not changed. Belgium might be obliged to mobilize on behalf of France's allies and thus become involved in a war starting in Central Europe.[1] The French interpretation of the Agreement was, from the Belgian viewpoint, simply out of the question. By now even the preservation of the Agreement, whatever the French interpretation of it, was impossible. Events in Belgium, the Quai d'Orsay was told, 'were moving in an accelerated rhythm . . .'.[2]

Time was running out. The Flemish Catholics had already passed their resolution calling for an end to the Military Agreement; the preliminary vote on Devèze's project was now imminent. On 25 February Secretary General Vanlangenhove met in Paris with his French counterpart, Alexis Léger, and told him, in effect, that the conversations were over. The only remaining question was whether the necessary declaration would be unilateral or bilateral. Léger agreed that the declaration would be bilateral. The Military Agreement would be denounced *in toto*, although the two countries would reaffirm their desire to continue staff talks. Léger felt that a new agreement ought to provide the basis for future staff contacts;[3] Vanlangenhove replied that this would only intensify the suspicions which they hoped to eliminate.[4] There was one last point. Vanlangenhove pointed out that van Zeeland would be asked in parliament whether the Military Agreement still existed. It was essential that he should be able to say 'No'. Léger agreed.[5]

Such was the end of the Franco-Belgian Military Agreement of 1920.

Staff once again indicated its hope that the Agreement would be preserved, although it seems to have viewed the Agreement as a technical convenience, not as a political arrangement. Kerchove to van Zeeland, 26 Feb. 1936, ibid., no. 170.

[1] The Agreement had provided for Belgian mobilization in the event of German mobilization. The Belgians always feared that if Germany mobilized against Poland or Czechoslovakia only, France would insist that this provision be put into effect.

[2] Kerchove to van Zeeland, 26 Feb. 1936, *DDB*, III, no. 169.

[3] Evidently the French wanted another agreement concerning staff contacts because they feared that some future Belgian government might repudiate the van Zeeland government's intention to maintain staff contacts. Eden to Ovey, 5 Mar. 1936, FO, 432/2/C1424/270/4.

[4] Foreign Ministry record of conversation held in Paris, 26 Feb. 1936, *DDB*, III, no. 171 and van Zuylen, *Les Mains libres*, pp. 337–8.

[5] Ibid., p. 338.

5. *Conclusion*

It is ironic that Vanlangenhove's last day in Paris, 27 February, was the day on which the military bill received its preliminary defeat in the Belgian parliament. Whether an announcement that the Military Agreement no longer existed would have prevented this defeat is doubtful, because there were other reasons for the bill's unpopularity. But there is no doubt that the preservation of the Military Agreement would have guaranteed the future defeat of any effort to strengthen Belgian defences. This, in turn, would have meant the end of the van Zeeland government.

One week after Vanlangenhove's visit to Paris there was an official exchange of identical letters which were dated 6 March and whose contents were reported by van Zeeland to a cheering Chamber of Deputies on 11 March—in dramatic and unexpected circumstances.[1] It is eloquent testimony to the unpopularity of the Military Agreement that even Hitler's march into the Rhineland on 7 March did nothing to moderate the enthusiasm which greeted the Prime Minister's announcement. Van Zeeland read the contents of the French letter. The only obligations now linking France and Belgium were those shared in the Locarno agreements and the League Covenant. The two countries did desire to maintain contact between the General Staffs 'in order to execute the obligations defined by the Rhine Pact of Locarno and to study the technical conditions for the eventual application of these obligations'.[2] Van Zeeland then read twice that part of the letter which said that staff contacts implied 'neither an obligation of a political nature nor an obligation as to the organization of national defence for either one of the interested parties'.[3]

Amidst all the enthusiasm one sceptical Fleming remarked apropos of maintenance of staff contacts: 'Nothing is changed. Everything is the same!' 'Pure comedy!' said another.[4]

---

[1] It is possible that the precise wording of the letters had not been agreed upon when the Germans remilitarized the Rhineland on 7 March and that the letters were predated so that the end of the Military Agreement would not appear the result of Hitler's initiative, which, of course, it was not. Ovey to Eden, 6 Mar. 1936, FO, 371/19850/C1456/270/4 and Charles to Baxter, 17 Mar. 1936, C2056/270/4.

[2] *Annales* (Chamber), 1935/1936, 11 Mar. 1936, p. 790. See also van Zeeland to Laroche, 6 Mar. 1936, *DDB*, III, no. 176.

[3] *Annales* (Chamber), 1935/1936, 11 Mar. 1936, p. 790.   [4] Ibid.

III

BELGIUM AND THE RHINELAND CRISIS

1. *Introduction*

Some historians attribute Belgium's return to neutrality in 1936 to the weakness of Britain and France during the Rhineland crisis and to the consequences thereof; others attribute it to the influence of King Leopold.[1] The first interpretation is misleading; the second is simply mistaken. Both neglect Belgium's earlier disillusionment with France and overlook the fact that the Franco-Belgian Military Agreement had ceased to exist before the Rhineland crisis even took place.

The standard interpretations are inadequate for another reason. It was domestic events—not international events or the influence of the King—which compelled the Belgian cabinet to accept the long-standing arguments of the Foreign Ministry and to pursue a policy of non-alignment. Because 1936 was so critical a year in international politics, it has been easy for non-Belgian historians to overlook or forget that 1936 was the most dramatic and dangerous year in the history of Belgium herself. By the same token, the British and French statesmen of the 1930s, who were overwhelmed with their own troubles, naturally failed to appreciate fully the domestic problems of a small power and tended to accept simple explanations—like the one involving King Leopold—for a development which they considered potentially disastrous. The failure to take into account Belgium's domestic crisis is one reason why her 'policy of independence' was regarded then and is sometimes regarded now with so little sympathy.

To argue that domestic events brought about the change in Belgium's foreign policy is not to deny that the calamitous drift

---

[1] The most remarkable exposition of the latter interpretation is the article by Rudolph Binion, 'Repeat Performance: a Psycho-historical Study of Leopold III and Belgian Neutrality', in *History and Theory* (Middletown, 1969), VIII, no. 2, 213–59.

of European politics in 1936 was of great significance for her. Events abroad were a major cause of the chaos in Belgian politics. Furthermore, disappointment with France and Britain —especially Britain—made all the more appealing a policy which events at home had made necessary. Hitler's violation of the Locarno agreements and the subsequent failure to negotiate adequate arrangements to replace them did provide the international framework within which the 'policy of independence' evolved. The Rhineland crisis and its frustrating aftermath had a profound impact on the thinking of Belgian statesmen. And the quiet but important role of Belgium in that crisis deserves a close examination.

Belgian and French writers have viewed this role from different angles. Belgians like to characterize their country's behaviour as unimpeachable. They point to the indecisiveness of France and Britain. They emphasize Belgium's willingness to fulfil her obligations and co-operate with strong measures against Germany. The French, on the other hand, contend that their little neighbour was all too reluctant to take such measures and that this attitude was among the factors which induced France to abandon her intention of meeting the Germans with force. There is some truth in both arguments. Of course Belgium would have joined France and Britain in taking sanctions. How could she have done otherwise? Belgium did, however, support the more conciliatory British position from the start. Her attitude would have handicapped the French if they had marched alone. But what evidence is there that the French ever really intended to march? The responsibility for the Rhineland fiasco was collective. Belgium's attitude was part of a larger tragedy. The margin of freedom within which Belgian diplomats negotiated had always been narrow. In 1936 it was narrower than ever.

2. *From the Events of 7 March to the Proposals of 19 March*

The remilitarization of the Rhineland was a surprise in Belgium. There were indications of German activity in the demilitarized zone. But it was precisely these clandestine violations which led van Zeeland to believe that an overt move was unlikely, because the Germans would have so little to gain from it.[1]

[1] Ovey to Eden, 29 Jan. 1936, FO, 408/66/C587/92/62 and Eden, *Facing the Dictators*, p. 374.

Political Director van Zuylen did not think the Germans would take such a risk, given the low level of their military preparations.[1] As late as 2 March Secretary General Vanlangenhove assured the French ambassador in Brussels, Jules Laroche, that the Foreign Ministry expected no trouble in the near future.[2]

The French naturally wanted to know what their little neighbour would do, if the unexpected did occur. By 7 March they should have had a fairly good idea.[3] Émile Vandervelde informed Laroche that in the event of a German move Belgium would be cautious and let the British and French handle the matter.[4] Paul Hymans expressed his doubts that either Britain or Belgium would be willing to march.[5] During his February visit to Paris van Zeeland indicated that Belgium intended to remain loyal to Locarno and to adjust her attitude to the cirstances of the moment.[6]

In other words, Belgium would take the line of least resistance. She would follow in the wake of France and Britain. If there was a policy conflict between them, Belgium would side with Britain. This was the safest course, especially since the British were unlikely to support any military operations in the Rhineland.[7] This was the safest course from a domestic viewpoint, too, for in March 1936 Belgium was in no mood to fight.

The reaction of the Belgian people to the remilitarization of the Rhineland was very calm. There was little demand for an immediate and vigorous response. The press pointed out that Hitler's complaints about the Franco-Soviet Pact had some

---

[1] Memorandum by van Zuylen, 14 Jan. 1936, *DDB*, IV, no. 3.

[2] Laroche to Flandin, 2 Mar. II, 1936, *DDF*, Ser. II, I, no. 263.

[3] What the French evidently did not know was that the Belgians had quietly suggested to the British that the whole matter be submitted to international arbitration before it generated a major crisis. There is no record of an official British reply to this proposal. Ovey to Eden, 3 Mar. 1936, FO, 408/66/C1181/4/18 and Memorandum by Vanlangenhove, 1 Feb. 1936, *DDB*, IV, no. 12 and Memorandum by Lantsheere, 24 Feb. 1936, *DDB*, no. 15.

[4] Laroche to Flandin, 1 Feb. 1936, *DDF*, Ser. II, I, no. 123.

[5] Laroche to Flandin, 12 Feb. 1936, ibid., no. 167. Both Hymans and Vandervelde were ministers-without-portfolio in the van Zeeland government.

[6] Foreign Ministry record of conversation held in Paris, 15 Feb. 1936, *DDB*, III, no. 163. See also van Zeeland to Kerchove, 24 Feb. 1936, IV, no. 16.

[7] 'The information we have received until now', noted Vanlangenhove, 'does not permit us to expect great firmness on her part.' Memorandum by Vanlangenhove, 1 Feb. 1936, ibid., no. 12.

justification and that the postwar status of the Rhineland had not been intended to endure for ever. What troubled Belgians most was the fashion in which the Germans had flouted legality. But few thought that this was sufficient cause for military sanctions, which meant exposing Belgian cities to German bombardment.[1] The nation was still involved in an unresolved debate about national defence, and France's reputation had sunk to a new low. No responsible government could commit Belgian troops to a joint expedition with the French, not without British participation.[2] The government would not have received much support for economic sanctions against Germany. The effects of the Rhineland crisis were bad enough for Belgian business as it was. A curtailment of trade with Germany, for whom Belgium was a creditor, might have been disastrous.[3] Paul van Zeeland had no support for any policy but a conciliatory one.

Van Zeeland's first official reaction to the events of 7 March was to associate Belgium with France's appeal to the League of Nations.[4] Privately, he informed the French that it would be difficult for Belgium to undertake military sanctions, lest they seem disproportionate to the threat.[5] The immediate reaction of the British did not make the prospect of military sanctions any more attractive, for it was obvious from the outset that they intended to negotiate. On 7 March Anthony Eden told the Belgians that he deplored Hitler's high-handed disregard for legality. But he thought that Hitler's stated willingness to negotiate new agreements with the western powers and his suggestion that Germany might return to the League of Nations ought to be taken seriously. Eden thought that Hitler's offer to

---

[1] *BPB*, no. 122, 23 May 1936, pp. 2–4; *The Times*, 9 Mar. 1936, p. 9; and Memorandum by Sussdorf, 23 Mar. 1936, in United States, Department of State, *Foreign Relations of the United States: Diplomatic Papers* (Washington, 1953), 1936, I, 264–5. (Henceforth this will be cited as *FRUS*.)

[2] The Quai d'Orsay received at least one report that Flemish troops could not be counted on: 'The Flemings always have been and still are profoundly anti-militarist . . . this is why most officers in the Belgian army are, fortunately, Walloon.' Riedinger to Maurin, 19 Mar. 1936, *DDF*, Ser. II, I, no. 468.

[3] *The New York Times*, 22 Mar. 1936, IV, p. 4.

[4] Van Zeeland to Kerchove, 7 Mar. 1936, *DDB*, IV, no. 27 and League of Nations, *Official Journal* (Geneva 1936), XVII, no. 4, Part I, p. 312. See also *Annales* (Chamber), 1935/1936, 10 Mar. 1936, pp. 758–9.

[5] Laroche to Flandin, 7 Mar. 1936, *DDF*, Ser. II, I, no. 302.

negotiate was 'one of the most important documents since the end of the war'.[1] This was hardly a call to battle. Van Zeeland, who throughout the crisis worried more about Anglo-French unity than anything else, quickly recommended to the French that they should not take a position so extreme as to risk an unfavourable reaction in London.[2] Several days later Political Director van Zuylen put it to the French more bluntly: 'The English do not wish to see a rotten branch restored. No one ever considered the demilitarization of the Rhineland to be a perpetual clause. It is necessary to save what remains of Locarno.'[3]

The Prime Minister's first public declaration on the Rhineland crisis was delivered to the Chamber of Deputies on 11 March, and it left no doubt that the government was ready to negotiate. Van Zeeland's position paralleled that of the British. 'It will be necessary to rebuild, it will be necessary to reconstruct', he said. The first condition for this was that everyone remain calm. But the most important thing was that the Locarno powers preserve their common front. If their unity broke down, 'the worst consequences are to be feared for us, for all the signatories, for the entire world, even for the future of civilization'. What was the role of Belgium? 'During the period of negotiations, we believe that our duty will be to support the common point of view; when at the beginning of discussions differences of opinion become apparent, it will be to do our best to mitigate and remove them.'[4]

Van Zeeland intended to serve as mediator between the British and the French. Because Anglo-French harmony remained the *sine qua non* of Belgian security, his role as 'honest broker' suited Belgian interests as well as international convenience. It is hard to imagine anyone better qualified for this task. During the Rhineland crisis van Zeeland was 'subtle, supple', and 'always soft-spoken', writes Paul-Boncour.[5] To Neville Chamberlain he seemed 'clear-headed, sensi-

---

[1] Cartier to van Zeeland, 7 Mar. 1936, *DDB*, IV, no. 21 and Eden to Ovey, 7 Mar. 1936, FO, 408/66/C1488/4/18.

[2] Laroche to Flandin, 8 Mar. 1936, *DDF*, Ser. II, I, no. 330.

[3] Laroche to Flandin, 11 Mar. 1936, ibid., no. 381.

[4] *Annales* (Chamber), 1935/1936, 11 Mar. 1936, p. 791. This was the speech in which van Zeeland announced the end of the Franco-Belgian Military Agreement.

[5] J. Paul-Boncour, *Entre deux guerres. Souvenirs sur la IIIᵉ République* (Paris, 1946), III, 43.

ble and agreeable'.[1] The Belgian Prime Minister was an ideal conciliator, and the Rhineland affair taxed his skill and patience to the fullest.

The foreign ministers of the Locarno powers[2] met in Paris on 10 March. Their first conversations revealed a fundamental difference of opinion. Van Zeeland was caught between Flandin's demand that there be no negotiations with the Germans before a restoration of the *status quo ante* and Eden's assumption that negotiations could begin after a formal protest. It was in delicate situations like this that van Zeeland excelled. First, he expressed agreement with Flandin's general sentiments, emphasized the precarious situation of Belgium, and made a plea for solidarity among the Locarno powers.[3] What precisely was the Belgian position? The dominating fact, said van Zeeland, was that war on behalf of the principle of the demilitarized zone was impossible. The Germans had made some interesting but inadequate proposals for replacing the guarantee which was contained in the Rhineland demilitarization. Of course, talks with the Germans could not begin in such a fashion that they would seem like a reward for treaty violations. Must the Germans evacuate the Rhineland before talks began? 'In this matter I do not share the opinion expounded by M. Flandin ...' It was essential that Britain and France agree on a policy that was both firm and conciliatory. The signatories of Locarno and the members of the League might agree on a proposal supported by the threat of military sanctions on the part of the Locarno powers and by the threat of economic sanctions on the part of the League. Whatever the final proposal, Hitler must not be forced to choose between a capitulation and war. In the last analysis, said van Zeeland, everything depends on the attitude of Britain. He remarked that he did not yet know exactly what that attitude was.[4]

Anthony Eden did not know either. He and van Zeeland met

---

[1] Keith Feiling, *The Life of Neville Chamberlain* (London, 1946), p. 279.

[2] It should be noted again that van Zeeland was Foreign Minister as well as Prime Minister of Belgium.

[3] Foreign Ministry record of conversation held in Paris, 10 Mar. 1936, *DDB*, IV, no. 41. See also *Survey, 1936*, pp. 282–3; Circular by Flandin, 11 Mar. 1936, *DDF*, Ser. II, I, no. 380; and Eden, *Facing the Dictators*, pp. 391–3.

[4] Foreign Ministry record of conversation held in Paris, 10 Mar. 1936, *DDB*, IV, no. 43.

alone and discussed what to do next. 'Van Zeeland and I were friends and had confidence in one another', writes Eden. 'Also, we were of the same generation; we had, therefore, no difficulty thinking out loud together, as he expressed it.'[1] Van Zeeland reminded Eden of France's stake in the Rhineland. A platonic condemnation of Germany, like the one at Stresa a year earlier, would not satisfy France. She would lose face; her European position would be compromised; her government would have trouble at home. Van Zeeland then elaborated a programme for beginning negotiations. Germany's illegality should be condemned. She should be required to withdraw some of the troops stationed in the Rhineland and not to build fortifications there. France and Belgium should receive supplementary guarantees. Specifically, Britain should announce that the Locarno agreements were still in effect and make more precise her commitment to defend Western Europe. She should do so in a fashion which would appeal to public opinion in both France and Belgium. Eden wondered if van Zeeland's programme would involve Britain in a permanent Anglo-Franco-Belgian alliance, if the Germans failed to co-operate. Van Zeeland 'demurred a little at this' and pointed out that a unilateral repudiation of a treaty by one power did not absolve the others of their obligations. If negotiations with Germany were to succeed, a firm British policy was essential. The key to the whole situation was in London. The next Locarno conversations and the impending meeting of the League Council ought to take place there.[2]

These ideas made sense to Eden. He and van Zeeland then persuaded Flandin that this was the best course to follow.[3] Before travelling to London, van Zeeland stopped for a day in Brussels, where he delivered his speech to the Chamber of Deputies. The Chamber's reception of his speech and the support expressed in the press assured him that his policy enjoyed almost unanimous support at home.[4] He departed for London

[1] Eden, *Facing the Dictators*, p. 393.

[2] Foreign Ministry memorandum, 10 Mar. 1936, *DDB*, IV, no. 44 and memorandum by Eden, 10 Mar. 1936, FO, 408/66/C1672/4/18.

[3] Eden, *Facing the Dictators*, p. 394.

[4] *BPB*, no. 122, May 23, 1936, pp. 6–7. See also Ovey to Eden, 13 Mar. 1936, FO, 371/19850/C1835/270/4.

intending to continue in his role as mediator between Flandin and Eden.

In London as well as in Paris van Zeeland was ready to support the French in matters of form and sentiment, while he inclined to the British position in matters of substance. He was sufficiently subtle to do this without being inconsistent. During his week in London van Zeeland co-operated with Flandin in the context of the League Council. He seconded the French in denouncing German illegality.[1] When it was suggested that the Council suspend its meetings until the arrival of a German representative, he energetically supported Flandin's argument that discussions should continue without the Germans. The French draft of a statement formally denouncing Germany was submitted with van Zeeland's approval.[2] When the British recommended that France and Germany submit their cases to the Hague Court, both Flandin and van Zeeland indicated that their countries did not wish to be bound by the decision of the Court.[3] Co-operation in matters like these was a safe way of preserving the appearance of Franco-Belgian unity of purpose.[4]

Van Zeeland tended to side with Eden in the meetings of the Locarno powers, where the real decisions were made. Must the Germans withdraw from the Rhineland before negotiations could begin? This was still the crucial question. Van Zeeland argued that Hitler should not be humiliated. Hitler was the kind of man who, if driven to extremes, might deliberately resort to war. Eden agreed. If there was a war and Germany was beaten, he said, what would the world have gained? Was it to be assumed that Germany would be taught a lesson by such means? Flandin replied that it was not France's purpose to teach the Germans a lesson. History had already demonstrated that they were slow learners. France wanted to show Europe that international law was still strong and collective

---

[1] League of Nations, *Official Journal* (Geneva, 1936), XVII, no. 4, Part 1, pp. 314–5.

[2] *Survey, 1936*, p. 299 and Massigli to the Quai d'Orsay, 17 Mar. 1936, *DDF*, Ser. II, I, no. 444.

[3] Foreign Office memorandum, 18 Mar. 1936, FO, 408/66/C2068/4/18.

[4] The attitude of Belgium and the role of her Prime Minister were the object of 'unanimous eulogies' in France, reported the Belgian ambassador there. The *Quai d'Orsay*, however, was not so impressed. Kerchove to van Zeeland, 14 Mar. 1936, *DDB*, IV, no. 46 and Kerchove to van Zeeland, 23 Mar. 1936, no. 48.

security still worth supporting. If this challenge was not met, Germany might turn on Austria and Czechoslovakia. Flandin explained that the French government was not contemplating anything like a general advance into the Rhineland, but rather the seizure of one or two key positions.[1] Moreover, the German troops in the Rhineland would be asked to withdraw only during the period of negotiation. France might be willing to legalize their eventual presence there, if the guarantors of the new arrangements—i.e., Great Britain and Belgium—made their obligations more precise and more automatic.[2]

For several days the discussions got nowhere. Flandin repeated his demand for a complete evacuation of the Rhineland. Eden and van Zeeland maintained that such a demand would invite a refusal. The Belgian insisted that Germany be made an offer which was moderate in her eyes and in the eyes of the world. On 14 March he presented the draft of a programme very similar to the one he had outlined for Eden during their private talks in Paris.[3] On 15 March Flandin wavered. He personally was willing to negotiate on the basis proposed by van Zeeland, he said. But the French government was not.[4] Several days passed before Flandin was able to accept the Anglo-Belgian position.[5]

Flandin and van Zeeland were in complete agreement on one vital matter. They wanted military conversations between Britain and her Locarno partners immediately.[6] They also wanted a new guarantee from Britain, for they could not leave London empty-handed. Flandin emphasized his need for something with which to do battle with the French public.[7] What he and van Zeeland had in mind was a letter addressed to the French and Belgian governments stating that, if negotiations with the Germans failed, Britain would carry out to the full her Locarno obligations, including the military ones. Did this mean,

---

[1] Luxembourg and the Saar were the two positions under consideration. General Staff memorandum, 11 Mar. 1936, *DDF*, Ser. II, I, no. 392.

[2] Memorandum by Eden, 13 Mar. 1936, FO, 406/88/C1806/4/18.

[3] Foreign Office memorandum, 14 Mar. 1936, ibid., C1861/4/18.

[4] Foreign Office memorandum, 15 Mar. 1936, ibid., C1918/4/18.

[5] The available French documents do not reveal when the French government took a position on this, if they ever did take one.

[6] Foreign Office memorandum, 18 Mar. 1936, FO, 406/88/C2069/4/18.

[7] Foreign Office memorandum, 14 Mar. 1936, ibid., C1861/4/18.

asked Eden, that Germany would be handed an ultimatum: 'Either you accept this, or there will be war?' Flandin admitted that he was no longer thinking of military sanctions, but rather economic sanctions milder than the ones applied against Italy. Eden noted that Flandin's words did not sound as tough as France's formal position. To this the Frenchman replied that he had gone as far as he could in conversation to meet the British position. There was a limit. If Britain did not give France and Belgium a letter of guarantee, agreement between them would be impossible. He might go home.[1]

Van Zeeland's diplomatic style precluded any departure threats on his part. But he wanted the British letter of guarantee as badly as Flandin. They could not say it outright. But they both intended to use the Rhineland crisis as the occasion for laying the foundations of a military alliance with Great Britain, the alliance which their countries had sought in vain since 1919 and which France and Belgium now needed desperately. Flandin later remembered that 'meeting followed upon meeting, and M. van Zeeland drafted one project after another with agreements which would confirm, extend, and make more precise the Treaty of Locarno.'[2] It is interesting to compare van Zeeland's draft proposal of 18 March with that finally agreed upon the next day. The former provided that if the Germans proved unco-operative, the British government would 'immediately take the most effective measures, economic and financial, military, naval and air to induce Germany to conform to the attitude which the Powers concerned have wanted her to adopt ...'.[3] This was too strong for the British. The wording adopted on 19 March was different. The British government would 'at once consider ... the steps to be taken to meet the new situation thus created' and would 'immediately come to the assistance of your Government, in accordance with the Treaty of Locarno, in respect of any measures which shall be jointly decided upon ...'.[4] Such nuances were important. This cautious wording reflected an ambiguous British attitude which soon became van Zeeland's major worry.

[1] Foreign Office memorandum, 18 Mar. 1936, ibid., C2069/4/18.
[2] Pierre-Étienne Flandin, *Politique française, 1919–1940* (Paris, 1947), p. 209.
[3] Memorandum drawn up by van Zeeland, 18 Mar. 1936, FO, 408/66/C2028/4/18.
[4] Proposals of 19 Mar. 1936, ibid., C2148/4/18.

But he was satisfied for the time being. The final proposals of 19 March closely resembled the programme which he had suggested in Paris. In fact the text of the final proposals was drawn up by him.[1] The French implicitly abandoned their intention of taking military sanctions, if they had ever had one. Negotiations would begin in return for a German promise not to increase the size of the forces already stationed in the Rhineland and not to build fortifications. An international force would be placed along a narrow strip of German territory. The old Locarno agreement would remain in effect until a new one was negotiated. From the Belgian point of view the most reassuring aspect of the new arrangement was that it did provide for Anglo-Franco-Belgian staff talks. This meant, in effect, that van Zeeland returned to Brussels with that which seventeen years of diplomacy had hitherto failed to obtain—the prospect of Anglo-Belgian military co-operation.[2]

Flandin has complained in his memoirs that van Zeeland was 'the instrument of the British' in forcing the French to give in.[3] This is not surprising. Van Zeeland's support for the more conciliatory British position was bound to provoke later criticism. Van Zeeland did not assume an heroic posture at these meetings. But it is hard to imagine any Belgian statesman conducting a substantially different policy; it is easy to imagine one of them conducting van Zeeland's policy less skilfully. His support for the British position followed necessarily from the state of Belgian politics and opinion. French Ambassador Laroche knew this. Shortly after the London meetings he informed Flandin that van Zeeland embodied 'the best we can hope for from Belgium in the present circumstances'.[4]

The Chamber of Deputies happened to have its annual foreign policy debate not long after the Prime Minister's return.[5] The tenor of this debate revealed how very satisfied with

---

[1] Flandin and Eden did make certain further revisions of van Zeeland's text. But, in general, it was his work. Foreign Office memorandum, 21 Mar. 1936, FO, 371/19896/C2193/4/18.

[2] For a complete published text of the proposals of 19 March see *Documents on International Affairs, 1936* (London, 1937), ed. by Stephen Heald and John W. Wheeler-Bennett, pp. 127–33. (Henceforth this will be cited as *DIA*.)

[3] Flandin, *Politique française, 1919–1940*, p. 201.

[4] Record of meeting held at Quai d'Orsay, 3 Apr. 1936, *DDF*, Ser. II, II, no. 17.

[5] *Annales* (Chamber), 1935/1936, 24 and 25 Mar. 1936, pp. 923–38, 941–63.

his diplomacy most members of parliament were. This did not mean that there was now national harmony in the matter of foreign policy; this was far from being the case.[1] However, almost every participant in the debate expressed admiration for van Zeeland's accomplishments. Most considered the proposals of 19 March an adequate provisional arrangement. The absence of the usual parliamentary acrimony was perhaps a tacit recognition that there was little Belgians could do or say until the fate of the proposed 'new Locarno' was known. Van Zeeland had made the best of a bad situation, which was the most Belgian statesmen ever did.

When the Prime Minister himself spoke to the Chamber of Deputies, he revealed a cautious optimism. Was the outlook for peace? 'I think so', was his answer.[2] He did not know whether Germany would accept the proposals of 19 March. If she did accept, the powers could negotiate a lasting settlement. If she rejected the proposals, Belgian security would be enhanced anyway because of the recent affirmation of Western unity. Van Zeeland concluded his brief talk on a philosophical note:

I assure you that those who were present at this meeting understand and will retain always this truth, of which I for one have always been convinced: that moral forces are of value not only in the spiritual world, but have direct and immediate effect in the real world as well.[3]

The one-time student of Thomistic theology would soon have his confidence in 'moral forces' put to the test. Such forces counted for even less than usual in 1936.

3. *Staff Talks*

The first blow to van Zeeland's optimism was the German response to the proposals of 19 March and the French reply to it, both of which illustrated clearly the obstacles to a 'new Locarno' or 'Western pact', as it was sometimes called. This is not the place for a lengthy exegesis of German and French differences. It is sufficient to note that in March and April 1936 there were two major stumbling-blocks to a Western pact. One was Germany's refusal to accept the conditions agreed on in

---

[1] 'Belgium is the ally of the ally of the Soviet', a Flemish Nationalist reminded his listeners. More significant were the words of the Flemish Catholic leader, van Cauwelaert, who expressed admiration for van Zeeland and simultaneously speculated about the advantages of 'voluntary neutrality'. Ibid., pp. 936, 948.

[2] Ibid., 20 Mar. 1936, p. 919.   [3] Ibid., p. 920.

London as necessary for beginning talks; her only concession was an offer not to reinforce the troops already stationed in the Rhineland.[1] This was not enough for the French, and they indicated that there would be no negotiations until the Germans conceded more.[2] The other stumbling-block was more fundamental and remained an issue until early 1937, when hopes for a Western pact finally died. The French insisted that any settlement provide for Eastern Europe as well as Western Europe. The Germans said they were willing to sign non-aggression pacts with both their Eastern and Western neighbours. But they rejected the French demand that any new settlement be placed under the supervision of the League of Nations. In plain language, the Germans wanted to use the negotiations for a Western pact as a device to separate France from her allies in Eastern Europe.[3] The French naturally found the German position unacceptable. A new Locarno was not imminent.

What troubled van Zeeland most was the persistent disagreement between Britain and France. On 19 March the British had formally promised that if the attempt to negotiate with the Germans failed, they would immediately consult with Paris and Brussels about appropriate measures 'to meet the new situation thus created'.[4] Did a new situation now exist? The French thought so. The effort to conciliate the Germans had failed, said Alexis Léger; it was now time for the Locarno powers to consider their next step.[5] The British disagreed. They felt that the door to negotiations was still open and that patience was the order of the day. 'We are still a little feverish', said Robert Vansittart, 'and perhaps it would be wise to give everyone time to calm himself somewhat.'[6] The British did not regard the proposals of 19 March as an ultimatum. The proposals were 'only the husk that contains the kernel', said The Times.[7]

[1] Note to the British Government, undated, DGFP, Ser. C, V, no. 207 and note to the British Government, 31 Mar. 1936, no. 242.

[2] Memorandum approved by the French Government, 6 Apr. 1936, DDF, Ser. II, II, no. 37.

[3] Survey, 1936, pp. 271, 332.

[4] Proposals of 19 Mar. 1936, DIA, 1936, pp. 127–33.

[5] Kerchove to van Zeeland, 25 Mar. 1936, DDB, IV, no. 57. See also Memorandum by Vanlangenhove, 2 Apr. 1936, no. 67 and Kerchove to van Zeeland, 3 Apr. 1936, no. 68.

[6] Cartier to van Zeeland, 25 Mar. 1936, ibid., no. 60.

[7] The Times, 21 Mar. 1936, p. 13.

What was van Zeeland's position? Ambassador Laroche was probably right when he reported that the Prime Minister simply did not know what procedure to follow next.[1] But van Zeeland was certain of one thing: the key to the situation was still in London. It was necessary to win time for Eden and not to embarrass him at home.[2] Van Zeeland's thinking on the indivisibility of peace, the impossibility of localizing a conflict, and the connection between settlements for both Western and Eastern Europe, was close to that of the French. But the British had to participate. Van Zeeland put it to Laroche this way:

... that which is necessary to obtain is that if peace is broken somewhere other than the Rhine, you can count on British support in maintaining or restoring peace; that is the way I see things; it is a matter of knowing what price is to be paid to obtain this support; I can't see it yet.[3]

As usual, van Zeeland took a position somewhere between those of Eden and Flandin. Like the former, he was not ready to close the door on negotiations with Germany. Like the latter, he was eager for another Locarno meeting. He therefore suggested to Paris and London that the Locarno powers convene for the purpose of examining 'whether it is necessary to consider that the effort at conciliation has failed'.[4] Eden agreed to a discussion at Geneva. But he indicated that he did not expect to enter into any new arrangements there.[5]

The Geneva meeting of 10 April was not as critical as the one in London. The acute phase of the crisis was over. The French were less intransigent. Flandin did argue that the effort at conciliation had failed and that it was now time to negotiate a treaty of mutual assistance. Eden replied that there was no urgency to conclude a definitive treaty. The British wanted first to send to Berlin a questionnaire designed to elucidate certain aspects of the German position. Flandin wanted an immediate study of possible economic sanctions. Eden rejected this. Van

[1] Record of meeting held at Quai d'Orsay, 3 Apr. 1936, *DDF*, Ser. II, II, no. 17.
[2] Ibid. It is interesting to note that Ambassador Laroche thought apropos of public opinion in Belgium that 'van Zeeland is in advance of it just as M. Eden is in advance of English opinion.' Laroche to Flandin, 6 Apr. 1936, ibid., no. 27.
[3] Laroche to Flandin, 9 Apr. 1936, ibid., no. 41.
[4] Van Zeeland to Cartier, 2 Apr. 1936, *DDB*, IV, no. 65 and van Zeeland to Kerchove, 2 Apr. 1936, no. 66.
[5] Cartier to van Zeeland, 4 Apr. 1936, ibid., no. 69.

Zeeland said little. He was asked to draw up the final communiqué which was a skilfully worded document.[1] It contained the British point of view, while making a gesture to French sensitivities. The German government 'have not made a contribution to the restoration of confidence indispensable for the negotiation of new treaties', it said. However, it would be necessary 'to explore all the opportunities of conciliation'. The communiqué concluded by saying that the British government had been delegated the task of clearing up a number of obscurities contained in the latest German memorandum.[2]

The undramatic results of this meeting suited van Zeeland's purposes perfectly. Just as the London meeting eliminated the possibility of military sanctions, this one ended the possibility of economic sanctions. The common front of the Locarno powers would remain intact, at least until the French general election, which was now less than a month away.[3] While the diplomats were waiting on the French electorate, the Foreign Office in London would have ample time to despatch its 'questionnaire' to Berlin. For all practical purposes, the Rhineland crisis was over.

Van Zeeland's hopes for the future were based on this paragraph of the proposals of 19 March:

The representatives of Belgium, France, the United Kingdom of Great Britain and Northern Ireland, and of Italy . . . undertake forthwith to instruct their General Staffs to enter into contact with a view to arranging the technical conditions in which the obligations which are binding upon them should be carried out in case of unprovoked aggression.[4]

Britain's pledge to defend Belgium not only compensated for what had been lost on 7 March. It also strengthened the hand of the van Zeeland government in domestic affairs. The debate about national defence was far from over, and Anglo-Belgian

[1] Memorandum by Flandin, 14 Apr. 1936, *DDF*, Ser. II, II, no. 68 and Minute by van Zeeland, 10 Apr. 1936, FO, 408/66/C3101/4/18.

[2] Communiqué issued by the Locarno Powers, 10 Apr. 1936, *DIA*, *1936*, pp. 210–11.

[3] Van Zeeland's communiqué was apparently a deliberate effort to 'bridge over' the French and British positions until this election. Morris to Hull, 14 Apr. 1936, *FRUS*, 1936, I, 287–8.

[4] Proposals of 19 Mar. 1936, *DIA*, *1936*, pp. 127–33.

staff talks were certain to have very salutary effects. Van Zeeland himself could never say this in so many words. But others could. Frans van Cauwelaert, the leader of the Flemish Catholics, described the situation thus: 'From the beginning we have explained that if an agreement with England like the one with France were concluded, we would not have harboured the same suspicions.'[1] In other words, Britain's pledge gave the proponents of military reform a better argument.[2]

It was therefore a glad occasion for the government when on 2 April Eden handed the Belgian and French ambassadors in London identical letters saying that the British government was ready to give its General Staffs instructions to enter into contact immediately with their French and Belgian counterparts. The wording of these letters resembled that of the letters exchanged by France and Belgium a month earlier: 'it is understood that this contact between general staffs cannot give rise in respect of either government to any political undertakings, nor to any obligation regarding the organization of national defence.'[3]

Enthusiasm in Brussels would have been more restrained, if anyone had paid close attention to the recent foreign policy debate in the British parliament. The prospect of staff talks came under heavy fire. Eden's words about Britain's traditional interests were clear and unambiguous.[4] But they were greeted with a barrage of criticism, and the most articulate critic was David Lloyd George. Staff talks, he said, had 'thwarted negotiations and precipitated war in 1914'.[5] Clement Attlee noted that the country was 'profoundly disturbed at the idea of these staff conversations'.[6] And so were many backbenchers disturbed: 'the boys won't have it,' Prime Minister Baldwin was told.[7] It is ironic that the arguments against staff talks were like the ones heard in the Belgian Chamber of Deputies during

---

[1] *Annales* (Chamber), 1935/1936, 25 Mar. 1936, p. 947.

[2] Defence Minister Devèze immediately recommended to the British that staff talks take place in Brussels on a bilateral basis. Ovey to Eden, 21 Mar. 1936, FO, 371/19896/C2199/4/18.

[3] Eden to Corbin and Cartier, 1 Apr. 1936, *DIA, 1936*, pp. 175–7. See also Eden, *Facing the Dictators*, p. 417.

[4] *Parliamentary Debates* (Commons), 1936, 310, 26 Mar. 1936, 1443.

[5] Ibid., 1480.   [6] Ibid., 1533.

[7] Ian Colvin, *Vansittart in Office* (London, 1965), p. 99.

the last sixteen years. The government's explanations were much the same, too. Neville Chamberlain was the Cabinet's spokesman. What would be the value of a promise to protect Belgium and France, he asked, if those countries did not know the nature of the promised assistance? Britain had accepted no new commitments. 'We ought to remember', he added, 'that we are in a situation in which it is impossible to eliminate all risks. You have to take lesser risks, perhaps, to avoid bigger risks hereafter.'[1] It was soon evident that the risks which Britain was willing and able to assume were small indeed.

Belgian and French staff officers travelled to London in mid-April with great expectations. For the Belgians this was the culmination of years of waiting. The conversations were concerned mostly with the creation of a British expeditionary force, its disembarkation on the continent, and its transportation to pre-arranged places of muster in Northern France. The Belgian and French officers were surprised to discover that the proposed expeditionary force would consist of only two divisions, that it would probably be ready to engage in battle by sometime between the twentieth and thirtieth day, and that it would be sent only 'if the London government decides to intervene . . .'. The British refused to say how or where their troops would be employed. The French and the Belgians attempted to enlarge the framework of the conversations. The former pointed out that the Maginot Line obviated the need for British troops in France; they could be used in Belgium instead. The Belgians endorsed this enthusiastically, while the British remained non-committal. The Belgians wondered whether the British could furnish them with raw materials and other means to assure the manufacture of armaments if Belgian factories were destroyed or occupied in the early stages of a war. The British replied that this question was outside the framework of their instructions; it would have to be referred to the two governments. The only encouraging aspect of the talks was that the British agreed to maintain contact through the services of military attachés.[2] Such was the content of the Anglo-Franco-Belgian staff talks of 1936.

The conversations in London did have one significant upshot, one on which the French had planned all along. Two weeks

---

[1] *Parliamentary Debates* (Commons), 1936, 310, 26 Mar. 1936, 1547.
[2] Schweisguth to Maurin, 20 Apr. 1936, *DDF*, Ser. II, II, no. 97.

earlier Ambassador Laroche had suggested to Flandin that the French could turn the conversations to great advantage 'in guiding the Belgian General Staff and in tipping the balance in favour of those who wish to defend Belgian territory at the frontiers'.[1] The French generals were themselves eager to resume the collaboration which 'the internal political situation of our neighbour has too long postponed'. The resumption of exclusive Franco-Belgian staff talks now 'could be presented to Belgian opinion as the logical result of the conversations with the British'.[2] It was indeed the logical result. If Britain's expeditionary force did intervene in Belgium, its doing so depended on French transportation and Franco-Belgian co-operation in making that transportation as efficient as possible. During the London talks the Belgians had acknowledged the need to pursue this matter further. After the talks the French generals had another argument. Because Britain's contribution in the early stages of a war would be so paltry, Franco-Belgian co-operation was all the more crucial. While France and Belgium were fighting alone, the outcome of the entire war might be decided.[3] Belgium's ambassador and military attaché in Paris recommended that talks begin soon. And the ambassador thought they should have 'a practical and genuine character, in contrast to the infrequent and almost theoretical contacts of preceding years.'[4]

The French did not have to wait long. In mid-May the new Belgian Chief of Staff, General van den Bergen, was on his way to Paris to meet with his French counterpart, Gamelin. The meeting's purpose was to work out the details for the movement of French troops into Belgium. The plan elaborated on 15 May was for an immediate French response to a Belgian appeal. An advance guard would move northward without delay and would be followed later by an entire French army. The Belgian forces south of the Meuse River would be placed under French command. Most of the combined Franco-Belgian forces would

---

[1] Record of meeting held at Quai d'Orsay, 3 Apr. 1936, *DDF*, Ser. II, II, no. 17.
[2] Schweisguth to Maurin, 20 Apr., 1936, ibid., no. 97.
[3] Kerchove to van Zeeland, 23 Apr. 1936, *DDB*, IV, no. 76. By now France's generals were very sensitive to Belgium's internal problems. The Belgian military attaché in Paris reported: 'If for reasons of domestic policy or any other reason certain modalities must be envisaged (the place of the meeting, etc....), the French General Staff is ready to conform.' [4] Ibid.

be concentrated on the Albert Canal, which ran from Liège to Antwerp and was never far from the Belgian frontier. The defence of the canal would constitute the 'common shield of France and Belgium'.[1]

The French were delighted. At no time since the war had their collaboration with the Belgians been as complete and as intimate as it was now. Schweisguth, the French Deputy Chief of Staff, could inform his associates that no matter how diverse Belgium's political tendencies were, 'the General Staff in its present composition is certainly won over to direct collaboration with the French army'.[2] Years later Gamelin remembered that the timidity of the politicians was not shared by General van den Bergen.[3] It is no wonder that the French should be so determined to take advantage of the new situation. The strategic importance of Belgium was increasing in direct proportion to the growing menace in the East. A French General Staff memorandum came straight to the point:

The precedent of 1914 showed that in the interest of our country the aid given Belgium could not be too rapid or too powerful. Speed and power will be all the more necessary in a future conflict in which the adversary will have motorized and mechanized units, and in which our aid will be really effective only if by its semi-instantaneousness it permits the Belgians to hold the fortified line they are building along the frontier.[4]

Van Zeeland certainly recognized the force of such arguments. Shortly after the Franco-Belgian staff talks he indicated his satisfaction with their results.[5] If the defence of Belgium at the frontiers had any chance of success, it presupposed massive

[1] Record of military conversations, 15 May 1936, *DDF*, Ser. II, II, no. 217. Gamelin was willing to put the French forces north of the Meuse under the command of King Leopold. He indicated, however, that this was a decision which could be taken by the French government only.

[2] Memorandum by Schweisguth, 18 July 1936, ibid., no. 480.

[3] Gamelin, *Servir*, II, 216, 239. Gamelin notes also that after Belgium was clearly committed to a policy of non-alignment, van den Bergen expressed the hope that Franco-Belgian military collaboration would continue none the less. It appears, however, that a visit to Brussels in July 1936 by Schweisguth was the last formal contact between the General Staffs until Oct. 1939. See Laroche to Delbos, 16 July 1936, *DDF*, Ser. II, II, no. 462 and Memorandum by Schweisguth, 18 July 1936, no. 480.

[4] General Staff memorandum, 9 July 1936, ibid., no. 419.

[5] Laroche to Flandin, May 1936, ibid., no. 236.

assistance from other countries. Belgium could not resist the Germans alone. This was self-evident. A national redoubt behind the Scheldt River might hold out. But not the entire frontier. These few months in 1936—just before domestic events compelled van Zeeland to dissociate Belgium from France— were the only time when the concept 'integral defence of the frontier' was plausible.[1] By the same token, if France's defensive strategy ever had a prospect of success, it was during these months. The Maginot Line, which did not cover France's north-eastern frontier, made Belgian co-operation essential. And France now had it. This was the only constructive result of the Rhineland crisis.

But the Belgians were uneasy. No matter how productive Franco-Belgian co-operation was, it did not compensate for the frustration which followed the staff conversations in London. The Belgian General Staff did not conceal its disappointment from the French.[2] King Leopold's aide-de-camp, van Overstraeten, noted in his diary that the programme discussed in London was 'meagre.' He noted also that the British were not yet anticipating any measures for the defence of the Belgian coastline.[3] The Foreign Ministry was concerned about this, too. Secretary General Vanlangenhove felt that the ideal arrangement was one in which Belgium could count upon French assistance on land and British protection on water (which protection had been available in 1914). He was interested also in Britain's capacity to supply Belgium with certain basic war materials like gunpowder and petrol for aircraft.[4]

While the army and Foreign Ministry worried about these fundamental military problems, van Zeeland and his cabinet worried about a fundamental political problem. Continued collaboration with the French presupposed collaboration with the British. The Flemish leader, van Cauwelaert, had reminded van Zeeland of that in the recent foreign policy debate. The government could never persuade the Chamber of Deputies to tolerate Franco-Belgian collaboration outside the framework of a more

[1] The German General Staff's official description of Belgian defences, which was written after the fall of Belgium, tacitly recognized this. Oberkommando des Heeres, General Stab des-Heeres, *Denkschrift über die belgische Landesbefestigung*, pp. 250–1.

[2] Laroche to Flandin, 16 July 1936, *DDF*, Ser. II, II, no. 462.

[3] Van Overstraeten, *Albert I. Léopold III*, pp. 218–9.

[4] Memorandum by Vanlangenhove, 6 June, 1936, *DDB*, IV, no. 82.

comprehensive arrangement which included the British. As long as the military reform project was outstanding, the Chamber of Deputies had a most effective lever with which to force the government to do its bidding. Ambassador Laroche informed the Quai d'Orsay that van Zeeland was 'very preoccupied with the indecisiveness which reigns in London, and he sees in it a possible source of serious difficulty'.[1]

Van Zeeland's first opportunity to appeal to his friend Eden in person was a reunion of the Locarno powers at Geneva in mid-May.[2] Van Zeeland was very frank. He said that time was working against them. The German presence in the Rhineland was becoming an accomplished and accepted fact; German rearmament was progressing fast. This was dangerous for Belgium. Would Britain consider bilateral staff talks with Belgium? The French certainly would not mind, especially since they had already indicated that the British would give military assistance to the Belgians, not to them. Anglo-Belgian staff talks need not take place on a formal basis; contact could be maintained through military attachés. A number of matters might be discussed. Airfields to be designated for the use of British aircraft was one of them. Another was the type of aircraft used by the Belgian Air Force. The Belgians might use the type employed by the Royal Air Force. Strategic problems could be discussed, too. Van Zeeland explained that for domestic reasons the Belgian army could not operate between two sections of the French army. If the British army assisted Belgium, ideally it would deploy on the left of the Belgian army. If Britain did not send an army to Belgium, the Belgian army would none the less remain to the left of the French army. British support could be given at sea. Van Zeeland also called attention to the Belgian munitions industry's proximity to the German frontier. It could be lost in the early stages of a war, and Belgium would thus have to depend on her allies for war materials. Van Zeeland emphasized that he was not asking for any new political commitments. Since Britain had already undertaken to help

[1] Laroche to Flandin, May 1936, *DDF*, Ser. II, II, no. 236.
[2] Because the French government in office was no longer in power, no formal decisions could be taken at this meeting. Lagarde to Flandin, 12 May 1936, ibid., no. 201 and Kerchove to van Zeeland, 8 May 1936, *DDB*, IV, no. 80 and Silvercruys to van Zeeland, 8 May 1936, no. 81.

Belgium, it was a good idea to make the technical arrangements for that help in advance.[1]

Eden expressed doubt that this was an appropriate time for such talks. Any intimation that Britain and Belgium were involved in them might handicap the negotiations with Germany. But, he said, he would seriously consider van Zeeland's proposals and reply to them in due course.[2]

This was not the answer van Zeeland wanted. He returned to Brussels disappointed, worried, and determined to see Eden again soon. On 22 May, two days before the Belgian general election, the Belgian embassy in London conveyed to Eden the message that Prime Minister van Zeeland wished to pay a quiet visit to London.[3] Eden did not know what to make of this. He figured that van Zeeland wanted to pursue further the matter of Anglo-Belgian staff talks and to discuss the lifting of sanctions against Italy. But what useful purpose would this visit serve, especially since van Zeeland might be out of office within a few days? But van Zeeland was his friend:

I don't want to be too discouraging because M. van Zeeland has been a good friend in the past and may be useful again in the future, and because it is healthy to parade Anglo-Belgian solidarity from time to time. It is most important not to give offence to my one really useful collaborator in Western Europe.[4]

The British embassy in Brussels was instructed to tell van Zeeland that Eden would be glad to see him in any capacity, but that he, van Zeeland, might find it convenient to wait a little longer before making definite arrangements for his visit.[5]

It was tragic for both Britain and Belgium that 'a little longer' now meant 'too long'. Time was running out for Belgium.

4. The Aftermath: the Attitude of Italy

Van Zeeland had always insisted on moderation and patience in the effort to create a new Locarno. But now he wanted fast results. The change in his attitude is quite striking. In late May he told a visiting American diplomat that whenever Europe was

[1] Memorandum by Eden, 14 May 1936, FO, 408/66/C3689/4/18.   [2] Ibid.
[3] Eden to Ovey, 22 May 1936, FO, 432/2/C3817/687/4.
[4] Minute by Eden, 3 June 1936, FO, 371/19852/C4016/687/4.   [5] Ibid.

headed towards war, there came a time when events passed out of the control of statesmen. That moment had not arrived, but it was approaching rapidly. It was necessary to make one last effort to organize Europe in a system of security.[1] About the same time he told Ambassador Laroche with regard to the next meeting of the League of Nations: 'This time there can no longer be any question of delay. Any new postponement could lead straight to disaster.'[2]

Van Zeeland's frantic wish for a last attempt to bring Germany to the negotiating table in circumstances favourable to the Western powers made the role of Italy seem more important than ever. The Italians had initialled the proposals of 19 March, but they later refused to sign them on the grounds that the continuation of League sanctions against their enterprise in Ethiopia made it impossible for them to do so.[3] Van Zeeland shared the view of most Belgians that Italian support in Western Europe was more important than the outcome of the war in Africa. The Rhineland affair reinforced this opinion. At first, van Zeeland's tact precluded his expressing this opinion outright. He could not risk offending the British during the immediate aftermath of 7 March. For a time he confined himself to worried remarks about the effects of the Ethiopian question on Anglo-French relations.[4] But by late May his patience was wearing thin. He told Laroche that although it was necessary to avoid a disavowal of what the League had undertaken, it was essential also to forget the past.[5] Shortly before the League convened in late June, he was more to the point. The first thing to be done at this meeting was to bring Italy into harmony with the other Locarno powers. This meant lifting sanctions and inviting her to sign the proposals of 19 March.[6]

The League meeting was a grim affair. 'Wretched days', writes Anthony Eden.[7] To raise the sanctions against Italy was to

[1] Memorandum by Bullitt, 20 May 1936, *FRUS*, 1936, I, 306–8.
[2] Laroche to Flandin, May 1936, *DDF*, Ser. II, II, no. 236.
[3] Chambrun to Flandin, 27 Mar. 1936, ibid., I, no. 518 and Quai d'Orsay memorandum, 4 June 1936, II, no. 271.
[4] Laroche to Flandin, Apr. 1936, ibid., II, no. 91 and Morris to Hull, 14 Apr. 1936, *FRUS*, 1936, I, 287–9 and Memorandum by Bullitt, 20 May 1936, 306–8.
[5] Laroche to Flandin, May 1936, *DDF*, Ser. II, II, no. 236.
[6] Laroche to Delbos, 27 June 1936, ibid., no. 362.
[7] Eden, *Facing the Dictators*, p. 437.

register the worst defeat ever sustained by the League. Van Zeeland was elected President of the League Assembly because of his parliamentary ability:

... the famous atmosphere of Geneva had deteriorated into something that was little better than a miasma of pharisaical hypocrisy; but the air of unruffled blandness which Monsieur van Zeeland succeeded, almost to the end, in imparting to the proceedings, was so unnaturally forced as to produce the very opposite of the effect that was intended. . . .[1]

For all his blandness the Belgian Prime Minister was desperately determined to bring the Italians into the Western camp and thus to pave the way for a new Locarno.

Van Zeeland proposed to the French and British the following course of action. Sanctions would be lifted. Italy would then be invited to attend a meeting of the Locarno powers whose purpose would be to obtain Italian approval of the proposals of 19 March. If this approval was obtained, the meeting could then be enlarged to include the Germans. The Germans would thus be confronted both with a 'policy of fair play' and with a warning that non-co-operation would mean the reconstitution of the Stresa Front. It was ten to one that Hitler would accept this invitation. If he refused it, the situation would at least be clarified to the extent that Germany would be put on the defensive. Eden agreed to van Zeeland's proposal. So did France's new Prime Minister and Foreign Minister, Léon Blum and Yvonne Delbos, who were very eager for another Locarno meeting. Of course, the two French Socialists were not exuberant at the prospect of doing business with Mussolini. Italy, they said, was not likely to be a 'solid stone' in the edifice about to be created. Van Zeeland replied that they all should see to it that this 'stone' did not become part of another edifice.[2]

As always, Eden and Van Zeeland had a private conversation. Van Zeeland said that this was the right psychological moment to begin negotiations with Germany. The Blum government was prepared to go further to meet German demands than any of its predecessors. Its domestic difficulties

---

[1] *Survey 1935*, II, 490.
[2] Memorandum by Spaak, 30 June 1936, *DDB*, IV, no. 85; Memorandum by Spaak, 30 June 1936, no. 86; and Eden to Foreign Office, 1 July 1936, FO, 408/66/C4721/4/18.

would make it all the more interested in some diplomatic success. The raising of sanctions against Italy and new evidence of Anglo-French friendship would give the Germans some second thoughts. If they were invited to negotiate on a basis of full equality and were made a simple offer, it would be hard for them to refuse.[1] Eden was impressed. 'I have considerable confidence in M. van Zeeland's judgement', he reported to the Foreign Office.[2]

It was decided that Brussels was the best location for the proposed Locarno meeting. The Italians would feel more comfortable there than in London. The British and French would be more comfortable there than in Paris, which was too reminiscent of the Hoare-Laval deal. Van Zeeland was therefore given the assignment of arranging the formalities.[3]

He was quickly disillusioned. The Italians refused his invitation, saying that the existence of mutual assistance arrangements in the Mediterranean and the failure to invite the Germans made the invitation unacceptable.[4]

What next? The Belgians and the French still wanted the Locarno meeting to take place. The Belgians did not feel that Italy's refusal made necessary a modification of the programme outlined at Geneva. The meeting would demonstrate again the unity of the three powers and their unwillingness to bow before the 'moral blackmail' of Mussolini. It was necessary to end this period of uncertainty.[5] Both the Belgians and the French wanted another chance to induce the British to resume staff talks.[6]

The British cabinet had its own ideas. It did not share Eden's

---

[1] Eden to Foreign Office, 3 July 1936, ibid., C4804/4/18.
[2] Ibid.
[3] Massigli to Quai d'Orsay, 3 July 1936, *DDF*, Ser. II, II, no. 386 and Laroche to Delbos, 17 July 1936, no. 473.
[4] Chambrun to Delbos, 12 July 1936, ibid., no. 431; Chastel to Spaak, 12 July 1936, *DDB*, IV, no. 94; and *Ciano's Diplomatic Papers* (London, 1948), ed. by Malcolm Muggeridge, pp. 14, 15, 17. The mutual assistance arrangements here referred to were negotiated in late 1935 by Britain, France, and certain other Mediterranean powers for the event of Italian aggression. See *Survey, 1935*, II, 248-71.
[5] Ovey to Eden, 13 July 1936, FO, 408/66/C5105/4/18; Ovey to Eden, 14 July 1936, 371/19909/C5158/4/18; and Ovey to Eden, 16 July, 1936, C5223/4/18.
[6] Delbos to Laroche, 8 July 1936, *DDF*, Ser. II, II, no. 405 and Laroche to Delbos, 16 July 1936, no. 462.

enthusiasm for van Zeeland's programme. Were the Western powers forming a bloc against Germany?[1] The cabinet drew a sharp distinction between a Locarno meeting for the purpose of concerting the policy of the Western powers and one for the purpose of extending an invitation to Germany.[2] It would be a bad mistake to give the Germans cause to suspect that a common front was being formed against them.[3] When the Italians declined the invitation to come to Brussels, the British again raised the question of the Locarno meeting's purpose. Would not the absence of both Germany and Italy tend to force the two of them together?[4]

Eden—probably against his own better judgement—informed the French and the Belgians that the purpose of any meeting *à trois* should be to pave the way for a meeting *à cinq*.[5] The French did not like this. They had suspected all along that a conference in two phases—one which included the Germans in its second stage—would give the British a chance to slip out of their formal engagements.[6] 'In reality', said Delbos, 'if we must announce that the July 22 meeting has no other purpose than to invite Germany to a new conference and to conclude a new treaty of mutual assistance, that would be to admit implicitly that we are making a *tabula rasa* of the past . . .'[7]

It is hard to tell what the Belgians really thought. In such situations they always went along with the British, and they did so again.[8] They did not have a choice. Nor did the French now have one. The meeting would take place on British terms, and it would take place in London.[9]

[1] Extract from Cabinet Conclusions 48(36)6, 1 July 1936, FO, 371/19908/C4788/4/18.
[2] Extract from Cabinet Conclusions 50(36)2, 6 July 1936, ibid., C4975/4/18. See also Colvin, *Vansittart in office*, p. 106.
[3] Laroche to Delbos, 8 July 1936, *DDF*, Ser. II, II, no. 407.
[4] Corbin to Delbos, 15 July 1936, ibid., no. 450.
[5] Eden to Cartier, 16 July 1936, *DDB*, IV, no. 96.
[6] Delbos to Laroche, 8 July 1936, *DDF*, Ser. II, II, no. 405.
[7] Kerchove to Spaak, 9 July 1936, *DDB*, IV, no. 90.
[8] Spaak to the Belgian Embassy in Paris, 17 July 1936, ibid., no. 97 and Laroche to Delbos, 17 July 1936, *DDF*, Ser. II, II, no. 473.
[9] Eden to Cartier, 16 July 1936, *DDB*, IV, no. 96 and *Survey, 1936*, p. 348. London was chosen as the site of the meeting instead of Brussels so that the Germans would be less suspicious, so that Blum would have a chance to meet Baldwin, and so that Britain could more easily maintain her leadership. Extract from Cabinet Conclusions 53(61)1, 16 July 1936, FO, 371/19910/C5315/4/18.

The meeting lasted one day and was devoted mostly to haggling about the wording of the concluding communiqué.[1] It called for a five-power conference which would negotiate a new Locarno. This, it was hoped, would facilitate a subsequent 'general settlement'.[2] For all its brevity this meeting was significant. Any expectation that the British intended to make more permanent their provisional military arrangements with the Belgians and the French now had to be abandoned. 'The situation created by the German initiative of March 7', as the communiqué politely put it, was now virtually accepted as a *fait accompli*. The French had, in effect, abdicated their leadership in continental affairs to the British.

Paul van Zeeland had worked for four months to preserve the Anglo-French *entente*, and he had had considerable success. In fact, he had had too much success. By helping consistently to bring the French around to the British position, he had undermined the prospects for success of his other major goal: negotiations with Germany in favourable circumstances. Those negotiations, if they ever took place, would take place on British terms. This meant that Belgium and her Western neighbours would not be negotiating from a position of strength.

This was a tragedy for Belgium, just as it was for France and Britain herself.

5. *Conclusion*

Prime Minister van Zeeland turned over the Belgian Foreign Ministry to Paul-Henri Spaak in mid-1936.[3] By that time the international conditions which had been the basis of Belgian security had changed or were being transformed rapidly. Most Belgians had regarded the remilitarization of the Rhineland as inevitable sooner or later. By the same token, German rearmament was accepted as the natural right of a great power. What worried Belgians most was the inability or unwillingness of the

[1] Foreign Office record of conversations held in London, 23 July 1936, FO, 408/66/C5449/4/18 and C5450/4/18 and Quai d'Orsay record of same, *DDF*, Ser. II, III, nos. 18 and 19.

[2] Communiqué issued by the Three Power Conference, 23 July 1936, *DIA, 1936*, pp. 218–19. See also *Survey, 1936*, pp. 348–50.

[3] Spaak had been present as Foreign Minister at the June meeting of the League and the July Locarno meeting. But he was still getting acquainted with his job and let van Zeeland do the talking.

other great powers to provide an effective counter-weight to German dynamism. The European balance of power was shifting, and Belgium was bound to be seriously affected.

One clear indication of change was the drift of Italy into the German camp. Since the beginning of the Ethiopian affair Belgium had hoped for the restoration of the Stresa Front. Until the June meeting of the League it was assumed in Brussels that Italy would eventually join the Western powers. Italy's fears for Central Europe and her economic interests suggested to the Belgians that she had little to gain from co-operation with Hitler's Germany.[1] Then came the Austro-German 'gentlemen's agreement', which went a long way towards removing the principal obstacle to German–Italian friendship. This happened almost simultaneously with Italy's refusal to attend the Locarno meeting. Who could doubt that Germany and Italy were partners in at least a *de facto* alliance? What made such an alliance especially ominous for bilingual, multi-party Belgium was its ideological overtones. German–Italian collusion in the Spanish Civil War, which broke out in July, strengthened the impression that Europe was indeed splitting into two camps.

A political scientist has noted that small states 'are in grave danger when caught on the wrong side of a balance turning in favour of an antagonized local Great Power'.[2] In mid-1936 there were some solid reasons for wondering if Belgium was being 'caught on the wrong side'. One of them was the decline of French influence and prestige. Seen from one angle, the advent of Léon Blum's Popular Front was to Belgium's advantage, because for all practical purposes it meant the end of Anglo-French friction. On the other hand, a Socialist government in a France which was allied to the Soviet Union could only reinforce the feeling in Belgium that Europe was dividing along ideological lines. Moreover, Blum and his colleagues had had to deal with serious domestic disorders, so serious that one might legitimately ask whether France could still resist Germany effectively. This worried van Zeeland. After all, he said, France did represent the *status quo*. Could she still defend it?[3] Paul-Émile Janson, a prominent Belgian Liberal, put it this way:

[1] Laroche to Delbos, 27 June 1936, *DDF*, Ser. II, II, no. 362.
[2] George Liska, *International Equilibrium* (Cambridge, 1957), p. 417.
[3] Memorandum by Bullitt, 20 May 1936, *FRUS*, 1936, I, 306–8.

'Do you believe that the Belgians who were in Paris in 1936, and who were forced to carry their luggage on their own shoulders because of a strike of hotel porters are not to be excused if they possess some misgivings about France?'[1]

Of all the spectres haunting the Belgian Foreign Ministry in mid-1936 none was so unsettling as the indecisiveness of Great Britain. Belgium had hoped to compensate for the remilitarization of the Rhineland with a British promise to commit troops to the continent in the event of war. After the staff talks in London the apprehensions began. The smallness of the proposed expeditionary force, the reluctance of London to complete the plans for its deployment, and perhaps a lingering fear that Britain might not send troops to the continent at all were a cause of understandable forebodings. And there remained that tenacious fear which had troubled the Foreign Ministry for years: 'Certainly England could not tolerate aggression against France or Belgium, but she would not support the policy of France in Central and Eastern Europe.'[2] If Belgium and France became involved in war against Germany which began in Central Europe and in which the British remained neutral, Belgium was faced with certain disaster.

Such was Belgium's situation during the early months of the period which Churchill called the 'loaded pause'.[3] Belgians had good reason to be frightened. What made Paul van Zeeland and his government all the more desperate was that, suddenly and without warning, the very forces dividing Europe now threatened Belgian unity itself.

[1] Quoted in Reynaud, *In the Thick of the Fight*, p. 155. Janson was van Zeeland's successor as Prime Minister in October 1937.
[2] Van Zuylen, *Les Mains libres*, p. 361. See also Laroche to Flandin, Apr. 1936, *DDF*, Ser. II, II, no. 91.
[3] Churchill, *The Gathering Storm*, p. 207.

IV

THE MAY ELECTION

1. *The End of the First van Zeeland Government*

In early April 1936 van Zeeland reported to the Chamber of Deputies about the domestic accomplishments of his government, which was now facing an election. This was a triumphant moment for him. Almost everyone recognized the success of his economic experiment, and the Chamber gave his brief talk an enthusiastic ovation.

Van Zeeland's message was simple and straightforward. As long as the country was in the grip of an economic crisis, he said, it was natural to blame every problem on the crisis itself. But now that the critical period had passed, it could be seen that Belgium's problems involved far more than the state of the economy; they involved the very structure of the economy. Many weaknesses were inherent in the system long before the crisis began. Whereas the government had until now concentrated on reviving the economy, it would now undertake a fundamental reform of the whole system. This reform would be so basic and so momentous that it could not be realized without a modification of the political structure of Belgium. Belgium's institutions had to be brought up to date. The importance of these changes was such that 'on their resolution depends the fate of several generations'.[1]

Van Zeeland was confident about the future. During the last year, he said, the country had demonstrated exceptional maturity. Amidst the economic and international crises there was evidence of both moral and material recovery. Rancour and distrust did still exist. There was no point in concealing the disarray in Belgian political opinion or in assuming that Belgium could remain impervious to outside influences. But it was necessary to find a working consensus and to take advantage

[1] *Annales* (Chamber), 1935/1936, 1 Apr. 1936, p. 1273.

of the 'ardent and disinterested forces which are in ferment among the young'. Belgium could solve her problems in her own fashion and according to the lessons of her own history. But this would happen only in a spirit of national harmony.[1]

This was the Prime Minister's message as the Chamber of Deputies concluded its annual session. Although his achievements were already impressive, he felt that his work of 'national renovation' had only begun. It remained to modernize the economy, ameliorate social conditions, and to make the government more efficient. Van Zeeland had not begun a revolution, wrote one observer. He began instead the adaptation of Belgium to the revolution which the modern world was undergoing without knowing it.[2] The beginning of this adaptation had been a great success.

Before van Zeeland could continue his work, his government had to submit its record to the electorate. For the leaders of a coalition which was at the height of its prestige, the prospect of an election should have been most gratifying. The election of 1932, which had taken place in the depths of the Depression, had produced no significant changes. Now prosperity was returning. The government coalition still functioned smoothly; van Zeeland was able to tell the Chamber of Deputies that all but a few cabinet decisions had been taken unanimously.[3] Was there any reason to think that the three major parties and their coalition would not emerge from the election even stronger?

One reason was that van Zeeland's tripartite government had been constituted for the purpose of economic renovation only. Now that this had been largely accomplished, there was no guarantee of government unanimity in other matters. To be sure, many young politicians did share a belief that a basic reform of the social and political structure of their country was badly needed. But it did not follow from this that young Catholics, Liberals, and Socialists would continue working together harmoniously once the cohesion created by economic crisis had been weakened.

There was another cause for concern. The election campaign

[1] Ibid.

[2] Pierre Nothomb, 'Le second cabinet van Zeeland', in *La Revue générale* (Brussels, 1936), 69th year, p. 226.

[3] *Annales* (Chamber), 1935/1936, 8 Apr. 1936, p. 1273.

would have been a rather quiet affair, had it not been for the flamboyant and noisy antics of the Flemish Nationalists and the Rexists, a new party which had been organized only a few months earlier. Extremists like these were troublesome at any time. But in 1936 bilingual Belgium could afford even less than usual to flirt with political adventurers. Although the three major parties had no cause to fear for their majority, marginal gains by splinter groups would undermine the prestige of the government. Substantial gains would play havoc with the delicate machinery of the coalition system. The government took no risks. In order to prevent the extremists from consolidating their support, the date of the election was moved from October ahead to May.[1]

Shortly after the remilitarization of the Rhineland, van Zeeland made some observations about parliamentary government to the American ambassador in Brussels. It was proving all too ineffectual in meeting crises, he complained. If it were to function effectively in the future, certain changes had to be made. The Prime Minister noted ruefully that those countries which faced elections in the near future were far worse off than those which did not.[2]

He did not know how right he was.

2. Rexism and Flemish Nationalism

In November 1935 a young man named Léon Degrelle forced his way to the podium during a meeting of one of the constituent organizations of the Catholic party and denounced its leaders as 'rotten'. Such charges were not new. An irritated Belgian public was already accustomed to hearing about illicit connections between politicians and high finance.[3] But Degrelle's raucous conduct was something new, and this incident marked the formal separation of Degrelle and his devoted followers from the Catholic party. Thus was launched the most spectacular adventure in Belgian political history.

[1] Höjer, Le Régime parlementaire belge de 1918 à 1940, p. 246.
[2] Morris to Hull, 1 Apr. 1936, FRUS, 1936, I, 271–2.
[3] The most celebrated scandals involved the directors of two large co-operative banks run by the Socialist and Catholic parties, respectively—the Banque Belge du Travail and the Boerenbond. Van Zeeland himself felt compelled to resign in late 1937 because of an innocent connection with a bank scandal. See J. Wullus-Rudiger, En marge de la politique belge (Brussels, 1957), p. 226.

The sudden prominence of Degrelle and his movement was a surprise to contemporaries, and even today the phenomenon of 'Rexism' is a little difficult to explain.[1] Belgium should have been one of the countries least susceptible to the charms of right-wing extremism. For over a century her political and social life had developed peacefully and gradually along constitutional and liberal lines. With the recent exception of the Flemish Nationalists, members of Belgium's large middle class had sought change through parliamentary methods alone. During the most dismal days of the Depression Belgians continued to vote for representatives of the traditional parties. Against this background it was easy to minimize and even overlook the malaise into which many ordinary Belgians had fallen by 1936 and to underestimate the political potential of an extraordinary character like Degrelle.

The *Chef* [Leader] himself was the major asset of the Rexists, so much so that a recent historian of the movement concludes that 'throughout its brief history, Rexism remained essentially a one man show'.[2] One of Degrelle's closest associates remarked that Rexism without Degrelle would be like a car without a motor.[3] Although his intellectual resources were unimposing, Degrelle was gifted with boundless energy, a magnetic personality, and a flair for public speaking. His admirers talked about his 'Rex appeal' and regretted that Belgian women could not vote. Degrelle was a born demagogue. His complete lack of scruple enabled him to identify his cause with nearly every element in Belgian society. The worker, the lower-middle-class *rentier* and shopkeeper, the disgruntled nobleman, Degrelle had something for all of them. 'To some he represented himself as more Catholic than the Pope, to others more

---

[1] The name 'Rexism' was derived from the name of the Catholic publishing house which Degrelle managed in the early 1930s. The best scholarly description of Rexism is Jean-Michel Étienne's *Le Mouvement rexiste jusqu'en 1940* (Paris, 1968). Shorter accounts are Jean Stengers, 'Belgium', in *The European Right* (Berkeley, 1965), ed. by Hans Rogger and Eugen Weber, pp. 127–67; Eugen Weber, *Varieties of Fascism* (Princeton, 1963), pp. 122–9; and André Buttgenbach, 'Le mouvement rexiste et la situation politique de la Belgique', *Revue des sciences politiques* (Paris, 1936), LIX, 511–54.

[2] Stengers, in *The European Right*, ed. by Rogger and Weber, p. 137.

[3] Étienne, *Le Mouvement rexiste*, p. 30. The best biographical sketch of Degrelle is in Pierre Daye's *Léon Degrelle et la Rexisme* (Paris, 1937).

Royalist than the King.'[1] Night after night growing crowds paid to hear him shout about 'rotten' politicians and 'banksters' and the system which permitted them to govern.

Degrelle's remarkable flexibility and his broad appeal were in no way hindered by his party's platform, which was very vague. Rexism was not noted for the quality of its ideologues, and the party programme was not fully worked out until after the election. One observer noted that Degrelle's followers did not know what they wanted, but they wanted it badly.[2] Degrelle himself talked about the integrity of the family, the Church, and the professions. He promised to restore the 'popular community' in which the party system would be replaced by a hierarchical, corporative arrangement. He liked to contrast the legitimate interests of the *pays réel* with those of the decadent *pays légal*. His use of these concepts reflected the influence of Charles Maurras, who was one of Degrelle's heroes.[3] Whatever the contents of its programme, Rexism remained for its devotees 'a mystique, a state of soul'.[4]

Degrelle's plans for Belgium's future had very little to do with his popularity. Most of his talk and most Rexist propaganda were strictly negative, and herein lay the attraction. Degrelle convinced his adherents that Belgium's social malaise and class struggle were artificial and had been caused by a political, social, and economic system based on a misunderstanding of natural law.[5] Although it was vague and muddled, Rexism's categorical critique of the whole system was especially effective in 1936. Even the solid accomplishments of van Zeeland's government could not erase the memory of fifteen years of unimaginative and sometimes ineffective government. Many Belgians remembered that van Zeeland's triumphs would not have been achieved without the use of 'special

[1] René Hislaire, 'Political Parties', in Goris, ed., *Belgium*, p. 106. See also Buttgenbach, in *Revue des sciences politiques* (Paris, 1936), LIX, 518–19.

[2] Charles to Eden, 15 June 1936, FO, 432/2/C4339/202/4.

[3] Many young Belgians had been impressed with Maurras's writings and those of other reactionary French writers. The French right-wing press was widely read in Belgium, too. For a description of the intellectual background of Rexism, see Stengers in *The European Right*, ed. by Rogger and Weber, pp. 142–4 and B. S. Chlepner, *Cent ans d'histoire sociale en Belgique* (Brussels, 1958), pp. 336–43.

[4] Buttgenbach, in *Revue des sciences politiques* (Paris, 1936), LIX, 520. See also pp. 530–42.

[5] Ibid., p. 521.

powers'. It is possible that many voted for Rexist candidates in 1936 not because they wanted a Rexist victory, but because they hoped that a substantial vote for the Rexists would make a sobering impression on the parliamentary representatives of Belgium's other parties.[1] The Belgian electorate knew that Degrelle's charges of corruption in high places had some foundation. Fifteen members of parliament were induced not to seek re-election because of them.[2] Collusion between politicians and financiers seemed particularly menacing to the one part of the population which had been adversely affected by van Zeeland's devaluation of the franc—lower-middle-class *rentiers*.[3] Finally the Rexist appeal was always most forceful among the young, many of whom were disgusted with the indecisiveness of the politicians and for whom a rejection of the whole system seemed the only way to get results.

Needless to say, Degrelle played on middle-class fears of socialism and communism. In 1936 the danger seemed all too real to cautious and conservative Belgians who daily read newspaper accounts of the French Popular Front's electoral success and the disorders which followed it. 'After Spain, France; after France, Belgium', intoned *Le Peuple*, the official paper of the Socialists.[4] This kind of prediction was blood-curdling for most Belgians. Of course, Liberals and Catholics could talk about the red menace, too, but Degrelle could go one step further. Socialism and communism were only one aspect of the problem, he told his audience. It would be necessary to rid Belgium of the liberalism which produced them. 'To break the neck of Communism will get us nowhere', he said, 'if we do not also break the neck of the social selfishness which gave it birth.'[5]

Degrelle always insisted that his movement was different from Nazism and Italian fascism. In some respects his assertion was true. He never openly rejected the concept of democracy. His party was not militaristic and usually avoided violence. His followers kept their sense of humour. In fact, a good deal of

[1] Harold Callender, 'Fascism in Belgium', *Foreign Affairs* (New York, 1937), XV, no. 3, 557–8.
[2] *The Times*, 22 May, 1936, p. 13.
[3] Ibid., 21 May, 1936, pp. 17–18.
[4] Quoted in ***, 'Les élections du 24 mai', *La Revue générale* (Brussels, 1936), 69th year, p. 716.
[5] Quoted in Weber, *Varieties of Fascism*, p. 125.

---

opera bouffe characterized the whole performance. But Degrelle's ideas about corporatism, his rabid anti-Marxism, his talk about a national revival, and his plans to increase the authority of the state did lend him a certain resemblance to Hitler and Mussolini—and especially the latter. Belgian memories of the First World War and Occupation were too vivid for Degrelle to make much ado about Nazi accomplishments. Most Rexists viewed Nazi race doctrines with scepticism.[1] There is no evidence of any tangible German support for the Rexists.[2] Italian fascism was a different matter. There were no unpleasant memories of the Italians, and Degrelle's programme bore a closer resemblance to Mussolini's. The *Duce* subsidized his Belgian admirers and granted them the use of Italian radio facilities when the same was forbidden them in Belgium.[3] But this sort of support meant nowhere near as much as the simple example of the success achieved by authoritarian Italy and Germany, while the Western democracies stumbled from one crisis to another.

Degrelle had another advantage. International affairs and Belgium's role in them quite naturally caused fear and confusion among Belgian voters. The Rexists capitalized on this by expressing views close to those of the Flemish Nationalists. Degrelle argued that Belgium ought to stay outside every diplomatic combination. He never advocated international cooperation with the Germans, but he did reserve his greatest disapprobation for the French. 'As for contemporary French foreign policy', he wrote, 'we ought to avoid it like the plague.'[4] 'France was a magnificent country', he said, but her politicians were 'Jewish adventurers, marxists, masons . . .'[5] Degrelle's advocacy of neutrality was hardly an innovation. It was simply

---

[1] *Le Pays réel*, 26 Aug. 1936, p. 3. It should be noted, however, that the Rexists showed more interest in anti-Semitism and were more open in their praise of Germany (although it remained qualified) after their electoral set-back in 1937. See Léon Degrelle, *Degrelle avait raison. Recueil de textes écrits par Léon Degrelle entre 1936–1940* (Brussels, 1941), pp. 35–7.

[2] De Jong, *The German Fifth Column in the Second World War*, p. 199 and GFMA, 1727/3325/E008157 (which is a note by the editor of this collection of German documents to the effect that there is no evidence of such support).

[3] De Jong, *The German Fifth Column*, p. 199 and Count Galeazzo Ciano, *Ciano's Hidden Diary, 1937–1938* (New York, 1953), trans. by Andreas Mayor, p. 11.

[4] Degrelle, *Degrelle avait raison*, p. 33.

[5] Louise Narvaez, *Degrelle m'a dit . . .* (Paris, 1961), p. 308.

a vulgar manifestation of a feeling now shared by most Belgians. Degrelle was too smart a politician not to make the most of the growing conviction that Belgium's salvation lay not in choosing sides, but in avoiding the impending struggle altogether.

Degrelle had an insurmountable handicap. Despite his flair for being all things to all men, no amount of histrionics would ever render him Flemish. This was the 'Achilles heel' of Rexism, and it was a cause of its eventual failure. Although Degrelle published a newspaper in Flanders and had a handful of followers there, Rexism was essentially a Walloon affair. Right-wing radicalism had no less appeal in Flanders than in Wallonia. But by 1936 Flemings had several such movements from which to choose, and they were exclusively and wholly Flemish.

The radicalization of Flemish nationalism, which began years before the birth of Rexism, was the result of many factors. Government inefficiency, corruption, and the like aroused as much dissatisfaction in Flanders as in Wallonia. Moreover, the instincts of most Flemings were profoundly anti-Marxist. The possibility of being drowned in a flood of Walloon and French Socialism induced many Flemings to look for ways to insulate themselves from the danger. But more important—and here Flemish nationalism had nothing in common with Rexism—there remained the unsolved problem of giving the Flemish people and their language equality within the Belgian community. The passage of the new language laws in the early 1930s was a step forward.[1] The general election of 1932 did register a setback for the Flemish Nationalists. But Flemings thought that the new laws were being implemented too slowly, if they were being implemented at all. Some wondered whether the problem required a more radical solution. The upshot was that by the mid-1930s there existed a motley collection of parties and programmes which did not augur well for Belgian political stability or, for that matter, Belgian unity.

The first significant Flemish group to reject outright national unity and democracy was the *Verbond van Dietsche Nationaal-solidaristen* (*Verdinaso*)—the Union of *Dietsch* National Solidarists—which was founded by Joris van Severen in 1931. The

---

[1] It will be recalled that these laws gave the Flemish language legal equality in every dimension of Belgian government.

goal of *Verdinaso* was the restoration of *Dietschland*—the union of Flanders with the Netherlands. This notion later gave way to that of the *Dietsche Rijk*—a restoration of the Netherlands of the sixteenth century, which had included Wallonia. 'No intelligent man still believes in democracy', van Severen told his followers; the *Dietsche Rijk* would be authoritarian and constructed along corporative lines.[1] *Verdinaso* was extra-parliamentary and never had many members. Those it did have were usually young men who found satisfaction in the uniforms, parades, and discipline which *Verdinaso* offered. Like Rexism, *Verdinaso* was a 'one man show'. Van Severen's powerful and colourful personality maintained the devotion of his followers despite the twists and turns of his ideological position.[2]

Among van Severen's favourite targets for abuse was the much larger organization of the Flemish Nationalists. As far as he was concerned, the *Vlaams Nationaal Verbond (VNV)*—the Flemish National Union—was only a squalid imitation of his own outfit. It was in this connection that van Severen made his influence felt. After their losses in the 1932 election the Flemish Nationalists were hyper-sensitive to this kind of criticism. When Staf de Clerq and his associates organized the *VNV* in 1933, they naturally sought to minimize the ideological attractions of *Verdinaso* and to offer Flemings something more exciting than hackneyed ideas about parliamentary democracy.[3] The leaders of the *VNV* were soon flirting with fascism. De Clerq called himself *De Leider*. Nazi salutes, parades, and all the paraphernalia of a fullfledged fascist movement became part of the *VNV*'s style. But the *VNV* never quite succeeded in producing a coherent programme, and its members held a wide variety of opinions. A contemporary described the Flemish nationalism of this period as 'a heterogeneous thing, amazingly flexible, always in motion. It is more voluntaristic than intellectual, more an attitude than a distinct concept.'[4] It is not surprising that

[1] Stengers, in *The European Right*, ed. by Rogger and Weber, p. 151.

[2] Ibid. See also Wullus-Rudiger, *En marge de la politique belge*, pp. 222–5 and Willemsen, *Het Vlaamse-Nationalisme 1914–1940*, pp. 346–60.

[3] Ibid., p. 350, and Stengers in *The European Right*, ed. by Rogger and Weber, pp. 153–4.

[4] Edgar de Bruyne, 'Le mouvement flamand et les tendances fédéralistes', *La Revue générale* (Brussels, 1937), 70th year, pp. 459. See also Wullus-Rudiger, *En marge de la politique belge*, pp. 233–6 and Willemsen, *Het Vlaamse-Nationalisme 1914–1940*, pp. 322–46.

the standard history of Flanders characterizes the extremism of the 1930s as 'more destructive than constructive, more confused than purposeful'.[1]

In so far as it was a radical, authoritarian movement, Flemish nationalism, like Rexism, was a 'straw fire' caused by the psychological and social dislocations of the 1930s. Unfortunately, the story does not end there. Whereas Rexism soon faded away, the *VNV* did not. Unlike their Walloon counterparts the Flemish Nationalists could rely on relatively consistent electoral support because of legitimate Flemish grievances.[2] It was as 'integral, radical *Flamingants*' that they sustained their popularity; it was as *Flamingants* that they remained very dangerous.[3]

Just as van Severen's little group caused the *VNV* to be more radical, so in turn did the *VNV* have an impact on Flemish Catholics. Most Catholics thought that the *VNV*'s fascist antics were sheer buffoonery. But its appeal to the nationalist sentiments of Catholics was very effective. In the mid-1930s there appeared a concept which not only provided a bridge between Nationalists and Catholics but also gave *Flamingants* of every stripe a practical programme around which to unite. This was the concept of 'federalism', which at first attracted the support of a few Louvain intellectuals and which soon won wide popular support. Strictly speaking, it was not a new idea. There was talk about a federal solution to Belgium's problems even before the First World War. By the 1930s some of the talk was coming from Wallonia.[4] But most of it came from Flanders. There were numerous schemes for a federal Belgium. Most of them left to the central government only matters relating to national defence, foreign policy, and the economy. All other matters would be handled by regional legislatures. Flanders and Wallonia would have a common monarch, but the functions of the King's ministers would be divided regionally.[5]

---

[1] Max Lamberty *et al.*, *Geschiedenis van Vlaanderen* (Brussels, 1949), VI, 251.

[2] In the elections of 1939 the Flemish Nationalists preserved the gains made in 1936, while the Rexists lost almost all of their support.

[3] Max Lamberty *et al.*, *Geschiedenis van Vlaanderen*, p. 252.

[4] Dr. Jur. W. Houtman, *Vlaamse en Waalse Documenten over Federalisme* (Schepdaal, 1963), pp. 116–7, 135–45 and Wullus-Rudiger, *En marge de la politique belge*, pp. 268–72.

[5] De Bruyne, in *La Revue générale* (Brussels, 1937), 70th year, pp. 461–5.

Whatever the nuances of the various proposals, their very existence meant that there now was a practical compromise between the proponents of *Dietschland* and Catholics who were still loyal to Belgium. While moderate Nationalists toned down their talk about a union with the Netherlands, there was growing agitation in Catholic circles for a 'concentration of Flemish forces around the federal idea'.[1]

Federalism was frightening to those who cherished Belgian unity. Some wondered how long a federal Belgium could survive. Precisely because of their differences, Flanders and Wallonia had always complemented one another economically and politically. It was hard to see how a Flemish peasant or a Walloon labourer would benefit from the division of his country. Others wondered how a Socialist would fare in conservative, clerical Flanders and how a conservative Catholic would fare in more industrialized, anti-clerical Wallonia. Extremists of the right would be far more potent in the north, while the left might get the upper hand in the south. Because of her two languages and location Belgium had always been vulnerable to outside influences. A federal Belgium would be even more vulnerable, and 1936 was not an ideal year to throw the doors wide open. It is no wonder that federalism seemed so dangerous.[2]

And it is no surprise that Paul van Zeeland appealed so often for national harmony and consensus. His appeals were more than mere election rhetoric.

3. *The Election*

Once the date of the elections had been moved ahead to May, the Prime Minister was more confident. It was very unlikely that the Rexists would have much success, he said.[3] Little happened during the campaign to ruffle his confidence, despite the commotion caused by the Rexists and Flemish Nationalists. Because the three major parties were partners in a successful

---

[1] Willemsen, *Het Vlaamse-Nationalisme 1914–1940*, p. 259. See also pp. 258–62 and Wullus-Rudiger, *En marge de la politique belge*, pp. 254–6.

[2] De Bruyne, in *La Revue générale* (Brussels, 1937) 70th year, p. 467. See also Louis de Lichtervelde, 'Réflexions sur le fédéralisme', *La Revue générale* (Brussels, 1936), 69th year, pp. 294–312, and Claeys-van Haegendoren, *25 Jaar Belgisch Socialisme*, pp. 424–6.

[3] Laroche to Flandin, May 1936, *DDF*, Ser, II, II, no. 236.

coalition, they were content to magnify their own roles in the van Zeeland government without attacking one another. The presence of a common enemy in Rexism was another reason for the parties to minimize their differences, and their leaders indicated they were ready to enter a new tripartite government.[1] The most fateful election in Belgian history was thus preceded by a deceptively quiet campaign. Foreign policy received little attention. The Rhineland crisis had just passed, and most agreed that van Zeeland had represented Belgium's interests skilfully. One thing did suggest that the Prime Minister might be over-confident: Léon Degrelle's rallies were the best attended.[2]

The results of the 24 May election were sensational. Although the Rexist organization had been founded only months earlier, it won one-tenth of the vote—a very large percentage by Belgian standards. The Rexists' twenty-one seats in the Chamber of Deputies, which had two hundred seats in all, made their representation nearly as large as that of the Liberals. The Flemish Nationalists doubled their representation from eight to sixteen seats. The Communists had had three seats; they now had nine. The traditional parties retained their majority. But all three lost ground. The principal loser was the Catholic party, which forfeited sixteen seats in the Chamber of Deputies.[3]

The significance of these changes was more far-reaching than one would suspect at first glance. Twenty-five per cent of the electorate voted for parties committed to a basic change in the structure of the Belgian state. This perhaps seems a modest percentage when measured by the standards of certain other countries. But in mid-1936 there was good reason to fear that Belgian voters would continue their drift to the extreme right and extreme left. This could be fatal for a bilingual country sandwiched between Hitler's Germany and Blum's France. The election not only strengthened the position of the extremists. It also undermined the capacity of the three major parties to cope with the new situation. The Catholics and

[1] Höjer, *Le Régime parlementaire belge*, p. 247.
[2] *The Times*, 23 May, 1936, p. 13.
[3] Roger E. de Smet, *et al.*, *Atlas des élections belges* (Brussels, 1958), pp. 28–9. The results of the 24 May election were confirmed in the provincial elections of 7 June. See *BPB*, no. 123, 2 Sept. 1936, p. 16.

Liberals together no longer constituted a majority. These two parties had dominated Belgian politics since the war, and tripartite governments were common only in times of crisis. Because the Catholics were the Rexists' main victim, most of their losses were sustained in Wallonia; this meant that the balance within the Catholic party had shifted in favour of the Flemings. Ironically, the Liberals, who had lost the fewest votes, had lost the most influence. The weight of this small, Walloon-dominated party had often been decisive in government crises. But now a Liberal-Catholic or, for that matter, a Liberal-Socialist coalition no longer had a majority.[1] The Liberals could no longer emerge from every governmental crisis with key cabinet posts such as the Ministry of Defence and the Ministry of Foreign Affairs.

Catholic losses had another consequence. The Socialists, despite their own set-back, were now the largest single party. It was unfortunate that this happened at a time when middle-class Belgians were terrified by the spectre of Socialism at home and abroad. After the election the leaders of the Socialist party behaved with moderation. But most Belgians were less impressed with the responsible attitude of men like Émile Vandervelde than they were by the occasional radical appeals for a 'popular front'.[2] 'The country does not want this at any price', said elder statesman Paul Hymans.[3] Nor did the country want a Socialist-dominated cabinet to conduct a foreign policy parallel with that of Popular Front France.

May 1936 marked the beginning of a chaotic period in Belgian political history. The Socialists were more confident and made bolder demands. The Liberals, denied their customary influence, became more rigid in outlook and more reluctant to participate in any government oriented towards the left. The Catholics, too, were worried about the drift to the left. Flemish Catholics naturally wanted to win back the allegiance of those voters who had defected to the Nationalists, and they were more attracted to federalism than ever. All these divisive

[1] Buttgenbach in *Revue des sciences politiques* (Paris, 1936), LIX, 511–14 and Höjer, *Le régime parlementaire belge de 1918 à 1940*, p. 248.

[2] Talk about a popular front lasted until September, when the trade unionists formally rejected the idea. *The Times*, 23 July, 1936, p. 14; 16 Sept., p. 11.

[3] Comte Capelle, *Au service du roi* (Brussels, 1949), I, 231–2.

tendencies within the three major parties were manifested at the very moment when extremist inroads had made their co-operation in a tripartite government a virtual necessity.[1] The three parties did share a common fear of Rexism. But fear was hardly a sufficient basis for a new government programme.

The general election of 1936 damaged the prestige and effectiveness of the Belgian government at a moment when those qualities were most needed.

4. Van Zeeland's Second Government

The days following the election were very discouraging. The worst blow fell when the French general strike movement suddenly spread to Belgium during the first week of June. Strikes spread from one industry to another, until in mid-June the movement came to a climax with a strike in the massive mining industry. The strikes took place without the approval of the Socialist party. Their spontaneity as well as their connection with events in France made them all the more frightening.[2] It is astonishing that during these critical days party haggling deprived Belgium of a new government. A breakdown in inter-party co-operation was bad at any time. In June 1936 it was a sign of irresponsibility.

Almost everyone agreed that Belgium needed another tri-partite government and that van Zeeland should lead it. Since the three major parties were now busy blaming one another for the results of the election, van Zeeland, who had never been a member of a party, seemed all the more ideal as head of the next cabinet. Belgians were therefore shocked when he refused to form a new government. It is hard to tell whether his refusal was just a tactical manœuvre designed to make his own indispensability more obvious or whether he really wanted to leave political life.[3] It is not hard to think of reasons why van Zeeland might no longer have a burning desire to be Prime Minister of Belgium.

[1] A Catholic-Socialist cabinet was precluded by the attitude of Catholic conservatives. Höjer, Le régime parlementaire belge, p. 248. See also pp. 255–7.
[2] The Van Zeeland Experiment, p. 133; Baudhuin, Histoire économique de la Belgique, I, 514; The Times, 16 June, 1936, p. 17.
[3] There is evidence for both explanations. See Hymans, Mémoires, II, 763; Capelle, Au service du roi, I, 226–7; Laroche to Flandin, May 1936, DDF, Ser. II, II, no. 236; and Charles to Eden, 3 June, 1936, FO, 432/2/C4025/202/4, and Memorandum by Eden, 14 May 1936, 408/66/C3689/4/18.

King Leopold had no choice but to call on the leader of the largest party, Vandervelde, to form a new government. Catholics and Liberals were willing to participate in another government which included Socialists. But they were unwilling to have the former President of the Second International as their Prime Minister.[1] After several wasted days of futile bargaining the old Socialist indicated that he was unable to form a government, and he simultaneously recommended that the King again call on van Zeeland.[2]

Whether he had anticipated this all along or whether he felt a sense of obligation, van Zeeland accepted. The parties now should have closed ranks, especially since van Zeeland had their agreement on the outline of a new government programme —grudging though it was. Their acceptance of it was probably prompted by sheer fear of the alternatives.[3] But they continued to haggle among themselves—this time over the number of portfolios to be given to each party and over personalities. Van Zeeland thus despaired of forming a cabinet and asked the King to relieve him of the task. Leopold was furious. The behaviour of the parties seemed to him the height of folly. For the second time in his controversial reign the King of the Belgians felt it necessary to intervene in a crisis.[4] He summoned the party leaders to the Royal Palace and lectured them like schoolboys: 'It is unbelievable', he said, 'that questions of politics and personalities could prolong the crisis, when the parties are in agreement on a programme.'[5]

Leopold was right. The general strike was still spreading, and it was essential that there be someone to negotiate with the strikers. Van Zeeland agreed to make a last effort. On 13 June he announced that Belgium finally had a new government.

All things considered, van Zeeland must have been rather

---

[1] Charles to Eden, 11 June 1936, FO, 432/2/C4268/202/4.

[2] Höjer, *Le Régime parlementaire belge*, pp. 249–50 and Capelle, *Au service du roi*, I, 227–32.

[3] The Council of the Liberal Party later formally expressed its reservations about the new government. Höjer, *Le Régime parlementaire belge*, pp. 251–3.

[4] Leopold's first intervention was in March 1935 when he called van Zeeland from outside parliament to form a new government.

[5] Quoted in Höjer, *Le Régime parlementaire belge*, p. 251. See also G. H. Dumont, *Léopold III. Roi des Belges* (Saverne, 1946), p. 174 and Capelle, *Au service du roi*, I, 233.

pleased with the government which emerged from the crisis. He had nudged both the cabinet and its programme leftwards without losing the support of the Catholics or the Liberals. There were fewer Catholics in the cabinet than before, and the Liberals no longer occupied so many influential positions. The controversial Devèze was replaced as Minister of Defence by a non-party technician—General Henri Denis.[1] The composition of the new cabinet clearly reflected the increased influence of the Socialists. Henri de Man was now Minister of Finance, and his friend Spaak was the new Minister of Foreign Affairs. It was a radical cabinet, and van Zeeland eliminated any doubt about its intentions when he presented the new government's programme to the Chamber of Deputies.[2]

The programme elaborated by van Zeeland on 24 June was the most ambitious ever presented to the Belgian parliament. The first section of the Prime Minister's declaration dealt with social reforms and reflected the effects of the general strike. The new government had come to terms with the strikers almost immediately, and this part of its programme was presented, in effect, as a *fait accompli*.[3] But a higher minimum wage and a forty-hour week were only a beginning. The government's ultimate goal was 'the amelioration of the standard of living of the whole population and especially that of the working masses'.[4] In order to accomplish this, Belgium must continue her economic recovery. The government would initiate new public works projects, seek new foreign markets, and so on. The most controversial part of the programme returned to a familiar theme: 'It is essential to reform our political institutions in such a way that they can respond to the new tasks of an economic and social nature with which they

[1] Devèze's retirement was a foregone conclusion. He was so distrusted by Socialists and Flemish Catholics, as well as a number of generals, that he had become a real liability. He realized this, and before the election he indicated that he intended to continue his fight for military reform from the floor of the Chamber of Deputies, not from the Defence Ministry. *L'Indépendance belge*, 30 May, 1936, p. 1 and Van Overstraeten, *Albert I. Léopold III*, pp. 219–22.

[2] For an analysis of the new cabinet see Höjer, *Le Régime parlementaire belge*, pp. 252–3.

[3] Van Zeeland later said that the strike had simply speeded up what the government would have done anyway. *Annales* (Chamber), extraordinary session, 1936, 26 June 1936, p. 57.

[4] Ibid., 24 June 1936, p. 22.

will have to deal.'[1] The parliament itself must be made more
efficient; the number of senators and deputies had to be
reduced; measures must be taken to hasten parliamentary
decisions on government budgets. The executive branch would
be made stronger, too. The government intended to explore the
possibility of introducing a referendum. It hoped to create a
'council of state' for reviewing legislation about to be presented
to the parliament. The government proposed also the establish-
ment of an 'economic council' which would consist of representatives from the chambers of commerce and the various
professional groups and which would advise the government in
economic matters.[2] Of course, steps would be taken 'to purify
the moral atmosphere of the country'—a reference to the recent
financial scandals.[3] Before concluding his statement, van
Zeeland remarked that the government did not expect blind
confidence in a programme so extensive; this or that aspect of it
could be modified after serious discussion.

Such was the programme of Belgium's new government. 'We
are convinced that it will open to our country a new era of
prosperity and calm', said the Prime Minister—brave words
when said to an assembly so disorderly that the Rexists and
Flemish Nationalists nearly prevented him from speaking at
all.[4] Van Zeeland thought that Belgium could successfully
undertake basic structural reforms, but his expressions of
optimism were always cautious. Returning to the Chamber to
participate in the hectic debate which followed his opening
presentation, he said this:

Gentlemen, I for one refuse to believe that the Belgian government
cannot adapt itself by an effort from within. I have no illusions.
When we look around us in Europe, we see, alas, that in most
instances reform and re-adaptation of the institutions of the last
century has had to be accomplished from without and by violence.[5]

As far as van Zeeland, de Man, Spaak, and their colleagues
were concerned, the new government and its programme
represented Belgium's best chance to avoid a dictatorship.[6]

[1] Ibid., p. 24.
[2] 'This is the first step on the road to corporatism', shouted a Socialist. 'Très
bien, très bien', the Rexists shouted back. Ibid.
[3] Ibid., p. 25.   [4] Ibid.
[5] Ibid., 26 June 1936, p. 61.   [6] Van Kalken, *Entre deux guerres*, p. 82.

Perhaps they were its last chance. Events in neighbouring countries suggested that time was running out fast.

5. *A New Foreign Policy*

Many Belgians were bewildered and worried by the brevity of the new government's statement on foreign policy, especially since the relative increase in Socialist influence might have important consequences. The declaration of 24 June said only this: 'In international affairs the government will pursue the same policy, one inspired by the desire to assure the country security and peace, while observing the most complete independence as well as the obligations of international collaboration.'[1] No wonder people were baffled! And they would be baffled again and again in the coming weeks by other such pronouncements. The government had to be vague. The fate of the new Locarno remained to be seen. Van Zeeland presented his programme to the parliament only one week before he went to Geneva with high hopes of arranging Italian participation in the next Locarno meeting. Furthermore, obscure statements of intention served to conceal other difficulties. Foreign policy had played a role in the formation of the new government, and amidst all the domestic commotion it was doubtless prudent to leave this sensitive matter in the background as long as possible.

The May election was bound to have an impact on the direction of Belgian foreign policy. It had benefited those who wanted a policy of non-alignment and undermined the influence of those who did not. The decline in Walloon Catholic and Liberal power was in direct proportion to the increase in Flemish Catholic power. The latter were very blunt about their conditions for participating in the new government: they would participate only if it recognized 'the necessity of safeguarding the complete independence of the country and of avoiding all obligations which could expose our country to indirect involvement in conflicts and complications between the other powers.'[2] Because this was now the view of most Belgians and because the still undecided military reform question would give the Chamber of Deputies an opportunity to impose that view on the government, it would follow that

---

[1] *Annales* (Chamber), extraordinary session, 24 June 1936, p. 25.
[2] *L'Indépendance belge*, 4 June, 1936, p. 3.

van Zeeland had no choice but to commit his second government unambiguously to a 'policy of independence'.

This would indeed have been the case, if the leadership of Belgium's largest political party had not been regarding France in a whole new perspective. The notion of an international 'popular front' against the fascist menace had its attractions for a Socialist like Émile Vandervelde, who until the advent of Léon Blum had never been enthusiastic about Belgium's special connection with France. The old Socialist was now having some second thoughts. This was embarrassing for van Zeeland, because Vandervelde was determined to be Belgium's new Foreign Minister, a position to which his past and his role as leader of the largest party clearly entitled him.[1] Given his ambition as well as the general atmosphere in Belgium, he should have maintained a discreet silence. But Vandervelde was not the man to allow ambition to prevent him from stating his convictions, and shortly after the election he informed a Parisian journalist that Belgian Socialists would seek to identify Belgian foreign policy with that of Popular Front France.[2] Vandervelde's words were not well received in Flemish and conservative circles. One Walloon paper complained that there was no need to give satisfaction to 'some anti-fascist or pro-soviet mystique'.[3] Vandervelde as Foreign Minister would have been a real problem for van Zeeland. It was the Prime Minister's good fortune that certain other prominent Socialists had a less controversial point of view. In fact, he had had one of them in mind all along.

'Dear friend', he had said to Paul-Henri Spaak a few weeks earlier, 'if we win the approaching election . . . I will ask you to become Minister of Foreign Affairs.'[4] This was a strange choice. It seemed so to Spaak himself, who was then only thirty-seven years old and who assumed that the elderly Vandervelde was the natural choice. Spaak had had no training for this post; he had travelled little; he knew no language except French; and he had a reputation for being a rabble-rouser.[5] Why was he appointed? He later wrote that 'it is to my attitude in the military

---

[1] Hymans, *Mémoires*, II, 766, and Spaak, *Combats inachevés*, pp. 27–8.
[2] *BPB*, no. 123, 2 Sept. 1936, p. 3.
[3] Ibid.   [4] Spaak, *Combats inachevés*, p. 26.
[5] Ibid., p. 27.

question that I owed this flattering promotion'.[1] Spaak had worked actively within the Socialist party leadership to bring about its support of the Devèze reform project. Vandervelde, as befitted his anti-militarist past, was lukewarm about military reform. Henri de Man, Belgium's other leading Socialist, had ideas of his own: he wanted Belgium to imitate the Swiss system of regional recruitment and short-term service. Thus, by process of elimination, Spaak became his party's leading exponent of a strong army and its leading candidate for Foreign Minister, since military and foreign political questions were so closely connected.

Van Zeeland must have had other reasons for selecting Spaak. Because Vandervelde wanted the Foreign Ministry and because the Socialist party was entitled to this portfolio, Spaak was a politically convenient alternative. Despite his years as a left-wing fire-brand, his decorous and moderate behaviour during the last year had won him the confidence of Belgium's older politicians.[2] Although he was inexperienced, he was obviously one of the ablest men in Belgian public life. His brand of Socialism suggested that there was little conflict between his personal predilections and Belgian national interest. It was no coincidence that Spaak and de Man, the two leading proponents of a Socialism adapted to Belgium's special needs, had a more flexible approach to international politics. Both were convinced that the pressure of domestic events as well as the new realities of the European situation made a change in the direction of Belgian foreign policy necessary. De Man had been advocating such a change since late 1935.[3] It is impossible to ascertain precisely when Spaak was brought around to this point of view. His memoirs seem to suggest that he gave little thought to foreign affairs until the day he actually set foot in the Foreign Ministry.[4] But common sense suggests that van Zeeland would never have relinquished this important office at such a critical moment to anyone whose views were not close to his own or to anyone who had no views at all. Be that as it may, by July 1936 Spaak was able to say, in stark contrast to most of his

[1] Ibid., p. 33.
[2] Hymans, *Mémoires*, II, 767–8.
[3] Hendrik de Man, *Gegen den Strom* (Stuttgart, 1953), p. 225.
[4] Spaak, *Combats inachevés*, pp. 27, 37–8.

party comrades, that in the matter of foreign policy he had forgotten his ideological preferences.[1]

Belgium's new Foreign Minister had a heavy responsibility: the redefinition of his country's international status. Spaak's inexperience caused him to rely heavily on the two highest permanent officials of the Foreign Ministry, Secretary General Vanlangenhove and Political Director van Zuylen. Spaak admired them both, and he discovered that they complemented one another nicely. He later recalled that Vanlangenhove was a man of discernment, moderation, and patience and that he possessed an 'excellent diplomatic style'.[2] Perhaps it was his style which led the French to believe that his views were more congenial to the interests of France than those of his colleague van Zuylen. In 1936 the French still associated van Zuylen with everything they disliked about Belgian foreign policy.[3] Perhaps they did so because of his style. Spaak remembers him as the 'grey eminence' of the Foreign Ministry and as possessing 'a subtlety of spirit which bordered on Machiavellianism and a certain taste for intrigue'. Van Zuylen had a capacity for anticipating all the dangers which might threaten Belgium, 'even if they were imaginary'.[4] One suspects that in 1936 van Zuylen needed little imagination to produce a whole catalogue of gloomy scenarios. Regardless of the impression he and Vanlangenhove made on the French, their advice to Spaak was, for all practical purposes, identical, and it was essentially the same as that given Spaak's predecessors since 1930. Spaak had to listen to them carefully not only because of his own inexperience, but also because the demands of domestic policy now paralleled those of foreign policy.[5]

When Spaak began his long career as Foreign Minister of Belgium, his country's international obligations and connections

---

[1] *BPB*, no. 123, 2 Sept. 1936, p. 4. See also Huizinga, *Mr. Europe*, pp. 77–86.

[2] Spaak, *Combats inachevés*, p. 37.

[3] Laroche to Delbos, 9 July 1936, *DDF*, Ser. II, II, no. 416 and Gazel to Delbos 11 Aug. 1936, III, no. 128.

[4] Spaak, *Combats inachevés*, p. 38. Spaak was surprised to discover that his advisers in the Foreign Ministry were 'rather badly disposed towards France', a fact which he attributes to the condescension with which France had treated Belgium.

[5] Van Zuylen, *Les Mains libres*, p. 363.

were multiple and very complex.[1] In some respects it was not
completely clear what they entailed. There were Belgium's
obligations to the League of Nations and, in particular, the
obligations which accrued from article 16 of the League
Covenant. Was Belgium obliged to grant right of passage to an
army acting under League auspices? No one knew for certain.
In the aftermath of the Ethiopian fiasco the League had begun
a formal inquiry into the nature of the Covenant and its
obligations. The Belgian Foreign Ministry could thus leave this
matter in the background for the time being, using Belgium's
membership in the League only as evidence that she had no
intention of returning to 'neutrality'. Later on, when Belgium
had severed her other connections, the French did use the
League Covenant and article 16 as the only remaining device
by which they could impose their will on Belgium and as a way
of demonstrating to their allies in Central Europe that Belgian
territory could still be used as the 'spring-board' for military
enterprises launched on their behalf. The French interpretation
of article 16 caused plenty of trouble later, but in mid-1936 the
Belgians were not particularly concerned about it.

   Nor were they much concerned about what remained of
Belgium's bilateral connection with France. When Paris and
Brussels formally abrogated the Franco-Belgian Military
Agreement of 1920, they had exchanged letters expressing their
common desire to continue staff talks 'for the purpose of
executing the engagements defined by the Rhine Treaty of
Locarno . . .'.[2] Although some members of the Chamber of
Deputies considered this 'pure comedy'—verbal camouflage
for an alliance—the fact is that Belgium's connection with
France had already been formally subordinated to Locarno and
involved no other political obligations. The French later
revealed that they had their own ideas about this, too. But in
mid-1936 the Belgians took it for granted that their special
relationship with France would end as soon as their country
disentangled itself from Locarno, which itself now seemed a
mixed blessing.

   When Belgium signed the London proposals of 19 March, she

---

   [1] The best concise description of Belgium's international status in 1936 is in
Raemaeker, *België's Internationaal Beleid, 1919–1939*, pp. 344–9, 363–6.
   [2] Van Zeeland to Laroche, 6 Mar. 1936, *DDB*, III, no. 176.

had reaffirmed her Locarno commitments. In fact, she extended them, because the proposals of 19 March entailed more reciprocity on her part than had the original arrangement. Belgium was now a guarantor of Great Britain as well as France. Both the London proposals and the British 'letter of assurance' of 1 April (which provided for the tripartite staff talks) made Britain's co-operation against unprovoked aggression contingent on a reciprocal assurance from Belgium. These arrangements were provisional. It was hoped that they would be replaced soon by a more permanent arrangement, ideally one which included the Germans and one which would thus serve as a 'new Locarno'. By mid-1936 it was obvious that no 'new Locarno' was imminent. The upshot was that Belgium was, willy-nilly, a member of a *de facto* alliance against Germany —one which had been rendered dangerous and ineffectual by Britain's refusal to make a solid military commitment.

This was the international position of Belgium after the Rhineland crisis. It was a position fraught with danger. If war broke out between France and Germany, Belgium was bound to be involved. Belgian involvement in any war save one of self-defence was fraught with domestic dangers. Vanlangenhove wrote that 'an insidious propaganda would blame the Government for having sacrificed it [Belgian territory] to foreign interests; national unity could be compromised by it, and we would be subjected at the end of the conflict to the gravest dangers'.[1] In other words, no matter who won the war, Belgium might pay for her own participation with the loss of her national unity. Hardly an inviting prospect! In April—i.e., before the national election took place—Vanlangenhove was already looking for alternative arrangements. How could Belgium make the best of a bad situation? Belgium could try to mediate the quarrels of the great powers, in the hope of preventing war from breaking out at all. But the scope for action in this respect was limited. It was more important that Belgium try in advance to keep any war away from her territory, which would become a theatre of war (1) if a great power believed that it was to its strategic advantage to strike at its principal enemy through Belgian territory, or (2) if a great

[1] Memorandum by Vanlangenhove, 25 Apr. 1936, *DDB*, IV, no. 77. Cf. with Memorandum by Vanlangenhove, 2 Feb. 1931, ibid., II, no. 233.

power had reason to believe that Belgium was linked to that enemy. The risk of Belgian involvement in a war could be limited (1) if Belgium strengthened her national defences so as to render them at least a serious obstacle to any potential aggressor, and (2) if Belgium pursued an independent foreign policy, one which precluded exclusive connections with any great power and one which would give no great power reason to number Belgium automatically among its enemies.[1] Finally, there should be no doubt that if Belgian territory was violated, Belgium would receive the prompt assistance of the other interested great powers and, in particular, that of Britain. But preparations for this assistance should not be made in such a fashion as to increase the chances of Belgian involvement in a war. Any military discussions should be carried on with 'prudence and discretion'.

A small country, when dealing with great powers, should appear prudent. Its obligations should be limited to those which are strictly indispensable. It is desirable that it preserve until the last moment its freedom of decision; if it takes up arms, it must be evident that it does so exclusively for the defence of the country. Upon that depends the unanimous *élan* of the nation, such as happened in 1914, and the maintenance of national unity.[2]

Vanlangenhove drew the conclusion that if the great powers did negotiate new treaties of mutual assistance, Belgium's frontier should be guaranteed without formal reciprocity on her part. To use the formula which soon became familiar: Belgium should be guaranteed but not a guarantor.

These were the thoughts of the Secretary General of the Foreign Ministry weeks before Spaak's arrival. They corresponded to the thoughts of the Political Director, van Zuylen.[3] After the May election the logic of these arguments was all the more compelling. Vanlangenhove welcomed the new Foreign Minister with still more arguments, if there was now any need for argument. In early July he pointed out that the efforts of the great powers to create a new system of security were not likely to succeed. Their various conceptions of a satisfactory arrangement were in fundamental opposition. The problems to be

---

[1] Memorandum by Vanlangenhove, 25 Apr. 1936, ibid., IV, no. 77.
[2] Ibid.   [3] Van Zuylen, *Les Mains libres*, pp. 358–63.

solved were very complex, and the general atmosphere was not conducive to their solution. France was still entangled in an alliance system which exposed her to serious dangers, and both she and Britain had lost prestige. Indeed, 'Europe is in a more unstable condition than twenty-five years ago'. Because the situation was so dangerous, Belgium must be strong and united at home: 'For this purpose it is necessary that our international status be simple and clear; that it cease to be an object of controversy and suspicion among a large segment of public opinion.' Belgium could no longer shoulder the obligations of the Locarno agreements; they were incommensurate with her limited resources and involved her in excessive risks. Those risks were not so formidable in 1925, which had seemed the threshold of an age of conciliation. Those days were now over. The most Belgium could do was defend her own frontiers. In so doing she would render her neighbours a great service, because she would thus be defending their most vital and vulnerable regions. This would be Belgium's contribution to Western security.[1]

It is clear that Spaak and the van Zeeland cabinet accepted these arguments and formally decided that Belgium would not accept the role of 'guarantor' in any new treaty arrangements. What is not clear is precisely when the decision was taken. Spaak's first weeks as Foreign Minister were the weeks during which van Zeeland made his desperate last effort to get Locarno negotiations under way in circumstances favourable to Belgium.[2] Until the Italians and the British made their attitudes known, there was little that the Belgians could do or say. It is possible that the Belgian government postponed its decision until those attitudes were known. Spaak himself was unusually quiet for several weeks and deliberately avoided any speech-making in the Chamber of Deputies.[3] When a Flemish deputy complained that Belgium's international position was not yet 'morally irreproachable', the normally talkative Spaak replied: 'The honourable member knows that we are engaged in ticklish negotiations . . .; he knows full well that at such a moment the wisest course for a government is to insist on silence.'[4]

[1] Memorandum by Vanlangenhove, 7 July 1936, *DDB*, IV, no. 88.
[2] See above, Ch. III, pp. 77–80.   [3] Spaak, *Combats inachevés*, p. 82.
[4] *Annales* (Chamber), extraordinary session, 1936, 16 July 1936, p. 340.

The silence did not last long. By mid-July the decision was taken. 'The Brussels government had not yet officially notified the powers of its intentions', writes Baron van Zuylen. 'It believed it useful, however, to acquant public opinion with them.'[1] On 20 July, three days before the Western powers met in London, Spaak made his public début as Foreign Minister.

'I want the foreign policy of Belgium to be placed firmly under the sign of realism', said Spaak. 'I want only one thing: a foreign policy which is exclusively and wholly Belgian.'[2] He did not wish to cast aspersions on those who had hoped after the World War to achieve security through an ideal system of international law. But now the 'beautiful dreams' were gone. Spaak wanted international law to descend from the 'admirable but inhuman heights to which the statesmen of 1918 raised it', and he hoped that nations would be asked 'to obey laws made for men and not for angels'. Of course, he was not going to turn his back on international law, but it must be brought up to date. While respect for international law did help the world to avoid conflict, such considerations should not lead to adventures in which the very basis of civilization could be destroyed. 'I must say that I tremble at the strange pacifism which does not hesitate to make war in order to demonstrate better a love of peace.' A country could make war only when its own vital interests were at stake. Furthermore, a Belgian Foreign Minister had always to remember certain factors: the geographical location of the country, the existence of her two populations, and the smallness of her resources.

In 1914 that which allowed us to resist, that which gave us complete unity, was the fact that Flanders and Wallonia understood the cruel injustice of which we were the object. If we have to realize again the difficulties and horrors of war, it is essential that the same situation present itself. It is essential that our people in their entirety have the absolute conviction that we have done nothing wrong or imprudent.[3]

In conclusion Spaak said that Belgium would co-operate within the limits of her resources with any realistic efforts to consolidate

[1] Van Zuylen, *Les Mains libres*, p. 363.
[2] *BPB*, no. 123, 2 Sept. 1936, p. 4. Spaak was speaking before the Foreign Press Union in Brussels. See also Spaak, *Combats inachevés*, pp. 42–5.
[3] *BPB*, no. 123, 2 Sept. 1936, p. 4.

the peace of the world. However, while this great task was incomplete, Belgium had every right to expect her neighbours to assure her tranquillity and security.[1]

This was a notable performance for a young and untried Foreign Minister. The speech was couched in generalities, but it was hard to miss the point. The Rexists were 'pleasantly surprised'; it was a 'Rexist speech', noted Degrelle's *Le Pays réel*.[2] Flemings were gratified, too. Spaak had revealed 'a good tendency for our foreign policy', said one Flemish paper.[3] An influential Walloon paper expressed the hope that the Foreign Minister would use the same kind of language at the impending Locarno meeting in London.[4] But one important segment of Belgian opinion had serious reservations. Spaak was soon summoned to appear before the General Council of the Socialist party. 'Mr. Spaak is still the hot-head of the party', noted one Catholic paper with relish.[5]

The hierarchs of Belgian socialism were not amused. 'You talk like Hitler', said Senator Henri Rolin, who must have been thinking about Spaak's distinctions between celestial and terrestial law.[6] Fernand Brunfaut, who was one of the most outspoken Socialists in the Chamber of Deputies, complained that Spaak's speech had had the unfortunate effect of encouraging all those who wanted a *rapprochement* with Hitler and disaffection from Popular Front France.[7] The beleaguered Spaak replied that these charges were false. He had not betrayed the idea of collective security. What he had meant was that 'our attitude will not be the same when a conflict breaks out at our frontiers as when one breaks out in South America'. The whole thing was just a misunderstanding. 'Jugez-moi sur mes actes!'[8]

The party leaders accepted this, and the next day *Le Peuple* reported that the incident between Spaak and the General

---

[1] Ibid., p. 5. This last remark was possibly a reference to the new idea that Belgium would be guaranteed, but not a guarantor.

[2] *BPB*, no. 123, 2 Sept. 1936, p. 5.

[3] Ibid.   [4] Ibid.   [5] Ibid., p. 6.

[6] *Le Peuple*, 28 July, 1936, p. 3. Rolin was one of Belgium's most ardent supporters of the League, and he frequently represented his country at Geneva.

[7] Ibid.

[8] Ibid. Spaak was amused to learn that copies of the message asking him to appear before the General Council had been sent to Léon Blum and Yvonne Delbos. Spaak, *Combats inachevés*, p. 47.

Council was closed.[1] Remembering the abruptness with which this affair ended, one of Spaak's party comrades was later moved to ask: 'Did the orchestra leader play a measure for nothing? The course of events was to show that Spaak . . . had in reality very ably tested the terrain in a skilful, prudent and tenacious policy.'[2] Spaak had indeed 'tested the terrain' and had discovered that it was rough. After this episode the government showed more respect for the sensitivities of Belgium's largest party. Spaak's subsequent pronouncements were always more cautious. It is possible that the aura of sanctity with which he and van Zeeland surrounded the 'policy of independence' and their frequent expressions of loyalty to the League and collective security were a direct result of Spaak's embarrassing confrontation with his own party. In the following weeks it was always difficult for them to couch their conception of Belgian state interest in language which was satisfactory to everybody.

For Paul van Zeeland it was especially difficult and especially embarrassing, too. After all, he had been the great friend of collective security, and he was at the moment an active partisan of a regional security agreement. He had been the President of the last League Assembly. He and Anthony Eden were close friends, and his tastes and instincts resembled those of Léon Blum. Van Zeeland was much more at home in the elegant world of international politics than in the rough-and-tumble world of Belgian politics, which the ebullient Spaak enjoyed immensely. It is hard to escape the impression that he found most regrettable that which domestic pressure compelled him to do. Shortly after Spaak's speech, French ambassador Laroche tried to sum up the Prime Minister's attitude in this way:

M. van Zeeland's thought is difficult but not impossible to understand. It certainly seems that he is convinced that his country cannot do without Franco-English assistance, which he considers the best protection against a German threat; that, on the other hand, he wants to receive the maximum and give the minimum . . .[3]

[1] *Le Peuple*, 28 July 1936, p. 1.
[2] Louis Pierard, 'Notre politique extérieur', *Le Flambeau* (Brussels, 1937), 20th year, p. 580.
[3] Laroche to Delbos, 22 July 1936, *DDF*, Ser. II, III, no. 14.

Van Zeeland's remarks to the French were ambiguous and almost contradictory. He told Léon Blum that he was surprised and irritated by Spaak's speech.[1] He told Laroche that the commotion caused by the speech was a 'tempest in a teapot'. Belgian policy had not changed. She was still loyal to the principles of collective security. She was not contemplating a return to guaranteed neutrality. 'But...' Van Zeeland's protestations of fidelity to collective security were from now on always accompanied by a qualification. 'But understand me well: what I want to avoid is that Belgium be led to accept obligations disproportionate to her resources. A small country cannot obligate herself to the same extent as a great power.'[2] The French embassy was aware that van Zeeland was under Flemish pressure. In early August it reported that he did not share his Flemish cabinet colleagues' desire for Belgium to become a non-guarantor, but that he was giving in to them on this as well as other matters.[3] Weeks later Laroche was wondering what van Zeeland's 'genuine opinion' was.[4]

Whatever his opinion was, van Zeeland no longer had a choice. On 9 September he broke a long silence and delivered a radio address designed to prepare the public for the coming change.[5] Although his language was less flamboyant, his message was much the same as Spaak's. The world was passing through a period of violence in which people were attracted to extremist solutions of both the right and the left. Located at the hub of Western Europe Belgium simply could not 'play with fire'. If the country divided into two hostile ideological blocks, it would mean the beginning of a fratricidal struggle in which all would be lost. 'There is', he said, 'a logic in events which, at a certain moment, proceeds without human control.'[6] Belgium's salvation lay in the consensus represented by the three major parties and in the realization of a political equilibrium. Belgium had to be stronger and more independent than ever. What was meant by the concept 'independence'?

[1] Léon Blum, L'œuvre de Léon Blum (Paris, 1955), V, 8–9.
[2] Laroche to Delbos, 30 July 1936, DDF, Ser. II, III, no. 47.
[3] Gazel to Delbos, 11 Aug. 1936, ibid., no. 128. See also Laroche to Delbos, 22 July 1936, no. 14.
[4] Laroche to Delbos, 2 Oct. 1936, ibid., no. 307.
[5] Van Zuylen, Les Mains libres, p. 363.
[6] BPB, no. 124, 19 Dec. 1936, p. 15.

... we want to make this clear to all without distinction: if we are attacked, we will defend ourselves to the end; but with the exception of the precise and direct instance in which we are confronted by a direct and unavoidable obligation, we intend to take into account only considerations and goals which are entirely and exclusively Belgian; we will not agree to be the pawn of any diplomacy, any group or any tendency, whatever they be ... The interests for which the government is responsible are those of the Belgians; we will never allow these interests to be obscured by any foreign diplomatic combination, no matter what it is.[1]

If Belgium remained true to herself and the lessons of her history, he said, disorder would not prevail against her.

This speech, like Spaak's, contained mostly generalities; but its point, too, was hard to miss. Political extremism was threatening Belgium with chaos. The government had to find the *juste milieu*—a programme which would hasten the return of political stability without jeopardizing national unity. Belgian foreign policy thus could not favour one side or the other in Europe's political and ideological struggles. In a word, domestic equilibrium required a position of equilibrium in international affairs.

6. *Sounding out the British, Germans, and French*

All the talk about independence notwithstanding, Belgium's international status was still inextricably connected with the fruitless effort to negotiate a new Locarno. There was no way of knowing the nature of this pact, if one was to be negotiated at all. The Belgians did not know whether their 'independence' would be based on a general settlement in the West, as they would have preferred, or whether they would have to make individual bilateral arrangements with Belgium's various neighbours. Because the Locarno powers had agreed not to make unilateral pronouncements while negotiations for a new settlement were still under way, Belgium could not implement her new policy without the consent and co-operation of her neighbours. There was therefore little the Belgians could do but 'test the terrain', quietly inform the great powers of their wishes, and wait on events. It was in a cautious spirit that the Belgian delegation travelled to London for the 23 July meeting of the Locarno powers.

[1] Ibid., p. 16.

This was the meeting at which the three Western powers acknowledged the Rhineland remilitarization as an accomplished fact and invited the Germans and Italians to attend a five-power conference for the purpose of negotiating a new Locarno. While van Zeeland and Spaak quietly listened to the British and French haggle over the wording of the meeting's final communiqué, Political Director van Zuylen had a conversation with Orme Sargent, an under-Secretary at the Foreign Office. Van Zuylen asked if the British would object if Belgium accepted no obligations in the new Locarno save that of defending her own territory? Sargent replied that the British would have no objection. But the French would not be so amenable: 'They still have the underlying intention of availing themselves of your territory.'[1] The Belgians returned to Brussels confident of British support and forewarned about impending difficulties with the French.

During the next few weeks there was no indication that the proposed five-power conference would take place soon. The Germans and Italians said they were willing to participate,but they wanted adequate preparations to guarantee the success of the meeting—a polite way of revealing they were in no hurry to negotiate.[2] As foreign ministry officials headed for their annual vacations, what little diplomatic energy remained was expended on the difficulties arising from the Spanish Civil War.[3] The pause was most welcome in Brussels. The Belgians needed time to complete the preparations for implementing their new policy.[4] They made their next approach to the Germans.

[1] Van Zuylen, *Les Mains libres*, p. 363. See also Sargent to Ovey, 15 Aug. 1936, FO, 371/19849/C5666/202/4.

[2] Davignon to Spaak, 31 July 1936, *DDB*, IV, no. 101 and Chastel to Spaak, 31 July 1936, no. 102 and *The Times*, 1 Aug. 1936, p. 12.

[3] Needless to say, Belgium was a very willing adherent to the policy of non-intervention. It was more than a matter of her following the British and French lead. Belgian public opinion was so divided that anything but a policy of non-intervention was ruled out from the start: '. . . we can only adopt an attitude inspired uniquely by concern for the tranquillity of our country', said Spaak. *BPB*, no. 124, 19 Dec., p. 11. See also Laroche to Delbos, 4 Aug. 1936, Ser. II, III, no. 68 and Spaak to Gazel, 21 Aug. 1936, no. 191 (see the appendix to this document), and Hugh Thomas, *The Spanish Civil War* (New York, 1963), pp. 258, 281, 377.

[4] Neither the cabinet nor the Foreign Ministry had worked out Belgium's 'line of conduct' for the coming negotiations, the French and British were told. Memorandum by van Zuylen, 19 Aug. 1936, *DDB*, IV, no. 103 and Memorandum by van Zuylen, 9 Sept. 1936, no. 106.

Early in August the German *Chargé* in Brussels, Curt Bräuer, found himself with Spaak at the dedication of a monument. Considering the circumstances of their meeting, the *Chargé* must have been startled by the contents of the Foreign Minister's conversation. Belgium intended to show no preference for any European power, said Spaak. After Belgium's security had been provided for in a new treaty of guarantee, the Franco-Belgian agreement of 6 March could go.[1] Spaak assured Bräuer that a majority in the cabinet and most of the Belgian people were agreed to this. A possible formula for Belgium's new international status was for her to be guaranteed without being a guarantor. Since Germany's primary concern was that Belgium should not form the left wing of the Maginot Line or serve as an area from which the French could launch an attack, Berlin certainly could agree to Belgium's request. Spaak added that Belgium had no wish to be drawn into war because of her connection with France or because of the Franco-Soviet Pact. He hoped that Belgium would assume a position like that of Holland so that the two countries would have a basis on which to pursue a common foreign policy.[2]

Some weeks later Spaak had a conversation with Ambassador Richthofen. The Foreign Minister remarked that he could understand Germany's feelings about the Franco-Soviet Pact; Germany had good reason to be concerned about events in France. Belgium wanted only to pursue an independent policy. Spaak noted that her attitude was very different from what it had been at the end of the World War and that it was easy for anyone to see the direction in which Belgian opinion was moving.[3]

The drift of Belgian opinion was indeed easy to see, and the Germans were delighted. Since Ribbentrop's premature visit to Brussels in September 1935 they had done little overtly to encourage the new trend in Belgian foreign policy. 'We don't want to give the impression of wishing to separate you from France', said Ribbentrop.[4] Now that events in Belgium had

---

[1] Spaak was referring to the letters exchanged on 6 Mar. 1936, in which the French and Belgian governments expressed their desire to maintain staff contacts.

[2] Richthofen to Foreign Office, 4 Aug. 1936, GFMA, 717/1160/326535–9. This includes a memorandum by Bräuer.

[3] Richthofen to Foreign Office, 14 Sept. 1936, ibid., 155/141/127015–16.

[4] Davignon, *Berlin, 1933–1940*, p. 47. In May 1936 Ribbentrop made what

taken a favourable turn without urging from Berlin the Germans remained quiet. The Wilhelmstrasse simply informed Richthofen that it was pleased with the 'reasonable attitude' of the Belgian government.[1] The Belgians themselves knew without being told that their new policy would encounter little opposition from this quarter.

There was another quarter from which the Belgians expected plenty of opposition. They had been warned by the British, and they were warned by their ambassador in Paris, Kerchove de Denterghem, that government circles there were preoccupied with Franco-Belgian relations and that the Quai d'Orsay was *au courant* with the evolution of opinion in Belgium. Foreign Minister Delbos admitted to Kerchove that France was partly to blame for this state of affairs. But so was Belgium. Delbos complained that the Brussels government had made no effort to stop the publication of articles hostile to France, especially in the Flemish press. The ambassador reported also that there were other government officials and members of parliament who were badly informed and who assumed that Franco-Belgian friction was an upshot of unsolved economic and commerical problems. Then there was the military. In these circles, noted Kerchove, there were fears that the Belgians intended to let the German army pass without firing a shot.[2]

When Spaak read this despatch, he was furious. He said that the Quai d'Orsay ought to know that the Belgian Constitution guaranteed freedom of the press. With regard to economic and commercial grievances, said Spaak, the ambassador could go and tell his interlocutors that they themselves were the cause of the trouble they deplored. Spaak thought that the French military's doubts about Belgium's determination to defend herself were 'surprising' and 'insulting'.[3]

---

appears to have been an off-the-cuff offer: in return for a bilateral non-aggression pact Germany would make numerous concessions. Davignon, the Belgian ambassador, replied that Germany should stop hoping for Belgium to become another Poland. Evidently the matter was not discussed again. François-Poncet to Flandin, 30 May 1936, *DDF*, Ser. II, II, no. 260.

[1] Dieckhoff to Richthofen, 19 Sept. 1936, GFMA, 155/141/127017–18.
[2] Kerchove to Spaak, 25 Aug. 1936, *DDB*, IV, no. 104.
[3] Spaak to Kerchove, 12 Sept. 1936, ibid., no. 112.

This exchange certainly augured badly for a smooth and friendly transition to a policy of independence. Three decades later Spaak testified in his memoirs that he always loved France.[1] One suspects that at no other time in his long career was his love of France put to such a test as during the next several months. The surprises and insults were only beginning.

The Belgian Foreign Ministry's showdown with the Quai d'Orsay was now imminent. When in mid-September the British set the wheels of diplomacy back in motion by suggesting that a five-power conference be convened soon, the Belgians had no choice but to begin talks with the French immediately. A League of Nations meeting later in the month provided the occasion for doing so. The fact that the British had by now formally accepted Belgium's request to become a non-guarantor[2] did not mean that the French would resist any less tenaciously. Spaak took with him to Geneva both Vanlangenhove and van Zuylen, who would make the initial contact with the French and thus prepare the way for the Foreign Minister's own later intervention.

The two Foreign Ministry officials met with René Massigli, the Political Director of the Quai d'Orsay. Vanlangenhove elaborated for him the exigencies of Belgian politics. Flemish extremism, distrust of the Popular Front, the government's need to win support for the military reform project, were important factors in determining Belgian attitudes towards France. The dominant preoccupation of the government was to strengthen national unity. Vanlangenhove explained that the structure of Belgium was complex and that in this respect Belgium was very different from France. Van Zuylen argued Belgium's case from a different angle: France had everything to gain from a strong and united Belgium serving as a powerful barrier to German aggression. The gossip about Belgian intentions to retire to a national redoubt behind the Scheldt River was most offensive. Belgium would defend herself to the death.[3]

[1] 'I have always loved France and I still love her, but I confess that I have loved other countries at the same time. It has sometimes seemed to me that the Quai d'Orsay would not forgive me for that.' Spaak, *Combats inachevés*, p. 39.

[2] Memorandum of British Government, 17 Sept. 1936, *DDB*, IV, no. 117 and Memorandum by van Zuylen, 22 Sept. 1936, no. 120.

[3] Record of conversation held in Geneva, 24 Sept. 1936, ibid., no. 121. See also Quai d'Orsay memorandum, 25 Sept. 1936, *DDF*, Ser. II, III, no. 287 and van Zuylen, *Les Mains libres*, pp. 365–6.

Massigli did not give in. His argument took the Belgians by surprise. If Belgium became a non-guarantor, he said, the British would lose the use of Belgian air bases and would not be able to fly over Belgium in order to strike at the Ruhr. If Belgium tried to remain outside a war, British support for France would be worth much less. The two Belgians were nonplussed. Vanlangenhove admitted that this aspect of the problem had escaped his attention.[1] What he could not admit was that Belgium had tried for over a year to interest Britain in her air bases and other related matters and had received no response whatsoever. Furthermore, it seemed ironic that Massigli invoked air bases for Britain as the basis of his argument, since the British themselves had already agreed to Belgium's request. The Belgians accordingly assumed that this was a diversion, a way of delaying and embarrassing them, as no military experts had accompanied them to Geneva.[2] Whether or not this was the case, Massigli promptly saw to it that the Belgians receive French General Staff memoranda describing Belgium's importance in an air war and the need for technical preparations to assure quick and effective French intervention on the ground.[3]

Now it was Spaak's turn. He told Delbos that Belgian public opinion was undergoing a moral crisis. Flemish extremism was only part of the story. The Belgian middle class distrusted the Popular Front and feared that France was on the verge of serious domestic difficulties. Belgian opinion was worried about the Franco-Soviet Pact and the risks it might entail for France. If the Belgian government was to win acceptance of its military reform project, it had to refuse the role of guarantor in the new Locarno. Spaak emphasized that a strong and united Belgium capable of defending herself would be of great value to France. Delbos was unimpressed. It was especially hard for him to swallow the argument about French internal problems, which he thought was inane. He argued that Belgium's new policy would have a deplorable psychological impact on French public opinion. The position of both countries

[1] Record of conversation held in Geneva, 24 Sept. 1936, *DDB*, IV, no. 121 and Quai d'Orsay memorandum, 25 Sept. 1936, *DDF*, Ser. II, III, no. 287.

[2] Van Zuylen, *Les Mains libres*, p. 366. The British Air Ministry was in fact interested in the use of Belgium air bases. See below, Ch. V, p. 140.

[3] Quai d'Orsay memorandum, 30 Sept. 1936, *DDF*, Ser. II, III, no. 300 and Memorandum by Vanlangenhove, 3 Oct. 1936, *DDB*, IV, no. 123.

vis-à-vis the Germans would be weakened. The Belgian attitude was barely compatible with article 16 of the League Covenant. Finally, the military implications of the Belgian proposal must be studied more thoroughly. Delbos wanted to consult with the French General Staff, and he hoped that Spaak would reflect on this aspect of the problem. Spaak promised to do so. And the meeting ended.[1]

If Massigli's argument about air bases surprised the Belgians most, Delbos's invocation of article 16 worried them most. It suggested that France intended to use Belgian territory in a war against Germany waged on behalf of Poland and Czechoslovakia. Van Zuylen puts it this way: before the remilitarization of the Rhineland 'France still had a spring-board for attack in the demilitarized zone. Now the anxiety to preserve her eastern alliances induced her to return to the charge'.[2] That is how it looked to the Belgian Foreign Ministry, which was terrified at the prospect of involvement in a war beginning in Eastern Europe. Since the May election the Foreign Ministry knew that even a peacetime association with France was an intolerable domestic liability. It is easy to sympathize with the Belgians. But it is easy to sympathize with the French, too. Concern for their alliance system and its credibility as well as the other factors which Delbos outlined for Spaak made Belgium's request highly undesirable from their point of view. This was a tragic situation. Both sides were right. Yet their positions were incompatible. The Belgian and French delegations left Geneva without reaching agreement.

7. *Conclusion*

In early October Belgian diplomats had little reason to view the future with confidence. The French were unwilling to release Belgium from its obligations. The British were still indifferent to staff contacts. The Germans and Italians had little or no desire for a new Locarno. Any illusions that Europe was not dividing into blocs were giving way to the fact of German-Italian collusion in Spain. Italy's intimacy with Germany became all the more disquieting for Belgium when

[1] Memorandum of the French delegation at the League of Nations, 29 Sept. 1936, *DDF*, Ser. II, III, no. 296 and Kerchove to Spaak, 13 Oct. 1936, *DDB*, IV, no. 126.   [2] Van Zuylen, *Les Mains libres*, p. 367.

the following remarks appeared in the official Italian newspaper, *Il Giornale d'Italia*:

Let us put the problem of Belgo-Italian relations in the context most
simple and most intelligible for Belgians: the context of Locarno. We
assert that Belgium has destroyed, she also, with her policy towards
Italy, the spirit of Locarno and given Italy reason for a new attitude
with regard to Belgium.[1]

No matter how often van Zeeland and Spaak protested their
country's desire for 'independence', Belgium was still linked to
the West by what remained of Locarno, by the letters exchanged
on 6 March, and, according to the Quai d'Orsay, by the
stipulations of article 16. No new Locarno was in sight. The
French were intransigent. Belgium's diplomats had reached an
impasse.

And by early October Belgium seemed headed for the worst
domestic crisis in her history.

[1] Quoted in *L'Indépendence belge*, 29 Sept. 1936, p. 3.

V

KING LEOPOLD INTERVENES

1. *The Threat of Chaos*

Spring and early summer 1936 had witnessed some of the most critical events in modern Belgian history. The Rhineland crisis, the May election, and the general strike had left the country confused and exhausted. And now the government was determined to enact the most extensive and most radical programme ever presented to the Belgian parliament. What Paul van Zeeland and his associates wanted above all was a prolonged period of calm during which the parliament could consider the government's proposals and the traditional parties could reconsolidate their popular support.

The days following the June crisis offered some encouragement. The new government received a large vote of confidence, larger than the one given its predecessor.[1] Royal commissions of inquiry began examining some of Belgium's most pressing problems.[2] A major portion of the government's social legislation passed into law without delay.[3] These were real accomplishments. It seemed for a moment that the new cabinet would duplicate the successes of 1935. None the less, van Zeeland had staked the ultimate success of his second government on the achievement of institutional reform. This part of the programme had been hotly debated. When parliament was adjourned in mid-summer, Belgians found themselves amidst a post-election campaign which revealed again that many politicians had their own ideas about institutional reform.

Flemings were dissatisfied with that section of the government programme which dealt with the nationality question. It promised only that the existing laws would be enforced and that

---

[1] The size of this vote was undoubtedly more the result of fear than the result of enthusiasm. *Annales* (Chamber), extraordinary session, 1936, 27 June 1936, p. 84.

[2] Van Kalken, *Entre deux guerres*, p. 84.

[3] *Annales* (Chamber), extraordinary session, 1936, 27 June 1936, pp. 103–4.

the autonomous development of both the Flemish and Walloon cultures would be encouraged.[1] Vague promises like this were unconvincing, and more and more Flemings became convinced that cultural autonomy would remain unrealized without political and administrative autonomy. During the recent parliamentary debate one Flemish Nationalist said this:

Whenever one speaks of structural reforms of the state, for us Flemish Nationalists—and very soon I should be able to say 'for us Flemings' —it is not just a matter of politics and economics . . . but also a matter of nationality, because no lasting political reform and no lasting economic recovery will be accomplished without the foundation of this state having been made healthy.[2]

The possibility that 'we Flemings' might demand a division of Belgium along more than cultural lines was now a political reality. Flemish Catholics were too eager to win back Nationalist voters to overlook the potential of federalism. Many middle-class Flemings were temporarily willing to overlook the authoritarian tendencies of the Nationalists, especially after the general strike and the outbreak of the Spanish Civil War. And 'for the first time the federalists in the Catholic Party really had wind in their sails'.[3] Editorials, speeches, and conferences filled the summer months while Flemings seriously considered the 'concentration of Flemish forces around the federal idea'. It all culminated with a congress at which Flemings of every political stripe were represented. The congress formally declared itself in favour of 'the building of a Christian and popular order in Flanders' and 'independence and right of self-determination'.[4] The reception given this campaign was so enthusiastic that Catholic leaders soon decided to divide their party. In October the *Union catholique* gave way to the *Bloc catholique*, in which the *Parti catholique social* and the *Katholieke Vlaamse Volkspartij* were virtually independent.[5] The latter could now negotiate with the Nationalists and did not wait

[1] Ibid., 24 June 1936, p. 25.
[2] Ibid., 29 June 1936, p. 118.
[3] Willemsen, *Het Vlaamse-Nationalisme 1914–1940*, p. 261. See also p. 365.
[4] Ibid., p. 262. See also Wullus-Rudiger, *En marge de la politique belge*, pp. 256–9.
[5] Simon, *Le Parti catholique belge*, pp. 116–17 and Moyersoen, *Prosper Poullet en de Politiek van zijn Tijd, 1868–1937*, pp. 350–1.

long to do so. By the end of the year the *KVV* and the *VNV* had signed a 'preliminary agreement' in which the two pledged themselves to work for a corporative, federal Belgium.[1]

The drift of Flemish opinion and the division of the Catholic party were bad enough. What made the situation intolerable was the accelerated activity of Léon Degrelle and his Rexists. Degrelle assumed that he would owe his eventual triumph to the progressive radicalization of Belgian voters, some going over to the Communists and the rest coming over to his own camp.[2] His astounding success in the national election convinced him that this could happen soon. Shortly after the election he began a campaign of agitation designed to make it impossible for the parliament to function normally and thus to force new elections.[3] While the party ideologues tried to produce a coherent programme, Degrelle addressed ever-larger nightly rallies. Everything seemed to work to his advantage. Just as he had always been able to win support by dramatizing the horrors of the French Popular Front, he could now shout about the Spanish Civil War. 'I am more the brother of the Spanish Catholic than of the Belgian Communist', thundered Degrelle.[4] Many of his listeners, for whom the memory of the general strike was still vivid, were inclined to feel that way too.

No matter how large Rexist crowds became, there remained that formidable and stubborn obstacle—Flanders. Degrelle made some headway there because his views on foreign policy harmonized with Flemish desires to be *los van Frankrijk*.[5] But he had to make plenty of headway there, or his movement was doomed to certain failure. Degrelle knew that there was a way out of the dilemma. From the beginning the Rexists had talked about substituting a 'linguistic regime' for the present system. Later they expressed interest in administrative decentralization. By October they were more specific: 'The Belgian

[1] Willemsen, *Het Vlaamse–Nationalisme 1914–1940*, pp. 263–4 and Wullus-Rudiger, *En marge de la politique belge*, pp. 259–62.

[2] Foreign Office memorandum, 3 July 1936, GFMA, 717/1159/326392–6. Degrelle told a German acquaintance this.

[3] Buttgenbach in *Revue des sciences politiques* (Paris, 1936), LIX, p. 514.

[4] *The New York Times*, 25 Oct. 1936, p. 11. See also *Le Pays réel*, 20 Aug. 1936, p. 3.

[5] Ovey to Eden, 7 Oct. 1936, FO, 432/2/C7003/202/4. The French embassy in Brussels noted that the cry *Los van Frankrijk* was no longer confined to extremist circles. Gazel to Delbos, 11 Aug. 1936, *DDF*, Ser. II, III, no. 128.

state can be constructed durably and soundly only in a federal spirit.'[1]

It was inevitable that the opportunistic Degrelle would sooner or later bid for some sort of *modus vivendi* with the *VNV*. In fact, he now wanted an alliance, and he discovered that the leaders of the *VNV* were very responsive. Why not? thought de Clerq and his friends. They recognized that the Rexists were fighting for some of the very things which they wanted. Now that the Rexists had transformed themselves into federalists, they might steal a few more votes from the *VNV*. Together the Rexists and the Flemish Nationalists could control one-fifth of the seats in the Chamber of Deputies. De Clerq discovered that Degrelle was willing to make extensive concessions. Therefore, early in October the *Chef* and the *Leider* reached an agreement. Belgium would be reorganized on a federal and corporative basis; the Flemish branch of the Rexist organization would eventually merge with the *VNV*; the two groups would fight together against communism. The *VNV* stipulated that it was not sacrificing its hopes for a resurrected *Dietschland*, a reunited Flanders and the Netherlands, but it promised to pursue them within the boundaries of the existing state and under the auspices of the Belgian royal house of Saxe-Coburg—whatever this meant.[2] Such was the agreement between Degrelle and de Clerq, which the Rexists considered a 'miracle'.[3]

It is easy to see in retrospect how harmless and ineffectual the *Rex-VNV* alliance was. It actually did its participants serious damage. Degrelle, who had always made appeals to Belgian patriotism, was going to have a hard time explaining his association with a party whose longtime war-cry had been *België kapot*. The *VNV* made matters worse for the Rexists by assuring its own camp-followers that a federal state would be only the prelude to a *Dietsche* state.[4] By the same token, Flemish Catholics who had been attracted to the nationalist aspects of

[1] Quoted in Buttenbach, *Revue des sciences politiques* (Paris, 1936), LIX, 537.

[2] Charles to Eden, 16 Apr. 1937, FO, 432/3/C2923/145/4 and Richthofen to Foreign Office, 10 Oct. 1936, GFMA 1727/3325/E008160–9. See also Willemsen, *Het Vlaamse-Nationalisme 1914–1940*, pp. 246–7, 366–8. It should be noted that the terms of the agreement were not made public until the following April.

[3] Taeda, 'L'Astrolabe', *Le Flambeau* (Brussels, 1936), 19th year, p. 626.

[4] Wullus-Rudiger, *En marge de la politique belge*, p. 228. See also Buttenbach, *Revue des sciences politiques* (Paris, 1936), LIX, 538–40.

the *VNV*'s programme were now abruptly reminded of its anti-democratic tendencies.[1]

In October 1936, however, subtleties like these were lost in the general uproar caused by the alliance. 'We are five months past the election', said one deputy, 'and it seems as though we are in the midst of an election campaign.'[2] One of King Leopold's advisers later remembered that the political atmosphere was 'charged with electricity'.[3] The turmoil was intolerable for van Zeeland and his cabinet, which was awaiting the imminent return of parliament. If a few Flemish Catholics and Socialists defected to the *Rex-VNV* alliance, it might mean the fall of the government.[4] The threat of Rexism simply had to be met head on. The cabinet therefore selected the combative Spaak to launch formally the government's campaign against Degrelle.

'Yes', said the Foreign Minister, 'finally the government picks up the gauntlet which was thrown to it . . .' No one could deny that Degrelle was a formidable opponent. He had two valuable assets—personal dynamism and sex appeal. But that was all. His programme was 'power first . . . we shall see later'. In order to rid Belgium of this nonsense, the government must do more than govern well; it had to launch a genuine popular movement. Recent events had generated another danger: '. . . .the extraordinary alliance which has just been concluded by Rex and the Flemish Nationalists has again made the problem of national unity a primary object of our concern.' Spaak was optimistic. Degrelle would not attempt a *coup d'état*; he did not have enough 'shock troops' for that. The Foreign Minister estimated that within six months Belgians would have forgotten their fears of a dictatorship.[5]

Spaak underestimated the foolhardiness of his opponent. As if in direct response to the government's challenge, Degrelle soon announced that on 25 October two hundred and fifty thousand Rexists would 'descend' on Brussels and 'sweep out' the government.[6] The Socialists lost no time in replying: 'The

---

[1] Willemsen, *Het Vlaamse-Nationalisme 1914–1940*, pp. 369–70.

[2] *Annales* (Chamber), extraordinary session, 1936, 29 Oct. 1936, p. 387.

[3] Capelle, *Au service du roi*, I, 236.

[4] Ovey to Eden, 14 Oct. 1936, FO, 432/2/C7286/202/4.

[5] *BPB*, no. 124, 19 Dec., 1936, pp. 17–18 and *Le Peuple*, 17 Oct., 1936 p. 3.

[6] Taeda, *Le Flambeau* (Brussels, 1936), 19th year, pp. 631–2.

Rexists want street fights', said their newspaper. 'They shall have them.'[1]

Prime Minister van Zeeland was a very reserved individual. He did not relish a fight the way his young Foreign Minister did. Several days before the 'march on Brussels' he sombrely explained to a radio audience why the government had placed a ban on the march. Belgium could not accept the government of the streets. If agitation and disorder caught hold of Belgium, they would compromise all that the government had accomplished so far. Van Zeeland concluded his talk by noting how vain and irrelevant all the commotion was. It had nothing to do with the real issues facing the country: military reform, foreign policy, and the economy. 'Calm yourselves and think about the position which the country should take on these essential problems . . .'[2]

Considering the extent of the tumult in Belgium, it is amazing how little it all came to. Degrelle's 'march on Brussels' never materialized, not because of the government ban, which Degrelle disregarded, but because 25 October was a rainy day.[3] Likewise, the sun stopped shining on the Rexist enterprise altogether six months later—thus fulfilling Spaak's prediction with uncanny accuracy—when van Zeeland defeated Degrelle so thoroughly in a Brussels by-election that the *Chef*'s political future was shattered.

But this is not the point. Belgium's leaders did not know that Rexism's days were numbered. Nor did they know what the fate of the *Rex-VNV* alliance would be or what the spread of federalism portended. Statesmen usually frame their policies with a view to the worst conceivable course of events. The events of October 1936 suggested that Belgium was on the brink of a major disaster. This sequence of events was well under way when Belgium's senior diplomats patiently explained to the French that the structure of Belgium was complex, that the

---

[1] Quoted in *The Times*, 22 Oct., 1936, p. 16.

[2] *BPB*, no. 124, 19 Dec., 1936, pp. 20–21.

[3] Degrelle chartered fifty trains to bring his followers to Brussels. The government refused them permission to enter the city and set up police barriers along the highways so that cars could be examined. When Degrelle tried to harangue the faithful who did show up in Brussels, his loud-speaker failed to function. Then he was arrested. Ovey to Eden, 26 Oct. 1936, FO, 432/2/C7666/202/4.

public was undergoing a moral crisis, and that her government was determined to strengthen national unity.[1] This sequence was approaching its climax when King Leopold personally intervened in the political argument most likely to ruin the van Zeeland government from within—the argument about military reform—while Degrelle threatened to ruin it from without. These were grim days for Belgium. If the government had not pursued its policy of neutrality, the future might have been grimmer.

2. National Defence

While the attention of the Belgian public was diverted by the antics of the Rexists and Flemish Nationalists, the parliamentary mixed commission on national defence had quietly gone about its more prosaic business. Since the first van Zeeland government had temporarily buried the military question in this committee, everyone had been content to leave this explosive problem in the background. The second van Zeeland government would gladly have left it there for ever. National defence was not a bone of contention during the June crisis, and the new government's declaration stated simply that its attitude would 'be inspired by the conclusions arrived at by the mixed commission'.[2] Van Zeeland took one precaution when he formed his new cabinet: Defence Minister Devèze was replaced by an uncontroversial general who was unaffiliated politically. General Henri Denis was a wise choice. His persuasiveness and tact enabled him immediately to begin restoring confidence between the cabinet, the parliament, and the General Staff.[3] The general soon learned, however, that he needed more than tact.

The parliamentary mixed commission had been instituted not only to avert a crisis; it was also hoped that its investigations and proposals would dramatize the whole military problem in

[1] See above, Ch. IV, pp. 118–120ff.

[2] *Annales* (Chamber), extraordinary session, 1936, 24 June 1936, p. 25.

[3] By 1940 General Denis did more than any of his predecessors to strengthen the army. One reason for his success was his respect for the sensitivities of Flemish soldiers and members of parliament, something for which Devèze was not noted. Van Overstraeten, *Albert I. Léopold III*, pp. 220–21; Wullus-Rudiger, *Le Défense de la Belgique en 1940*, pp. 171–3; and Wullus-Rudiger, *La Belgique et la crise européene* (Villeneuve-sur-Lot, 1941), I, 312–13.

such a way that the three major parties could reach some sort of consensus. After thirty-seven meetings and the testimony of witnesses representing every shade of opinion, the members of the commission themselves reached agreement at least on general principles. The chairman summed up the work of the commission this way: '. . . we have found ourselves with almost the same proposed legislation that Minister Devèze presented earlier.'[1] In other words, after months of investigation most experts agreed that Belgium needed a permanent frontier defence. In September the commission published a resolution calling for the prolongation of the period of service to eighteen months; the motorization of the cavalry; the strengthening of the air force; the intensification and modernization of the demolition system along the frontier; and the authorization of the money necessary for measures to protect the civilian population. It was estimated that if this programme was accepted, the strength of the Belgian army would be increased by sixty per cent.[2]

Although the remilitarization of the Rhineland had dramatized Belgium's defence needs more vividly than a parliamentary commission could ever hope to, there was no indication that the traditional opponents of heavy military expenditures and burdens were much better disposed to a thorough-going reform than before. Furthermore, the national election in May had tipped the balance in their favour. There were those like the Flemish Nationalists, who voted against every government proposal and whose opposition was taken for granted. More decisive was the attitude of the Socialists, who were still loath to burden young Belgians with a long period of military service. But the most formidable obstacle of all was the stubborn Flemish refusal to support any defence project which might be put at the disposal of the French.

The Socialist position remained uncertain as late as mid-October. Spaak provided reliable support within the cabinet

---

[1] *Annales* (Chamber), 1936/1937, 1 Dec. 1936, p. 263. See also pp. 251–3; Van Overstraeten, *Albert I. Léopold III*, pp. 221–5; and Groupement national belge, *Contribution à l'étude de la question royale* (Brussels, 1946), p. 43. (Henceforth this will be cited as *Contribution*.)

[2] British Military Attaché in Brussels to Ovey, 16 Oct. 1936, enclosure in FO, 432/2/C7342/7284/4; *The Times*, 9 Sept. 1936, p. 11 and 29 Oct., p. 11; and *L'Indépendance belge*, 9 Sept. 1936, p. 1.

itself. This was, after all, a reason why van Zeeland made him Foreign Minister. But the attitude of the party leader Vandervelde, who was a minister-without-portfolio, was another matter. He said that after fifty years of opposition to compulsory military service he found it difficult to support a prolongation of military service. What if his party comrades provoked a crisis? Vandervelde thought a compromise possible. But the prospect of a crisis and another national election did not worry him: 'Catholics and Liberals would lose seats—Socialists, also Communists, would lose none.'[1] It goes without saying that Vandervelde's colleagues in the cabinet were not so sanguine.

The possibility of a Socialist defection was made more dangerous by the certainty of a Flemish defection, if certain ambiguities about Belgian foreign policy were not eliminated immediately. The mixed commission itself minced no words about this. 'Flanders does not want our military policy to move in the wake of France', said one commission report, which noted also that this attitude was shared by the working class, the middle class, and intellectuals alike.[2] The commission had called attention to the close connection between military and foreign policy. In early August it published this resolution:

Considering that to preserve the moral unity of the country it is essential to avoid the appearance that its military organization is directed in a permanent fashion against certain states, or linked to certain of them ... Recalling the declarations made by various foreign ministers ... [The Commission] expresses the opinion that the organization of national defence be inspired by the principles of our foreign policy.[3]

But most Flemings were not content with statements of principle like this one. They wanted more than 'platonic declarations', as one deputy called them.[4] As long as any obligations to France remained, Flemings would be dissatisfied and suspicious. But as long as the French refused to release Belgium

---

[1] Capelle, *Au service du roi*, I, 48.   [2] *Contribution*, p. 40.

[3] *Annales* (Chamber), 1936/1937, 1 Dec. 1936, p. 263 (quotation of the August resolution).

[4] Ibid., extraordinary session, 1936, 16 July 1936, p. 340.

from her obligations, the government would be confined to 'platonic declarations'.

The French attitude was not the only reason for not making public the details of Belgium's new foreign policy. Ever since Spaak's incident with the General Council of the Socialist party, the government knew that its policy was likely to get a cool reception from this quarter. The members of Belgium's largest political party re-emphasized their devotion to collective security in late September when a party congress resolved that there never had been and never would be any question of a return to neutrality or a breach of Locarno obligations. The Socialists wanted a policy of 'complete independence', too. But such a policy did not mean a passive attitude, but rather 'intense action' on behalf of the League and collective security.[1] This interpretation of 'independence' was in sharp contrast to that of most Flemings, for whom 'independence' meant strict neutrality.

It is easy to imagine the consternation of Van Zeeland and his cabinet as they contemplated the special session of parliament which was scheduled for late October for the purpose of dealing with national defence. 'I'm not fooling myself about the difficulties which I will encounter', said the Prime Minister.[2] The government was heading straight into a cul-de-sac. The loss of Socialist support for the military project was threatened in any event. A failure to announce the end of Belgium's obligations to France would guarantee the loss of Flemish support. But a unilateral abrogation of these obligations would alienate the Socialists (not to mention the French themselves). The situation bore a resemblance to the one existing when Defence Minister Devèze introduced his original proposals in early 1936. But then the Rexists and the Flemish Nationalists were no threat. And this time there could be no procrastination: in order to be effective in 1937 the military legislation had to pass through parliament by 1 December.[3]

This was the immediate background of the most notable event of the year.

[1] *Contribution*, p. 42. See also E. Ramon Arango, *Leopold III and the Belgian Royal Question* (Baltimore, 1961), p. 39.

[2] Gazel to Delbos, 1 Sept. 1936, *DDF*, Ser. II, III, no. 223. See also Laroche to Delbos, 21 Sept. 1936, no. 270 and Laroche to Delbos, 14 Oct. 1936, no. 346.

[3] *Contribution*, p. 43.

3. King Leopold's Speech

The King of the Belgians cannot have enjoyed his royal office much, even though he was immensely popular among his people.[1] Leopold III was a quiet, slightly aloof individual, whose love of solitude had been transformed into loneliness by the loss of his lovely wife Astrid.[2] He was always more comfortable in the world of the out-of-doors than in the world of politics. Golfing, skiing, and mountain climbing were the things he really liked. But they never interfered with his responsibilities, which he took very seriously. Indeed, his detractors later argued that he took them all too seriously. Yet his detractors rarely questioned his integrity. His leading opponent in Belgium's impending constitutional struggle, Spaak, later remembered that the King 'was serious, hard-working, reflective. He had a lofty idea of his duty and of his mission and even when he was, in my opinion, mistaken, his basic motives were never low.'[3]

Leopold's natural reserve and quiet interests were not the only causes of his discomfiture. Ever since his accession to the throne in 1934 he had seen more and more evidence of parliamentary incompetence and unreliability. The quarrel over military reform was only the most recent example. Leopold had twice felt compelled to intervene in government crises. In March 1935 he had called Paul van Zeeland from outside parliament to head a new government, and in June 1936 he had had to call Belgium's haggling politicians back to their senses. The King's active role in these episodes was well within the limits of his constitutional prerogatives. In fact, the Belgian

[1] For descriptions of Leopold, see Theo Aronson, *Defiant Dynasty* (Indianapolis, 1968), pp. 229–88; Alfred Fabre-Luce, *Une Tragédie royale* (Paris, 1948); Émile Cammaerts, *The Prisoner at Laeken* (London, 1941); and G.-H. Dumont, *Léopold III. Roi des Belges* (Saverne, 1946).

[2] The tragic death of Queen Astrid has provided the point of departure for the most recent and, in the opinion of the author, the most dubious interpretation of Belgian neutrality. Professor Rudolph Binion argues that Leopold drove his country to ruin in a neurotic re-enactment of the day he drove his car off the road and thus, in his own mind, became responsible for the death of his wife. According to Binion, Belgian neutrality from 1936 to 1940 was Leopold's effort to come to terms with his own sense of guilt through a re-living of the Küssnacht tragedy. The author wishes to suggest that his own work is at least a partial refutation of Binion's contention that without Leopold 'Belgium's policy of neutrality would never have been conceived or executed'. Binion, *History and Theory* (1969), VIII, no. 2, p. 238.

[3] Spaak, *Combats inachevés*, p. 62.

constitution granted the King more power than he was now accustomed to employ. He had the right to appoint and dismiss ministers, to adjourn parliament, and to refuse approval of legislation. Royal power in Belgium would have been un-limited were it not for a constitutional provision that no act of the King was effective unless counter-signed by a minister. The reason for these extensive royal powers was that the numerous elements of division in Belgium made it essential that a strong King stand above party and linguistic disputes. Only during the reign of the illustrious King Albert did the throne willingly cease to exercise its prerogatives.[1] But they still existed, and this made Leopold's impatience with parliamentary indecision all the more acute.[2] Moreover, there remained one area in which the King was active in practice as well as in theory. The Belgian constitution said this: 'The King commands the forces on land and on sea, declares war, makes treaties of peace, alliance, and commerce.'[3]

As commander-in-chief of the armed forces Leopold played an important role in defence planning. All plans were sub-mitted to him for approval before being presented to the cabinet.[4] For two years Leopold had reluctantly endured Albert Devèze, with whose strategic thinking he disagreed. It is no wonder that Leopold was unimpressed with Devèze's arguments for the 'integral defence of the frontier'. Among the King's principal military advisers, whom he inherited from his father, were General Galet and Colonel van Overstraeten, his aide-de-camp, who for years had been locked in battle with Devèze over the organization of Belgian defences. King Albert himself had thought that some of Devèze's ideas were 'absurd'.[5] A clash between the new King and his Defence Minister was avoided in 1934 only because Leopold felt it would be inoppor-

---

[1] Arango, *Leopold III and the Belgian Royal Question*, pp. 9, 19–22 and *Contribution*, pp. vi–vii.

[2] Leopold shared many of the ideas of van Zeeland, de Man, and Spaak on the need to strengthen the executive branch of the government. Huizinga, *Mr. Europe*, pp. 67–8, 73.

[3] *Contribution*, p. vi.

[4] Miller, *Belgian Foreign Policy between Two Wars*, p. 227. Here it is pointed out that Leopold's role as Commander-in Chief resembled that of the American Presi-dent.

[5] Van Overstraeten, *Dans l'étau*, p. 31. See also Wullus-Rudiger, *La Défense de la Belgique en 1940*, pp. 169–71.

tune to provoke the latter's resignation. He decided that Devèze's plans did have some potential, and he knew that the Flemish members of parliament would moderate the Defence Minister's excesses. On the other hand, Leopold and his advisers were delighted to have Devèze replaced in June 1936.[1]

One aspect of Devèze's strategic thinking did not lend itself so easily to parliamentary supervision. Belgium's close connection with France worried King Leopold. It had worried King Albert too. In 1930 Albert said that 'neutrality corresponds ideally to our position. Had it not existed, we would have had to invent it. It has rendered us inestimable services.'[2] Leopold's memory of his father's view was reinforced by the frequent advice of his closest advisers. Early in his reign his private secretary, Louis Wodon, assured him that the Franco-Belgian Military Agreement had no juridical value at all. Colonel van Overstraeten agreed. He argued that Belgium 'ought to try to remain independent, to seek support from England . . .'.[3] The Quai d'Orsay worried about Leopold and his entourage. It knew full well that the King was not surrounded by rabid Francophiles.[4] What it did not know was that the King got the same kind of advice from other quarters as well. For example, Belgium's most respected diplomat, Paul Hymans, told the young and inexperienced King that if his country became involved in a war against Germany as the ally of France without the support of Britain 'she would risk material destruction and the rending of her national unity'.[5]

Leopold accepted the advice. He told his ministers in 1934 that Belgium should follow a policy of equilibrium between France and Britain and that she could wield real influence in the military balance between France and Germany. Belgium

---

[1] Ibid., pp. 171–2 and van Overstraeten, *Dans l'étau*, pp. 44–5.

[2] Ibid., p. 25. See also Capelle, *Au service du roi*, I, 43; Hymans, *Mémoires*, II, 602; de Man, *Gegen den Strom*, p. 225; and Laroche to Delbos, 14 Jan. 1937, *DDF*, Ser. II, IV, no. 301. It is worth noting that after the policy of independence was a *fait accompli* the French embassy in Brussels reported that King Albert would have done what his son had done. De Man writes that Leopold felt he was the heir to his father's attempt to induce his ministers to abandon the 'disguised, quasi-military alliance with France.'

[3] Van Overstraeten, *Albert I. Léopold III*, pp. 107–8.

[4] Gazel to Delbos, 11 Aug. 1936, *DDF*, Ser. II, III, no. 128.

[5] Report by Hymans to Council of Ministers meeting under the presidency of the King, 24 Apr. 1934, *DDB*, III, no. 127.

should avoid 'the idea of participation in any war which does not concern us directly'.[1] Devèze's plans prompted him to warn the Foreign Minister about Belgium's 'progressive deviation' from her traditional policy.[2] 'Our diplomatic and military efforts should strive to keep away from us a war in which we would have everything to lose without the hope of the slightest gain', wrote the King. 'It has become apparent to me that M. Devèze nourishes the opinion that he would appeal for co-operation with the French army as soon as Germany concentrated troops in the Rhineland. I hardly believe that the Minister of Foreign Affairs shares this opinion.'[3]

It is obvious that King Leopold was won over to a 'policy of independence' at least two years earlier than many of his leading ministers.[4] But it is just as obvious that this was not extraordinary. The King's opinion was shared by almost all Flemings. It was shared also by many military men—'the school of General Galet'. And it was shared by an increasingly influential group in the Foreign Ministry led by Political Director van Zuylen, whose own thinking was much the same as that of Secretary General Vanlangenhove.[5]

Did Leopold's early conversion have any practical consequence? Probably not. His cabinet ministers do not appear to have paid much attention to his ideas, at least not until 1936, when they had some weighty new reasons to think that His Majesty had been right all along. Foreign Minister Spaak, who sometimes irritated the King by not submitting documents to the Royal Palace, was actually more responsive than most to Leopold's recommendations.[6] For example, in July 1936 Leopold sent van Zeeland a letter in which he outlined his ideas on the guiding principles of Belgian foreign policy. The King argued that it should be determined by three essential factors: the country's geographical position, its linguistic

[1] Capelle, *Au service du roi*, I, 25.

[2] Ibid., p. 27.

[3] Van Overstraeten, *Albert I. Léopold III*, p. 138.

[4] And at least one year before the accident at Küssnacht.

[5] Van Zuylen says *apropos* of the King's early support for a 'policy of independence': 'It is all to his honour . . .' Van Zuylen, *Les Mains libres*, p. 363.

[6] Leopold and Spaak, at this stage in their respective careers, enjoyed a pleasant personal relationship, and the King had confidence in his Foreign Minister. Spaak, *Combats inachevés*, p. 62; Capelle, *Au service du roi*, I, 63-4; and Huizinga, *Mr. Europe*, pp. 67-8.

division, and its modest resources. The Prime Minister passed the letter along to Spaak, and one week later the new Foreign Minister incorporated the King's ideas in his famous 'maiden speech'.[1]

This must have been most gratifying to Leopold, especially since he had not imposed his ideas on his cabinet ministers. Van Zeeland and Spaak accepted his ideas because domestic events had imposed them.

Leopold was not as satisfied with developments in the area of national defence. Although the mixed commission had completed its work, there were still no signs of consensus in parliamentary circles. The members of the cabinet were now arguing among themselves.[2] The passage of the new defence bill presupposed unity of purpose at least within the government itself. The King therefore concluded that the time had come for another royal intervention. He proposed to van Zeeland that he address to the cabinet a statement of principle describing the military and political position of Belgium in European affairs and designed to raise the whole problem above party rivalries. The speech would be designed solely to rally cabinet unanimity for the military project. Van Zeeland thought this was a good idea. If his government fell apart because of the military question, the only winners would be the Rexists and the Flemish Nationalists. Leopold's suggestion was very timely indeed. The Prime Minister accepted it and personally approved the text of Leopold's statement, most of which was written by Colonel van Overstraeten.[3] It was in this fashion that the King came to address the Belgian Cabinet on 14 October.

Leopold's speech was a remarkably lucid and concise description of the dilemma facing Belgium in 1936. Because it soon became the best known and, in some quarters, the most notorious Belgian document of the entire decade, the speech merits extensive quotation.

The King began by saying that it was his obligation to

[1] Capelle, *Au service du roi*, I, 46–7. See also van Overstraeten, *Albert I. Léopold III*, pp. 225–6.

[2] Ibid., p. 230 and Ovey to Eden, 14 Oct. 1936, FO, 432/2/C7286/202/4.

[3] Van Overstraeten, *Dans l'étau*, pp. 65–8; Capelle, *Au service du roi*, I, 48; and Spaak, *Combats inachevés*, p. 49.

maintain the independence and integrity of his country and that he was thus eager to preside over the cabinet as it prepared to submit its defence bill to the parliament. He noted that there were several reasons for military reform. Among them were the rearmament of Germany, the change in the methods of warfare, and the remilitarization of the Rhineland.

At the same time we have watched the foundations of international security being weakened by the infraction of treaties, even those freely entered into, and by the virtual impossibility, under present circumstances, of adapting the provisions of the League of Nations, so as to provide for the punishment of those infractions.

There was another reason for strengthening Belgium's defences.

. . . the internal dissension of certain states threatens to become enmeshed in the rivalries between the political and social system of other states, and to unleash a conflict even more desperate and more destructive than that from whose repercussions we are still suffering.

After reviewing the recent background of the military question, Leopold came to the most controversial and most significant part of his speech.

Our military policy, like our foreign policy, on which it is based, must aim, not at preparing for a more or less successful war, with the aid of a coalition, but at keeping the war away from our territory.
    The reoccupation of the Rhineland, by breaking the Locarno treaties both in letter and in spirit, has almost put us back in the same international position we occupied before the war. Our geographical position requires us to maintain an army large enough to dissuade any of our neighbours from making use of our territory to attack another state. In fulfilling this mission Belgium greatly assists in preserving peace in Western Europe, and *ipso facto* acquires a right to respect and eventual assistance from all states interested in peace.
    On these basic points I believe that Belgian opinion is unanimous.
    But our engagements must go no further. A unilateral policy will weaken our position abroad, and—rightly or wrongly—cause dissension at home. An alliance, even if purely defensive, does not lead to the goal; for, no matter how prompt the help of an ally would be, it would not come until after the invader's attack, which will be overwhelming. To meet this attack we would be alone in any case. Unless Belgium possesses a defensive system capable of resistance, the

enemy would penetrate deeply at the beginning, and the country would be devastated. After this stage is over, friendly intervention will certainly assure final victory; but the struggle will cover the country with destruction of which that of the 1914–1918 war would be but a feeble image.

For this reason, as the Minister for Foreign Affairs said recently, we must pursue an 'exclusively and wholly Belgian policy'. This policy must aim resolutely at keeping us outside the quarrels of our neighbours; such an aim is in keeping with our national ideals. It can be maintained by a reasonable military and financial effort, and it will gain the support of the Belgians, all animated by an intense and basic desire for peace. Let those who doubt the feasibility of such a foreign policy consider the proud and resolute example of Holland and Switzerland. Let them recall how decisively Belgium's scrupulous observance of neutrality weighed in our favour and in favour of the allies during the war and the settlement which followed.

Leopold concluded his speech with a plea to the three traditional parties to co-operate in supporting the defence bill: 'Thus you will have shown the country once again that the chief preoccupation of the government of national union is to place the higher interests of Belgium before everything.'[1]

Leopold's audience was very impressed. Émile Vandervelde was especially enthusiastic. He 'covered the King with flowers' and recommended that the royal speech be made public.[2] Leopold had never intended to publish his speech. But his ministers assured him that doing so would hasten passage of the defence bill, which the cabinet now adopted à l'unanimité complète, and the King agreed. Van Zeeland later wrote that the cabinet thus gave the speech the significance of an official government act and took full responsibility for it.[3] The Prime Minister and his associates were thoroughly pleased with themselves.[4]

Evidently it occurred to no one that King Leopold's speech was certain to make an impression abroad as well as at home.

---

[1] Declaration by King Leopold III, 14 Oct. 1936, DIA, 1936, pp. 223–7. For a French text of the speech, see DDB, IV, no. 128.

[2] Capelle, Au service du roi, I, 49 and Spaak, Combats inachevés, p. 49.

[3] Paul van Zeeland, 'La position internationale de la Belgique', La Revue générale (Brussels, 1939), 72nd year, p. 596. See also Rapport de la Commission d'Information institué par S. M. Le Roi Léopold III le 14 Juillet 1946 (Luxembourg, 1947), p. 12.

[4] Ovey to Eden, 16 Oct. 1936, FO, 432/2/C7342/7284/4.

4. *The Hectic Aftermath of the Royal Speech*

Considering the caution with which Belgian statesmen had always conducted their country's diplomacy, the hasty decision to publish Leopold's speech was uncharacteristically rash and inept. In fact, it was so inept that British Ambassador Ovey was moved to attribute it to van Zeeland's and Spaak's relative lack of experience in public life.[1] French Ambassador Laroche thought that the speech's having been *heard* rather than *read* might explain why even the Socialists in the cabinet, mesmerized like everyone else by the domestic and parliamentary aspects of the military question, failed to take into account the diplomatic repercussions of the speech.[2] Of course, the Foreign Ministry in Brussels had no chance to inform Belgium's representatives abroad of the contents of the speech or to provide them with an official interpretation. 'The surprise for us was great', remembered the Belgian ambassador in Berlin. 'We sensed a coming change in Belgian foreign policy. We did not expect to see it announced so publicly and without previous diplomatic preparations.'[3]

Although Belgium's neighbours had actually received ample indication of her intentions, the King's speech none the less did raise certain serious questions. Was Belgium unilaterally contracting out of all her obligations? It seemed that way to some. Or was the speech simply a statement of principle? If this was the case—as indeed it was the case—the speech still had made public all the delicate questions about Belgium's role in any new Locarno, her participation in staff talks, and the like. Part of the problem was the bluntness of Leopold's language. Because the speech was originally intended for the cabinet only, it made no concessions to international sensitivities. As one observer put it: 'The King's language seemed harsh to some because it was completely exempt from the solemn foolishness to which the deliberations at Geneva had accustomed people . . .'[4] By the time Belgium's embarrassed ambassadors were autho-

---

[1] Ovey to Eden, 21 Oct. 1936, ibid., C4984/4921/4.

[2] Laroche to Delbos, 22 Oct. 1936, *DDF*, Ser. II, III, no. 392. See also Laroche to Delbos, 21 Oct. 1936, no. 385.

[3] Davignon, *Berlin, 1936–1940*, p. 49. See also van Zuylen, *Les Mains libres*, pp. 370–1.

[4] ***, 'Le discours du Roi', *La Revue générale* (Brussels, 1936), 69th year, p. 536.

rized to say that their country still observed all her obligations and that the King's speech was in fact a statement of principle, the damage was done.

Even the British were irritated. 'When did kings begin throwing bombs around in public?' asked Anthony Eden.[1] London was well aware of the domestic background of the King's speech and had known for months what the Belgians wanted. At this juncture, only the Air Ministry was inclined to argue. It wanted the use of Belgian air bases, and it wanted the Royal Air Force to have direct access to German bombing targets.[2] The Chiefs of Staff Sub-Committee of the Committee of Imperial Defence had a different opinion. The Chiefs of Staff actually thought that Belgium's return to neutrality could be of great benefit to Britain. A well-armed Belgium would be a more effective deterrent to German aggression than the Belgium of 1914. The Chiefs of Staff argued that Germany would have no excuse for invading a neutral Belgium. If Germany did invade, then Britain would have a clear-cut justification for going to war.[3] The officials in the Foreign Office considered this particular line of argument exceptionally stupid.[4] On the other hand, they recognized the futility of any attempt 'to screw an unwilling Belgium', as Robert Vansittart put it.[5] What troubled the Foreign Office most was that the Belgians should make known their intentions in so high-handed and so categorical a fashion. The Locarno powers had agreed not to

[1] Laroche to Delbos, 3 Dec. 1936, *DDF*, Ser. II, IV, no. 85.

[2] Foreign Office memorandum, 25 Nov. 1936, Appendix to FO, 371/19851/C8425/270/4. See also Corbin to Delbos, 20 Oct. 1936, *DDF*, Ser. II, III, no. 377.

[3] Memorandum from the Chiefs of Staff, 20 Nov. 1936, FO, 371/19853/C8348/6597/4 and Memorandum from the Chiefs of Staff, 25 Nov. 1936, 19851/C8425/270/4. A 'trusted' Englishman informed the Germans that the War Office wondered whether a militarily strengthened Belgium might improve Britain's chances of staying clear of a war beginning in Central Europe. The same source informed the Germans that the only real opposition to Belgium's new policy came from the few who still pinned their hopes on collective security and from the Air Staff, who wanted the use of Belgian air bases. Bismark to Foreign Office, 20 Oct. 1936, GFMA, 717/1160/326572–8.

[4] Foreign Office minute, 20 Nov. 1936, FO, 371/19853/C8348/6597/4. This was the beginning of a serious argument between the Foreign Office and the Chiefs of Staff about the future of Belgium.

[5] Minute by Vansittart, 26 Oct. 1936, ibid., 19854/C7618/7284/4. See also minute by Sargent, 19 Oct. 1936, C7452/7282/4 and Ovey to Eden, 21 Oct. 1936, C7494/7284/4.

make unilateral pronouncements while they were still seeking a new settlement. The Foreign Office was naturally worried lest the already listless negotiations for a new Locarno be delayed even longer.[1]

All the Belgian Foreign Ministry could do was assure the Foreign Office that Belgium was abrogating none of her obligations.[2] Van Zeeland wrote an apologetic letter to his friend Eden explaining that 'imperious reasons of internal policy' had caused his government to publish the King's speech.[3] Eden graciously replied that he was looking forward to resuming his collaboration with van Zeeland.[4] The Foreign Secretary did not know that his troubles with Belgium had only begun.

British fears that the Belgians had unwittingly undermined the effort to reach a new settlement in Western Europe were borne out by the Italian and German responses to Leopold's speech. The Belgian embassy in Rome reported that the royal pronouncement had created a great sensation there. The Italians were pleased with it precisely because they figured it would slow down the Locarno negotiations.[5] 'The paradoxical situation in Europe is beginning to clear up', said *Il Giornale d'Italia*. 'The first to break the spell [of collective security] was Belgium.'[6]

The Germans were pleased too. It had been a long time since news from abroad had given them so much satisfaction.[7] The Belgian attitude justified their desire to go slowly in the Locarno negotiations, and it had dealt a serious blow to the French system of alliances. The German press interpreted Leopold's

[1] Eden to Ovey, 15 Oct. 1936, FO, 432/2/C7301/7284/4 and Eden to Ovey, 16 Oct. 1936, C7338/7284/4.

[2] Spaak to Cartier, 16 Oct. 1936, *DDB*, IV, no. 134 and Cartier to Spaak, 16 Oct. 1936, no. 135.

[3] Van Zeeland to Eden, 26 Oct. 1936, FO, 371/19854/C7601/7284/4.

[4] Eden to van Zeeland, 28 Oct. 1936, ibid.

[5] Chastel to Spaak, 16 Oct. 1936, *DDB*, IV, no. 141. See also Chambrun to Delbos, 17 Oct. 1936, *DDF*, Ser. II, III, no. 366. The Italians were ambivalent about the Locarno negotiations. On the one hand, they did not wish to abstain from 'Locarno II' for reasons of prestige. On the other hand, the Italians did not want to be associated with a bloc of northern states led by 'perfidious Albion' and unwilling to give them sufficient compensation for their adherence to any settlement. Thus, anything which might postpone their having to take a firm position was to their liking.

[6] Quoted in *L'Indépendance belge*, 17 Oct. 1936, p. 3.

[7] François-Poncet to Delbos, 20 Oct. 1936, *DDF*, Ser. II, III, no. 382. See also François-Poncet to Delbos, 17 Oct. 1936, no. 367.

speech as a staggering defeat for the Franco-Soviet *entente*.[1] Foreign Minister Neurath discreetly informed Ambassador Davignon that if the negotiations for a new Locarno failed, Berlin might be willing to conclude a bilateral pact of non-aggression with Belgium. Such a pact, he said, would improve German–Belgian relations in every respect.[2] Needless to say, Neurath was able to assure Davignon that the German government took no exception to the words of King Leopold.[3]

The French did take exception. The Paris press insisted that Belgium was guilty of treaty infractions as serious as those of Germany.[4] The Belgians had damaged France's entire system of alliances: 'The blow dealt by Leopold's speech had repercussions in every capital of Central and Eastern Europe . . .', said Pertinax.[5] They had weakened themselves and France militarily: 'Germany is the only certain beneficiary of this declared neutrality', wrote one military analyst.[6] They had embarrassed the Popular Front government by giving another propaganda weapon to the right-wing press, which tended to blame Belgium's apparent defection on the Franco-Soviet Pact and France's internal troubles.[7] 'Franco-Russian Treaty; international inertia; internal disorder; here is how France has nourished the anti-French propaganda of the *flamingants* and repulsed the sympathies of the Walloons', wrote André Tardieu.[8]

[1] *The New York Times*, 20 Oct. 1936, p. 24. See also *The Times*, 16 Oct. 1936, p. 14, and *DDB*, IV, no. 140. The American embassy in Moscow reported that Leopold's speech was a 'distinct shock' to Soviet diplomats and that it had caused them to fear that 'the foundations are already beginning to fall away from so-called collective security . . .'. Henderson to Hull, 28 Oct. 1936, *FRUS*, 1936, I, pp. 364–5.

[2] Davignon to Spaak, 17 Oct. 1936, *DDB*, IV, no. 143.

[3] Memorandum by Neurath, 16 Oct. 1936, GFMA, 155/141/127019–20. The German ambassador in Brussels, Richthofen, correctly reported that the royal speech was the culmination of a policy begun in 1931. However, he mistakenly reported that it meant a return to 'integral neutrality'—one more indication of the confusion generated by Leopold's words. 15 Oct. 1936, ibid., 717/1160/326566–9.

[4] *Survey, 1936*, p. 357.

[5] Pertinax, 'La nouvelle orientation de la politique étrangère belge: les répercussions diplomatiques', *L'Europe nouvelle* (Paris, 1936), 19th year, no. 976, p. 1056.

[6] G. Charlyvel, 'La nouvelle orientation de la politique étrangère belge: l'aspect militaire du probleme', Ibid., p. 1058.

[7] Kerchove to Spaak, 16 Oct. 1936, *DDB*, IV, no. 137. See also Miller, *Belgian Foreign Policy Between Two Wars*, p. 242.

[8] André Tardieu, *La Note de semaine 1936* (Paris, 1937), p. 180.

Léon Blum and his colleagues had been warned about the coming change in Belgian foreign policy, and, like the British, they were aware of the domestic considerations which made the change necessary.[1] But they had assumed that the Belgians would not broach the matter again until the new Locarno discussions began. Now they wanted explanations fast.

They got them. Spaak insisted that there was no question of Belgium's abrogating her obligations. Staff talks could continue. Belgium remained loyal to the League. Nothing had changed.[2] Van Zeeland offered the same interpretation of the King's speech. It was intended only to prepare public opinion, and in particular Flemish opinion, for the military reform.[3] Van Zeeland and Delbos soon communicated by telephone, and the French Foreign Minister quickly reported the conversation to the foreign affairs committee of the Chamber of Deputies: 'Van Zeeland told me that Leopold's words were purely a gesture and that the Franco-Belgian alliance would endure.'[4]

Despite the avalanche of assurances from Brussels, the Quai d'Orsay was angry. This was made clear to the Belgian ambassador in Paris. After all, said Delbos, during the recent conversations at Geneva the Belgians had agreed not to take any unilateral decisions. They had agreed also that the general staffs of both France and Belgium would be consulted before they pursued their policy further. Moreover, France had received a moral setback in the Little Entente and Balkan countries. Delbos hoped that the Belgians would quickly

---

[1] On the day that Paris received word of Leopold's speech, Léon Blum happened to have a meeting with Colonel Charles de Gaulle. The colonel suggested that Belgium had opted for neutrality because France lacked a professional, mechanized army (a suggestion which Belgian military men like van Overstraeten would have accepted as part of the truth). Blum did not argue, de Gaulle remembers, 'although he thought the motivations of the attitude in Brussels were more than strategic'. Charles de Gaulle, *Mémoires de Guerre. L'appel, 1940–1942* (Paris, 1954), p. 19.

[2] Laroche to Delbos, 15 Oct. 1936, *DDF*, Ser. II, III, no. 358. See also Memorandum by Vanlangenhove, undated, *DDB*, IV, no. 130.

[3] Laroche to Delbos, 15 Oct. 1936, *DDF*, Ser. II, III, no. 359.

[4] *The New York Times*, 22 Oct. 1936, p. 6. Delbos also told the committee that the royal speech was an 'internal political manœuvre to get the Flemish and Rexists votes behind a new army bill'. It is no wonder that the Flemish Nationalists should remind van Zeeland of his phone conversation with Delbos during the next parliamentary foreign policy debate. *Annales* (Chamber), extraordinary session, 1936, 28 Oct. 1936, p. 376.

eliminate any confusion about the meaning of the King's speech for the benefit of European public opinion.[1]

Whatever the true meaning of Leopold's speech, it was obvious that Belgium was still determined to become a non-guarantor of France. The Quai d'Orsay considered this dangerous, not because a Belgian guarantee was itself worth much, but because the French army wanted to use Belgian territory for the defence of France and was already implementing its plans to do so.[2] 'In reality', said Alexis Léger,

the situation will from now on be the following: Germany will always be free to violate the Belgian frontiers at the moment she pleases . . . As opposed to this, France will not be able to penetrate into Belgium until after a German attack and she will not be able to use Belgian access routes to Germany, as long as Belgium is neutral. It is an important trump-card which Belgium has just given Germany and it suffices to note the joy which is being manifested in that country . . .[3]

For Belgium to put France on the same footing with Germany would be a grave mistake, said Delbos, because

the danger of violation of Belgian neutrality is completely different from the French point of view and the German point of view. France is firmly determined never to attack Belgium and it is not the same with Germany. Therefore, measures of military protection intended to guarantee this neutrality ought to be different, according to the country to which they are directed.[4]

The Belgians could only offer more protestations of fidelity to their obligations and the news that Spaak intended to clear

[1] Kerchove to Spaak, 17 Oct. 1936, *DDB*, IV, no. 142. See also Delbos to Corbin, 21 Oct. 1936, *DDF*, Ser. II, III, no. 388.

[2] Two days before Leopold's speech Gamelin complained to the British military attaché that Belgium's desire to become non-guarantor would compel a change in the plan of campaign which he had been elaborating for the past few years, a plan to move both armoured and infantry divisions into Belgium at a moment's notice. If Belgium changed her international status, said Gamelin, France would have to change her strategy, since an operation of this magnitude could not be extemporized. Report by British Military Attaché in Paris, 13 Oct. 1936, enclosure in FO, 432/2/C7382/7284/4.

[3] Kerchove to Spaak, 16 Oct. 1936, *DDB*, IV, no. 138.

[4] Kerchove to Spaak, 17 Oct. 1936, ibid., no. 142. See also Kerchove to Spaak, 13 Oct. 1936, no. 126. It is interesting to note that Delbos was willing to let Belgium become a non-guarantor, provided that the military contacts were continued. The trouble with this was that the Flemish members of the Chamber of Deputies would certainly have interpreted this as evidence of an alliance.

up all the confusion in a parliamentary address. Their beleaguered ambassador in Paris quietly suggested that France
stop asking Belgium embarrassing questions about her future
commitments, lest a bad situation be rendered even worse.
Belgium now wished to pursue a 'policy of silence'.[1]

Two weeks after Leopold's speech the ambassador sadly
reported to Brussels that 'the euphoric love which France
entertained for Belgium . . . is definitely dead, and from now on
Belgians have become again, in this country, 'congenial
foreigners', instead of the brothers of heart and soul which they
have remained since the first German uhlan entered Belgium
on 4 August, 1914'.[2]

Paul van Zeeland and his associates were wondering if the
publication of the royal speech had been such a master-stroke.
The commotion the speech caused abroad might have been
compensated for somewhat if it had produced some solid
political assets at home. But it failed to do so. Of course, most
Belgians approved of it. But few thought that the King had
said anything new; he had only made more solemn a message
which van Zeeland and Spaak had delivered earlier. The royal
speech had still less impact because everyone's attention was
riveted on the Rexists, whose so-called 'march on Brussels' took
place only ten days after Leopold's intervention.[3] There was
another problem. Leopold's blunt language inevitably aroused
suspicions in Socialist circles. The King seemed 'to have made
rather short shrift of mutual assistance and collective security',
noted *Le Peuple*.[4] One Socialist member of parliament was more
to the point. He wanted to know 'the precise significance of the
word "neutrality", which appeared in the King's speech . . .'.[5]

Spaak sought to allay the misgivings. He told Socialist
audiences that Belgium was not rejecting the principles of

[1] Kerchove to Spaak, 30 Oct. 1936, ibid., no. 160. See also Kerchove to Spaak,
20 Oct. 1936, no. 147 and Delbos to Corbin, 21 Oct. 1936, *DDF*, Ser. II, III, no.
388.

[2] Kerchove to Spaak, 31 Oct. 1936, *DDB*, IV, no. 161.

[3] *BPB*, no. 124, 19 Dec. 1936, pp. 4–6; *The Times*, 21 Oct. 1936, p. 14 and 22
Oct. 1936, p. 16; and Miller, *Belgian Foreign Policy Between Two Wars*, pp. 240–41.
One segment of the Walloon press was actually hostile to the speech.

[4] *Le Peuple*, 17 Oct. 1936, p. 1.

[5] *Annales* (Chamber), extraordinary session, 1936, 28 Oct. 1936, p. 361. See also
BPB, no. 124, 19 Dec. 1936, p. 5.

collective security or the ideals of the League of Nations. Belgium was breaking none of her engagements.[1] He told the foreign affairs committee of the Senate that Leopold's speech had not meant a change in the direction of Belgian foreign policy; it was to be regarded only as the opening of the debate on military reform.[2] Émile Vandervelde seconded the Foreign Minister. He told a Socialist congress that the only reason Leopold had failed to mention loyalty to the League was that he had addressed his speech to a Cabinet for which this went without saying. The Socialists in the cabinet were not supporting a foreign policy which contradicted their party loyalty. This loyalty, said Vandervelde, came first.[3] Accordingly, the Socialist party published an official interpretation of the King's speech which promised its worried members that Belgium still maintained all her obligations.[4] Walloon Liberals who still valued Franco-Belgian friendship highly could breathe more easily, too. 'You see', said *L'Indépendance belge*, 'that nothing has changed.'[5]

The Flemish reaction to all these explanations was predictable. To one Flemish deputy it all seemed like three steps forward and two backward. This uncertainty, he said, was intolerable: The time has come to play with the cards down . . .'[6] The Rexists concluded that there was a difference between the King's speech and its subsequent interpretations and that Spaak had executed a 'pirouette' before the admonishments of the Socialist party.[7] The Brussels correspondent of *The Times* of London noted that there was plenty of fog surrounding Belgian foreign policy. He reported that the Foreign Minister had 'not yet made up his mind about the future'.[8]

On 28 October, one day after the government formally presented its military reform project to the parliament, Spaak made a last effort to clear up the muddle. Was Belgium turning her back on the League of Nations? Not at all, Spaak told the Chamber of Deputies. But there were certain imprecisions in

[1] *The Times*, 19 Oct. 1936, p. 13 and *Le Peuple*, 26 Oct. 1936, p. 3.
[2] *L'Indépendance belge*, 17 Oct. 1936, p. 1.
[3] *Le Peuple*, 26 Oct. 1936, pp. 1–2.   [4] *Contribution*, p. 44.
[5] *L'Indépendance belge*, 17 Oct. 1936, p. 1.
[6] *Annales* (Chamber), extraordinary session, 1936, 28 Oct. 1936, pp. 366–7.
[7] *Le Pays réel*, 17 Oct. 1936, p. 3.
[8] *The Times*, 22 Oct. 1936, p. 16.

the League Covenant, and there was nothing more dangerous than to accept obligations which were imprecise. This situation could not be allowed to last. What would be Belgium's role in the new Locarno? Spaak said that the Chamber could not ask him to bring it up to date on negotiations which were still in progress. Was Belgium returning to neutrality? Absolutely not, said Spaak, 'rather our foreign policy places us under the sign of independence'. The Foreign Minister assured his audience that there was no contradiction between his words and those of the King. 'In any case, I hope that this time you think I have said enough to clear up the ambiguities.'[1]

'You haven't said anything', shouted a Flemish deputy. The Flemish press agreed. All this verbiage was just a way 'to swindle the agreement of the Flemings for the eighteen months of service and the other overwhelming military burdens'.[2] Several days later the Socialists, who still abhorred a long period of compulsory military service, combined with the Flemings in a preliminary vote to defeat the government proposal for an eighteen month period of service—and they defeated it by a large margin of votes.[3]

Such was the aftermath of King Leopold's famous speech: anger abroad, confusion at home, and another set-back for the defence project. This could have meant the end of the van Zeeland government of national union, and the fall of this government at this particular time would have been a catastrophe for Belgium.

5. *The Secret Conversations of Blum and van Zeeland*

The success of Belgium's military reform and the survival of the van Zeeland government now depended on the French, and there was little indication that their attitude had become more flexible. Several days after the King's speech the Quai d'Orsay sent to Brussels a list of questions, and it seemed as though the

[1] *Annales* (Chamber), extraordinary session, 1936, 28 Oct. 1936, pp. 370–71. Apparently, this was the speech which the Quai d'Orsay was told would undo some of the damage done by Leopold's speech.

[2] *BPB*, no. 124, 19 Dec. 1936, p. 7.

[3] *L'Indépendance belge*, 4 Nov. 1936, p. 4, and *The Times*, 4 Nov. 1936, p. 13. It should be noted that the deputies did approve the other parts of the government's project.

two foreign ministries were on the brink of one of those discussions which proved nothing but how much misunderstanding there really was. Some of the anger generated by this whole episode stemmed from sheer confusion compounded by a certain lack of candour. In the past it had been the French who were evasive. Now the Belgians were evasive, because they feared being pinned down to anything which could embarrass their government at home. But as their ambassador in Paris pointed out apropos the French questions, 'even an elusive and evasive response would be worth more than a silence which will be interpreted here as inimical and not very friendly to France'.[1]

What was Belgium's conception of a French guarantee, if she herself wished no longer to be a guarantor of France? asked the Quai d'Orsay. France could effectively implement her guarantee of Belgium only if staff talks continued.[2] The Quai d'Orsay knew that the French General Staff was genuinely worried about this. The end of staff talks and the resultant failure to make technical preparations for Franco-Belgian collaboration would handicap any intervention of the French army in Belgium. Moreover, Belgium's return to neutrality would leave France in a situation in which some of her best troops—poised to march into Belgium—might be rendered useless in the early stages of a war if Germany attacked France only.[3] Hence the General Staff's fears were quite natural.

There was plenty of disagreement within the Belgian government and parliament on this important matter. Its existence perhaps accounts for Spaak's irritability: 'I don't understand why you don't stop asking us for precision on these different points . . .', he complained to Ambassador Laroche.[4] Actually, Spaak, like many others, thought that staff talks were useful no matter what the international status of Belgium was.[5] Common-

---

[1] Kerchove to Spaak, 20 Oct. 1936, *DDB* IV, no. 147.
[2] Kerchove to Spaak, 17 Oct. 1936, ibid., no. 142. See also Delbos to Corbin, 21 Oct. 1936, *DDF*, Ser. II, III, no. 388 and van Zuylen, *Les Mains libres*, pp. 372–3.
[3] Van Overstraeten, *Albert I. Léopold III*, pp. 235–6; Kerchove to Spaak, 17 Oct. 1936, *DDB*, IV, no. 142; and Memorandum by Vanlangenhove, 30 Nov. 1936, no. 178; Quai d'Orsay memorandum, 30 Sept. 1936, *DDF*, Ser. II, III, no. 300.
[4] Laroche to Delbos, 10 Nov. 1936, *DDF*, Ser. II, III, no. 463. See also Laroche to Delbos, 29 Oct. 1936, no. 422.
[5] Van Overstraeten, *Albert I. Léopold III*, p. 238.

sense considerations like Belgium's own lack of troop strength and the ever-present threat of invasion from the East suggested that some kind of co-operation with friendly neighbours was in order. The Foreign Ministry sought the opinion of the Belgian General Staff. Its Chief, van den Bergen, replied that staff talks were not essential. The French army's destination in Belgium would be determined by the military situation at the moment of entry. Belgian roads and railroads would be placed at French disposal almost instantaneously. In the last analysis, French assistance to Belgium would always be determined by the needs of French security—with or without staff talks.[1] These arguments strengthened the hand of King Leopold and his advisers, who were opposed to staff talks of any kind: they could 'only compromise us politically without being necessarily militarily', argued the King in an exhortation to Spaak.[2] Whether or not it was because of differences of opinion, no decision was taken—at least for the time being. The official reply to the Quai d'Orsay's question about staff talks simply evaded it. Staff talks could continue while a new Locarno was being negotiated. Nothing was changed in this respect. But: 'In the future Belgium will draw her inspiration from the circumstances and from her international status.'[3]

What was Belgium's interpretation of the obligations deriving from article 16 of the League Covenant? asked the Quai d'Orsay. If Germany attacked France only, would Belgium grant French troops 'right of passage' in accordance with article 16?[4] Of course, the Belgian Foreign Ministry assumed that the French intended to invoke article 16 on behalf of their allies in Central Europe, even if they did not say so. Since 1930 questions like this had caused endless argument between French and Belgian diplomats, and the questions always emerged when the Belgians had the least time to discuss them. The Belgians could accept no interpretation of article 16 which did not leave Belgian sovereignty intact. Their qualms

[1] Ibid., pp. 240–41. It should be noted, however, that in November 1936 Van den Bergen told Gamelin that the 'new circumstances would not trouble our relations or our eventual collaboration'. Gamelin, *Servir*, II, 239.

[2] Ibid., p. 239.

[3] Spaak to Kerchove, 12 Nov. 1936, *DDB*, IV, no. 166.

[4] Kerchove to Spaak, 17 Oct. 1936, ibid., no. 142 and Delbos to Corbin, 21 Oct. 1936, *DDF*, Ser. II, III, no. 388.

about the League and collective security were hardly peculiar to themselves. Secretary General Vanlangenhove wrote this:

... it is certain that the nations are not disposed to obligate themselves in a general and unconditional manner to apply such measures. It is only within the limit of regional agreements, in connection with precise hypotheses affecting their vital interests, that certain of them have proven ready to undertake obligations so formidable. Even within this restricted framework, Belgium has decided, for her part, no longer to accept such a burden, which exceeds the resources at her disposal.[1]

In other words, Belgium could not accept general obligations at the very moment she was unburdening herself of her more particular obligations. But an open repudiation of League obligations was certain to antagonize the Socialists. It is no wonder that the Foreign Ministry left this question open, too. It informed the Quai d'Orsay that Belgium remained a member of the League and intended to execute all her obligations. But it was desirable to clear up the uncertainties surrounding article 16. 'The Government of the King is thus in complete agreement with the French Government on the necessity of elucidating the matter of the interpretation of article 16.'[2]

The Quai d'Orsay asked this. What would be the new status of Belgium? Was Belgium returning directly or indirectly to the conception of perpetual neutrality which existed in 1914?[3] The Foreign Ministry replied that Belgium was repudiating none of her obligations. However, the obligations accepted in London on 19 March 1936 were binding only until a new Locarno was negotiated, and 'the Belgian Government cannot consider participation in the new Locarno as a guarantor'.[4] There was no ambiguity on at least this point.

The Foreign Ministry dispatched its aide-mémoire to Paris on 12 November. But domestic events were now moving too fast for Brussels to await a reply. The government had made a last review of the defence question. Was there any way in which the eighteen month period of service could be reduced? On 18

[1] Memorandum by Vanlangenhove, 28 Oct. 1936, *DDB*, IV, no. 159.
[2] Spaak to Kerchove, 12 Nov. 1936, ibid., no. 166.
[3] Kerchove to Spaak, 17 Oct. 1936, ibid., no. 142 and Delbos to Corbin, 21 Oct. 1936, *DDF*, Ser. II, III, no. 388.
[4] Spaak to Kerchove, 12 Nov. 1936, *DDB*, IV, no. 166.

November the cabinet revealed its answer: 'The government maintains its own formula, that of the eighteen months of service. It will be the duty of the Chamber to fulfil its responsibilities in this matter.'[1]

Paul van Zeeland found the aftermath of Leopold's speech very painful. He said that he was hurt and offended by the attitude of the French press and the Quai d'Orsay and that he was sad to see that his efforts of nearly two years had led only to this. He was 'profoundly convinced' that the permanent interests of France and Belgium were identical. 'I seem to have been misunderstood in Paris. This has been a great disappointment for me', he told Ambassador Laroche.[2] The ambassador wondered if van Zeeland was not deliberately exaggerating his bad humour. Perhaps he was. But the fact is that the Prime Minister had some good reasons to be gloomy and depressed. His domestic political troubles were far from over. He was overworked and still recovering from a recent illness. Van Zeeland compounded his real problems by tending to take set-backs too personally, a tendency which Laroche attributed to his relative inexperience in politics.[3] Like many successful businessmen and lawyers who enter politics fully expecting more success, van Zeeland found it difficult to accept failure. He had assumed that patience, persuasiveness, a spirit of compromise and so on could be applied as effectively in international politics as in business or in the academic world. But it had not worked out that way. Furthermore, it must have been personally humiliating to him that the untimely publication of the now notorious royal speech, which he himself had approved, had led to so much ill will and suspicion abroad.

It was especially galling to be criticized by the British. 'The blame which one can attribute to Belgium does not involve substance, but rather form', Robert Vansittart told van Zeeland.[4] In late November the Belgian Prime Minister travelled to London to address the International Chamber of

[1] *BPB*, no. 124, 19 Dec. 1936, p. 23.
[2] Laroche to Delbos, 7 Nov. 1936, *DDF*, Ser. II, III, no. 454.
[3] Laroche to Delbos, 10 Nov. 1936, ibid., no. 463.
[4] Memorandum by van Zeeland, 27 Nov. 1936, *DDB*, IV, no. 175.

Commerce—an institution which he undoubtedly found more congenial than the Belgian Chamber of Deputies—and he thus had a chance to talk to Eden and other Foreign Office officials. 'The French are worried', said Eden, who then recapitulated the French position for his visitor.[1] Van Zeeland replied that Belgium's policy served the best interests of both France and Britain, in so far as it would strengthen Belgium herself and thus help 'to immunize one of the nerve centres of the West'.[2] The British did not argue. They had never argued with the Belgians. What concerned them was not the substance of Belgium's policy, but rather the way in which that policy was being conducted. To repeat Vansittart's words: it was a matter of form.

Van Zeeland's problem was how to harmonize good form in international politics with necessity in domestic politics. The next vote on the military reform project was now scheduled for 2 December. The Belgian government could not simply announce Belgium's refusal to guarantee France in the new Locarno. That would have been bad form. But it could not go on quarrelling with the Quai d'Orsay. Any further delay would have conflicted with political necessity. Van Zeeland's only hope was personally to persuade Léon Blum to give in before the vote on the military legislation.

In late November Blum was surprised to hear via a 'rather sinuous chain of intermediaries' that Paul van Zeeland wanted a secret meeting.[3] The probable reason for the secrecy is that Flemings might have considered any such meeting evidence of

---

[1] Ibid., no. 174. See also Eden to Ovey, 30 Nov. 1936, FO, 432/2/C8592/7284/4.

[2] Memorandum by van Zeeland, 28 Nov. 1936, *DDB*, IV, no. 176.

[3] Blum, *L'Œuvre de Léon Blum*, V, 9. The dates of van Zeeland's meetings with Blum are a real mystery. In his memoirs Blum remembered only that it was 'around the first days of December'. Later in testimony given before a postwar parliamentary commission he thought it was in late December or early January 1937. The author has corresponded with Paul van Zeeland about this. He very courteously took the trouble to ascertain whether the records of the Belgian cabinet contain any allusion to these meetings. They do not, nor do the available French and Belgian diplomatic documents. Actually, the conversations, or at least one of them, had to take place before the vote on the defence bill (2 December). The only accounts of these meetings are in Blum's memoirs and in the testimony mentioned above. The former account is the earlier of the two, and it will therefore be followed. See *Les Événements survenus en France*, op. cit., I, 130–31 and Joel Colton, *Léon Blum. Humanist in Politics* (New York, 1966), pp. 206–7.

a 'diplomatic Canossa'.[1] Two meetings were arranged. One took place in a private Parisian residence; for the second meeting Blum travelled incognito to Brussels, where he met van Zeeland in the latter's home. At the first meeting van Zeeland represented Belgium alone, and at the second he was accompanied by Spaak. In both instances Blum had at his side Foreign Minister Delbos and Camille Chautemps, who was a minister-without-portfolio in the Popular Front government.

Blum later remembered that the language of the two Belgians was 'earnest, suggestive, and warm-hearted'. Their arguments contained nothing new. They said that a policy of independence would be to the advantage of both countries. Belgium's defences were in a bad way, and it was necessary to construct fortifications and build up the army. Only with a policy of independence could the government hope to receive support for all the necessary sacrifices. If the government maintained the existing arrangements, '*flamingant* opposition and obstruction would fatally shackle all its efforts'. On the other hand, the presence of a well-armed and united Belgium would mean that France could concentrate her efforts on her own frontier; indeed, France need not worry about her northern frontier at all. Of course, Belgium still expected to have France's unilateral guarantee.[2]

This moment was as painful for Blum as it was for van Zeeland. 'We had been in power only a few months', and despite all efforts to strengthen the edifice of collective security, 'we saw a new section of the façade crumble before our eyes, and, in the state of Europe at that time, we could hardly doubt that this fissure would lead to others.' None the less, Blum and Delbos knew full well that the Belgians had already made their decision and that it was irrevocable. 'The Belgians were our friends, and one could not hold friends in an alliance against their will.' Blum knew also that the British government would not have 'the slightest hesitation in giving the Belgian govern-

[1] Corbin to Delbos, 30 Nov. 1936, *DDF*, Ser. II, IV, no. 63. When van Zeeland met with Flandin in Paris in February 1936, the Flemish press called it 'the greatest blunder of Belgian foreign policy since 1918.' See above, Ch. II, p. 53 n.
[2] Blum, *L'Œuvre de Léon Blum*, V, 9–10.

ment its liberty'. In other words, he was ready to give in. Blum remembered having said this:

All right. France does not intend to compel you to remain in the alliance, nor could she, any more than Great Britain, refuse to continue her guarantee to you. But I want to warn you of something right now: you yourself will give this guarantee its strength and its worth. It will be valuable only to the extent to which we have together prepared to make it effective. There is something which France will not again undertake, the adventure of Charleroi. If the two countries have effectively concerted their action, the French army will enter Belgium. If not, it will remain in France . . .[1]

These secret meetings ended in a near disaster. Driving back to Paris after the second one, the French statesmen encountered an icy road. Because they were travelling incognito, they refused to stop. One of the cars carrying Blum's party skidded, plunged through the railing of a bridge, and was saved from destruction only because it crashed into an electricity pole. The scene of the accident was Compiègne.[2]

6. *The Passage of the Defence Bill*

'Today this policy of independence is consummated', Paul van Zeeland told a cheering Chamber of Deputies. He was making his final appeal for support of the defence project. Who would dare to make a distinction between the attitude of the government and that of the King? To deny that the government was pursuing a really independent foreign policy was 'to deny the light of day'. Of course, independence did not mean isolation, because Belgium remained a loyal member of the League. But Locarno was a different matter: 'We no longer intend to give France and Germany the guarantee which was set down in the Locarno agreements of 1925 . . .'[3]

That was enough. The military project was voted into law that very day.[4] And from that moment Belgian foreign policy was no longer the prisoner of domestic developments.

[1] Ibid., pp. 10–11.   [2] Ibid., p. 9.
[3] *Annales* (Chamber), 1936/1937, 2 Dec. 1936, p. 318.
[4] Ibid., p. 341. See also *L'Indépendance belge*, 3 Dec. 1936, p. 1 and *The Times*, 3 Dec. 1936, p. 13. In order to make the bill more acceptable to the Socialists the government allowed an amendment reducing the period of service to seventeen months.

VI

BELGIUM'S NEW INTERNATIONAL STATUS

1. *Unfinished Business*

Belgium's decision to return to neutrality was more a response to domestic pressures than a response to international events. Of course, domestic and foreign affairs were so closely connected in Belgium that it is difficult to make a sharp distinction between them or to know which frightened Belgian statesmen most. But the fact is that the Belgian government's four most significant initiatives—the elimination of the Franco-Belgian Military Agreement, the July decision to become a 'non-guarantor', the publication of King Leopold's speech, and van Zeeland's last-minute appeal to Léon Blum—were the immediate upshot of some domestic crisis. The Belgians had had little time to negotiate, and they had, in effect, presented their neighbours with a series of *faits accomplis*. The great powers had accepted Belgium's new policy in principle, but they had not yet agreed on the terms of her new international status. Was Belgium to be a signatory of the new Locarno? What form would the new guarantee of her integrity take? What about her role in future staff conversations or her interpretation of article 16 of the League Covenant? These were important questions. They involved Western European security as a whole and the future of France's entire system of alliances, or what was left of it.

The Belgians themselves had hoped that their country would achieve her new status within the framework of a new Locarno, a general settlement for Western Europe. But by the end of 1936 any lingering expectations of a new Locarno were giving way before Germany's refusal to negotiate on any but her own terms. All the familiar obstacles still existed. Berlin would not accept the Anglo-French demand that the new settlement be placed under the surveillance of the League Council and be structured in such a way as not to hinder the fulfilment of League obligations, i.e., the obligations of France to her allies in Eastern Europe.[1] Moreover, the general drift of events suggested that the longer Germany procrastinated, the less reason she would have to negotiate at all. The birth of the Rome-Berlin Axis in October indicated that the balance of power was still shifting in her favour. After the Germans signed the Anti-Comintern Pact with Japan in November, they had less reason to fear the Soviet Union and thus more reason to be confident in their dealings with the West.[2] In other words, when in November the British circulated two more notes among the Locarno powers in the hope of getting talks started, there was not one solid reason for optimism about a new Locarno.[3]

Despite this bleak prospect the Belgians had one cause for encouragement. By late 1936 both Britain and France had made clear publicly and unequivocally their commitment to defend Belgium, regardless of her foreign policy. On 20 November Eden said in a speech on rearmament that British arms 'may, and if the occasion arose, they would be used in the defence of France and Belgium . . .'.[4] One week later, when van Zeeland was visiting London, the Foreign Secretary made another declaration. Belgian integrity was a 'vital interest' of Britain, said Eden. The Belgians could count upon British help if ever they were the victims of unprovoked aggression.[5] The French government had no choice but to follow suit. Speaking before the Chamber of Deputies on 4 December, Foreign Minister Delbos said this: 'I wish to say in the name of the Government, that all the land, sea and air forces of France will be spontaneously and immediately used in the defence of Great Britain, in the event of non-provoked aggression. I say the same with regard to Belgium.'[6]

[1] Neurath to the Embassy in Great Britain, 13 Oct. 1936, *DGFP*, Ser. C, V, no. 596.

[2] *Survey, 1936*, pp. 364–6 and Colvin, *Vansittart in Office*, pp. 114–16.

[3] Memorandum of the British Government, 4 Nov. 1936, *DDF*, Ser. II, III, no. 439 and Memorandum of the British Government, 19 Nov. 1936, no. 513.

[4] Declaration by Eden at Leamington, 20 Nov. 1936, *DIA, 1936*, pp. 260–3.
[5] Ibid.

[6] Declaration by Delbos in the Chamber of Deputies, 4 Dec. 1936, ibid., pp. 274–82.

Such words were always great morale-boosters in Brussels. But they did not solve the Foreign Ministry's most pressing problem. How and when was Belgium going to sever her connection with the old Locarno? If the great powers had consented to Belgium's wishes for the future, they had not yet formally released her from her obligations. If the discussions about a new Locarno went on indefinitely, Belgium's association with France and Britain could be prolonged indefinitely. The Belgian government obviously could not maintain for long obligations which it was now publicly committed to terminate. A precise formula for the status of Belgium had to be found, and it had to be found soon.

2. *The Anglo-French Declaration*

The Belgians made their first concrete proposal in late November. During his visit to London van Zeeland suggested to Eden that it might expedite the effort to reach a general settlement if the negotiations were divided into two stages. During the first stage a preparatory agreement to respect Belgian integrity would be concluded. Van Zeeland argued that this could then become the nucleus of a subsequent, more comprehensive arrangement.[1] Eden promised to think it over. Three weeks later the Foreign Office sent to Brussels a memorandum asking that the Belgians should not take the initiative in the matter and recommending that van Zeeland talk it over with the French government.[2]

A discussion with the French was the last thing the Belgian Foreign Ministry wanted. On 24 December Brussels received an aide-mémoire from Paris which intimated that the impending discussion would be a lengthy one. It was no longer a question of Belgium becoming a guarantor in the new Locarno. The French aide-mémoire simply noted that if Belgium considered the existing Locarno arrangements provisional, they would none the less remain effective until a new treaty was

---

[1] Memorandum by Vanlangenhove, 26 Nov. 1936, *DDB*, IV, no. 173 and Memorandum by van Zeeland, 28 Nov. 1936, no. 176; and Eden to Ovey, 30 Nov. 1936, FO, 432/2/C8592/7284/4.

[2] Lantsheere to van Zeeland, 18 Dec. 1936, *DDB*, IV, no. 181. Eden wanted van Zeeland to find some pretext for a visit to Paris. It is clear that he knew nothing about the secret meetings of Blum and van Zeeland, the second of which probably took place about this time, i.e., late December.

signed. The Belgians naturally interpreted this as evidence of an intention to keep their country bound to France indefinitely, because no new treaty was in sight.[1] The aide-mémoire said that in order to make France's guarantee and military assistance to Belgium really effective, arrangements must be made in advance and staff contacts maintained. And it asked whether the Belgians might be interested in joining the French and British in an exchange of views on article 16 of the League Covenant and, in particular, its stipulation relating to the right of passage.[2]

'We considered it useless to prolong the discussion', writes Baron van Zuylen.[3] None the less, the questions remained.

Of the various issues still dividing Paris and Brussels, the meaning of article 16 was the most far-reaching in its implications. For the French it involved the preservation of their crumbling alliance system; for the Belgians it involved nothing less than the preservation of their national sovereignty. In November 1936 the Belgians had evaded a French inquiry about this by recommending that the two governments await an official League interpretation of article 16. Doubtless they did so knowing full well how little chance there was that the League would produce an interpretation favourable to the French viewpoint. Since the League's founding there had been an inconclusive argument about article 16.[4] Did it preclude neutrality or not? Because this question never received a definitive answer, the powers tended to interpret article 16 and, for that matter, the entire League Covenant in terms of national interest.[5] Before 1936 most small powers had regarded a strict observation of League obligations as the path to security. But then came the Ethiopian affair, which had served as the 'great eye-opener' for all who had placed confidence in the League and its sanctions system.[6] In July 1936 the foreign ministers of seven small

---

[1] Van Zuylen, Les Mains libres, p. 374.
[2] Kerchove to Spaak, 24 Dec. 1936, DDB, IV, no. 183.
[3] Van Zuylen, Les Mains libres, p. 374.
[4] Nils Örvik, The Decline of Neutrality (Oslo, 1953), pp. 122–3.
[5] For a description of French and British interpretations of the Covenant, see Wolfers, Britain and France between Two Wars, pp. 153–98.
[6] Örvik, The Decline of Neutrality, p. 172.

powers wished 'to place it on record that, so long as the Covenant as a whole is applied so incompletely and inconsistently, we
are obliged to bear that fact in mind in connection with the
application of article 16'.[1] Simultaneously, the League had
instituted a formal inquiry into the meaning of the Covenant
and the possibility of its reform.[2]

In 1936 there was no question of Belgium's joining the seven
'ex-neutrals' of the First World War, but their scepticism about
the value of the League's peace-keeping apparatus was ideally
suited to Belgian purposes. Because the questions raised by the
League inquiry were unlikely ever to be settled, individual
governments could adhere to that interpretation of article 16
which best fitted their own interests without incurring the
charge of violating the Covenant. The Belgian Foreign Ministry could dodge French questions by insisting that the matter
could be settled in Geneva only. The Belgian government
could make public increasingly flexible interpretations of article
16, confident that Socialist protests would be buried in an
avalanche of popular and scholarly counter-arguments.[3] When
the Belgians submitted their reply to the League's request for
suggestions and observations, they cautiously expressed the
hope that the obligations deriving from article 16 would be defined with more precision.[4] In his 2 December speech to the
Chamber of Deputies, van Zeeland was less cautious: until
article 16 was rendered more precise, Belgium would 'accept
no other interpretation than that which we ourselves intend to
give it, in the fullness of our sovereignty'.[5] In private, van

---

[1] Quoted ibid., p. 178. The seven states were Holland, Denmark, Norway,
Sweden, Finland, Spain, and Switzerland. See also William E. Rappard, *The Quest
for Peace* (Cambridge, 1940), pp. 321–2.

[2] F. P. Walter, *A History of the League of Nations* (London, 1965), pp. 709–20.

[3] The most articulate Belgian proponent of a strict interpretation of article 16
was Socialist Senator Henri Rolin, whose pamphlet provoked a reply from a
Catholic conservative, Louis de Lichtervelde. See Henri-A. Rolin, *La Belgique
neutre?* (Brussels, 1937) and Louis de Lichtervelde, 'La Belgique et la S.D.N.', in
La Revue générale (Brussels, 1937), 70th year, pp. 385–91. Two scholarly discussions
of Belgium's role in the League, the first of which argues that the 'policy of independence' did conflict with the Covenant and the second of which argues the
opposite are H. Tashin, 'Le statut international de la Belgique', *Revue de droit
international* (Paris, 1937), XX, 114–26 and Bernard de Franqueville, 'La position
internationale de la Belgique', ibid., XXIII, 21–73, 435–82.

[4] *L'Indépendance belge*, 14 Nov. 1936, pp. 1, 4. See also Miller, *Belgian Foreign
Policy Between Two Wars*, pp. 253–4.

[5] *Annales* (Chamber), 1936/1937, 2 Dec. 1936, p. 318.

Zeeland's message was essentially the same. He admitted to Eden during their November meeting that Belgium was bound by article 16 in some cases, but she reserved the right to decide when those cases had arisen.[1]

When the Quai d'Orsay tried to open another discussion of article 16, the Belgian Foreign Ministry evaded the issue again. It eventually had its own way simply by waiting and allowing the progressive breakdown of collective security to answer all the questions.

Belgium's participation in future staff conversations was still a source of uncertainty and disagreement within the Belgian government. The available evidence on this important matter is slim. It does appear, however, that by early 1937 there was a growing consensus that regular staff contacts were no longer desirable. Secretary General Vanlangenhove wrote that although there were advantages in studying and making technical preparations for eventual military co-operation, they were outweighed by the disadvantages: the maintenance of staff contacts might compromise the country politically.[2] In January Leopold's aide-de-camp, van Overstraeten, reviewed the problem with Spaak. He rehearsed the usual arguments: staff contacts would do nothing to halt an invasion at the frontier, and they would provide a potential invader with an excuse. For the first time on record Spaak admitted that these arguments were hard to refute.[3] Of course, a termination of formal staff contacts did not preclude exchanging information through the services of military attachés. Vanlangenhove was in favour of this.[4] So was van Zeeland, who thought also that Belgium should be free to exchange such information with Germany, if the latter wanted it.[5] On the other hand, King Leopold and his associates were opposed to exchanging confidential information with anybody and, as usual, were in sharp disagreement with the Ministry of

---

[1] Eden to Ovey, 30 Nov. 1936, FO, 432/2/C8592/7284/4. Eden indicated his acceptance of this interpretation three weeks later. Lantsheere to van Zeeland, 18 Dec. 1936, *DDB*, IV, no. 181.

[2] Memorandum by Vanlangenhove, 18 Dec. 1936, ibid., no. 182.

[3] Van Overstraeten, *Dans l'étau*, pp. 74–6.

[4] Memorandum by Vanlangenhove, *DDB*, IV, no. 182.

[5] Foreign Office memorandum, 6 May 1937, FO, 432/3/C3530/1/18.

Defence about this.[1] To complete the confusion, the Chief of the General Staff, van den Bergen, wanted to co-operate with the French. He was eager to pass along information to the British, and he did so—possibly on his own initiative.[2] Political Director van Zuylen said the one thing about this problem with which all the interested parties could agree: the less said about it, the better.[3] In fact, not much more was said, at least among the diplomats. The French embassy in Brussels advised the Quai d'Orsay that the best course was to wait patiently for a change in the Belgian attitude.[4]

It was going to be a long wait.

What made the confusing situation of early 1937 still worse for the Belgians, although they themselves were not fully aware of it at the time, was that the British had now concluded that the French had a good case against Belgium and that Britain's vital

[1] The French were now finding it hard to acquire military information from the Belgians. They attributed this to the influence of the King and his entourage, namely van Overstraeten and General Nuyten. This is an early example of Leopold's strict interpretation of the 'policy of independence'. Both the French and British were now associating him with everything they disliked about Belgian foreign policy, just as the French had once blamed everything on Baron van Zuylen. Laroche to Delbos, 7 Jan. 1937, *DDF*, Ser. II, IV, no. 255; Laroche to Delbos, 17 Feb. 1937, no. 459; and Ovey to Eden, 26 Feb. 1937, FO, 432/3/C1658/181/4.

[2] This is a most interesting matter about which not enough will be known until more documents are available. In November 1937, after all the questions about Belgium's international status had been settled, Spaak revealed to the British Belgium's willingness to convey information to them about Belgium's defences. In February 1938 van den Bergen presented the British with a map showing Belgian military dispositions. A little later he conveyed to them another map showing the places which could be held by a 'friendly air force'. He even suggested that Belgium's frontier ground observation posts be linked to London by telephone, just as they were *already linked to Paris by telephone*. British Ambassador Clive had the impression that van den Bergen was acting without authorization in order to avoid the use of Foreign Ministry channels. This suggests that Spaak and his colleagues were still arguing about this. The author wishes to note that he found no other evidence of a link between the Belgian frontier and Paris. Clive to Foreign Office, 4 Jan. 1938, FO, 371/21561/C72/68/4; dispatch from British Military Attaché in Brussels, 1 Feb. 1938, C707/68/17; Memorandum by British M.A. in Brussels, 10 Feb. 1938, C1008/68/4, Clive to Foreign Office, 15 Mar. 1938, C1776/68/4; letter from Foreign Office to Committee of Imperial Defence, 17 Dec. 1937, 21653/C841/37/18. See also Gamelin, *Servir*, II, 239 and Eden, *Facing the Dictators*, pp. 565–7.

[3] Ovey to Eden, 26 Mar. 1937, FO, 432/3/C2373/181/4.

[4] Laroche to Delbos, 7 Jan. 1937, *DDF*, Ser. II, IV, no. 255 and Laroche to Delbos, 17 Feb. 1937, no. 459.

interests were involved, too.[1] It is ironic that the British, who
had acquiesced to the change in Belgian foreign policy without
a protest and whose own half-hearted attitude about staff contacts had encouraged the change, should now deplore the consequences. For years the Belgian foreign and defence ministries
had wanted above all to establish the basis for close Anglo-
Belgian diplomatic and military collaboration. The British had
always refused. Perhaps they never realized that their collaboration with Belgium was the prerequisite for Belgium's collaboration with France. When Britain refused to co-operate with
Belgium, Belgium could no longer co-operate with France. And
the British Foreign Office regretted it. To be sure, wrote Eden,
the Foreign Office had agreed to Belgium's request no longer
to give a guarantee to France, 'but let there be no mistake about
it, we acquiesced unwillingly ... Franco-Belgian co-operation
was the basis of our policy and any break in it was bound in our
point of view to be most inconvenient.'[2] Robert Vansittart
agreed: if the Belgians thought that their new policy would provide them with security, they 'were indulging in a false and
dangerous form of self-delusion'.[3] And, for the first time, there
was a suspicion which later became 'common knowledge' and
the basis for a simple explanation of a great catastrophe: King
Leopold might be one of the 'comparatively pro-German
elements in Belgium today', wrote Eden.[4]

The Foreign Secretary disliked van Zeeland's recent proposal for a limited arrangement guaranteeing Belgium only.
Such a treaty would have an 'unpleasant resemblance' to the
famous neutralization treaty of 1839. Its existence would cause
the Belgians to be less inclined to co-operate with Britain and
France in the defence of Western Europe. Moreover, France
would not accept van Zeeland's suggestion unless it was accompanied by a separate Anglo-French treaty to replace the
present arrangements, and this 'might have the appearance of

---

[1] The Belgians did suspect that the Foreign Office was getting advice from the
Quai d'Orsay, as indeed it was. Memorandum by van Zeeland, 27 Nov. 1936,
DDB, IV, no. 174 and Foreign Office memorandum, 6 May 1937, FO, 432/3/
C3530/1/18.

[2] Draft of letter from Eden to Ovey, Mar. 1937, FO, 371/20697/C2165/181/4.

[3] Vansittart to Ovey, 21 Jan. 1937, ibid., 20678/C181/181/4.

[4] According to Eden, Spaak might be among these elements, too. Minute by
Eden, 29 Jan. 1937, ibid., C1081/181/4.

an Anglo-French alliance against Germany'. Co-operation between Britain, France, and Belgium 'forms the basis on which His Majesty's Government are at present conducting their negotiations for a new Western Pact of Mutual Guarantee'.[1] It was Britain's policy to make effective her own guarantee of Western Europe by enlisting the support of Belgium in the defence of the territorial *status quo* there.[2]

Eden's argument contains a contradiction, one which epitomizes the contradiction at the heart of British policy for years. Eden himself must have been painfully aware of it.

In discussing with the French the question of urging the Belgians to define the extent to which they are prepared to co-operate with France, I should make it clear that, although I sympathize with the desire of the French to remove the present uncertainty, I am not prepared to take part in any detailed discussions with regard to the actual French proposals (i.e., the communication of defence plans, and the preparation of positions in Belgian territory for French troops), since His Majesty's Government themselves do not wish to participate in such measures of co-operation. The latter desideratum I am satisfied that the Belgian Government would not in any circumstances grant.[3]

That 'latter desideratum' about the preparation of positions for French troops had been granted with enthusiasm in mid-1936, when there was the prospect that Britain herself would participate in such 'measures of co-operation'. One wonders whether Eden and the other officials of the Foreign Office knew the extent to which the attitude of their own government had contributed to the present situation. Perhaps they did.[4] There was certainly little they could do about it. The state of British

[1] It was precisely this tripartite co-operation which van Zeeland wanted so desperately in mid-1936 in order that the Western powers could negotiate with Germany from a position of strength.

[2] Memorandum prepared by Eden for the Cabinet, 5 Dec. 1936, FO, 371/19851/C8745/270/4.

[3] Ibid.

[4] For example, Eden indicated to the cabinet that British support of some co-operation between Belgium and her neighbours would 'strengthen the hands of those Belgians who are anxious to co-operate with us in the defence of Belgian territory . . .'. Ibid. In other words, Eden was aware of the dilemma faced by van Zeeland. It is worth noting in this connection that in June 1936 Eden told Baldwin that there was plenty to be said for an Anglo-Belgian military understanding. Foreign Office minute, 13 Aug. 1936, ibid., 19850/C5752/270/4.

public opinion, the Baldwin government's fear of antagonizing the Germans, the British military's notion that Belgian neutrality was desirable, all these left the Foreign Office scant opportunity to protect Britain's traditional interests. Be that as it may, the fact is that Britain wanted Western European co-operation without being willing or able to pay the price for it. This was a great tragedy for Britain, just as it was for all those who relied on her for support.

This leads to another aspect of this strange story. In May 1936 —two months after the remilitarization of the Rhineland—van Zeeland had called Eden's attention to one of Belgium's most serious military handicaps. He explained that part of the Belgian munitions industry was located near the German frontier and therefore would be abandoned in the early stages of a war. Could the British and Belgian governments discuss the supply of munitions from Britain to Belgium? Eden expressed doubts that this was an appropriate time for such a discussion.[1] Two months later the Belgians tried again. In July Spaak handed Eden a memorandum:

The supply of our Army is to a great extent and in certain important respects dependent on the co-operation of foreign countries. If this co-operation is not assured, the supply is precarious. The following cases may be cited as examples: gun-powder (*poudres de guerres*), of which our factories are unable to produce more than $\frac{1}{20}$ of our requirements; explosives, for which we have no national source of production; cartridges (infantry), of which we can produce only $\frac{1}{3}$ of our needs; petrol (for aeroplanes) of which the stock at our disposal represents at a maximum four day's consumption, while it is impossible, by reason of the prohibition to which the British importer is subjected, to increase this stock.[2]

The Foreign Office referred this document to the War Office, which then suggested that the Foreign Office itself should 'start the ball rolling'. The latter therefore referred the matter to a sub-committee of the Committee of Imperial Defence, which was expected to consider it at an October meeting. Instead, the sub-committee begged the question by means of a discussion on departmental procedures relating to all such re-

[1] Memorandum prepared by Eden for the Cabinet, 6 Jan. 1937, ibid., 19851/ C9088/270/4.   [2] Quoted ibid.

quests, and it made no response to Belgium's specific request.[1]
It was November, and the Belgians were still awaiting a reply.
Van Zeeland tried once more. Could Belgium's military
authorities please be allowed to make immediate arrangements
with their British counterparts for an agreed supply of certain
war materials in the event Belgium became involved in war
with Germany? Eden promised to make more inquiries, but he
warned van Zeeland that there could be difficulties in the way
of Britain's supplying war materials to anybody.[2]

The Foreign Office was embarrassed. The matter could not
be allowed 'to slide any longer'. Under-Secretary Orme
Sargent argued—and all his colleagues agreed—that if the
Belgian request was left in the hands of the military, it would
get nowhere. The military would take the position that Anglo-
Belgian talks could not take place on the grounds that they
would constitute staff conversations and thus violate Belgian
neutrality.[3] The Foreign Office therefore took the initiative. In
January 1937 Eden presented to the cabinet a memorandum
reviewing the whole problem and recommending on political
grounds that conversations between the Belgian military
attaché in London and the War Office be authorized. Britain
should 'endeavour in every possible way' to meet Belgium's
requirements.[4] The cabinet was willing to permit the Belgians
to state their requirements in more detail.[5]

Within two weeks the Belgians presented the War Office with
a long list of required war materials ranging from tanks and
aircraft to barbed wire and bandages.[6] At this juncture the War
Office suggested that the political implications be examined before Belgium's requests were conveyed to the technical experts.[7]
This was too much for the Foreign Office, whose patience had
now worn thin. Orme Sargent wrote that the important thing

[1] Ibid. and C.I.D. Sub-Committee on Defence Policy and Requirements
memorandum, 8 Oct. 1936, ibid., 19850/C7403/270/4.
[2] Memorandum prepared by Eden for the Cabinet, 6 Jan. 1937, ibid., 19851/
C9088/270/4.
[3] Minute by Sargent, 10 Dec. 1936, ibid., C8691/270/4.
[4] Memorandum prepared by Eden for the Cabinet, 6 Jan. 1937, ibid., C9088/
270/4.
[5] Extract from Cabinet Conclusions 1(37)7, 13 Jan. 1937, ibid., 20678/C318/
181/4.
[6] Memorandum from the Belgian Military Attaché, 6 Feb. 1937, ibid., C1055/
181/4.   [7] Inskip to Halifax, 6 Feb. 1937, ibid.

was 'to check the Belgian tendency towards isolationism . . .'. Anglo-Belgian collaboration with regard to war materials was a good way to do so. 'There are no further political considerations . . .,' said Vansittart. 'Let the supply officers get down to it.' Eden agreed.[1]

The Belgians submitted their list in January 1937. The British cabinet authorized a reply to it in February 1938.[2] The Belgian ambassador in London received that reply in July 1938.[3] Its substance is not as significant as the fact that over two years had passed since van Zeeland first brought the matter to Eden's attention. And, of course, by 1938 Belgium's international status was no longer under discussion. The available Belgian documents contain few allusions to this matter. It is impossible to know precisely what impression it made on Belgian statesmen. But it takes no great leap of the imagination to suggest that the impression must have been a bad one. It is hardly surprising that the Belgian government concluded that the advantages of being closely associated with Britain were outweighed by the disadvantages of being compromised politically by that association.

Great Britain bears a heavy responsibility for Belgium's strict interpretation of her neutrality policy. Those who later attributed that responsibility to Belgium alone and to her King did Belgium a grave injustice.

To return to Belgium's dilemma in early 1937. She was still tied to Locarno. The British and the French were in no hurry to release her from those obligations. Belgian diplomats were faced with a situation now very familiar to them, namely a total impasse. One wonders how they would have slipped out of it gracefully, if they had not received some assistance from Berlin.

The background of Hitler's offer to Belgium (and Holland) in his speech of 30 January 1937 is obscure. Did the initiative

[1] Foreign Office minute, ibid.

[2] Extract from Cabinet conclusion 4(38)8, 9 Feb. 1938, ibid., 21561/C936/68/4. A memorandum by Inskip indicated that Britain could supply Belgium certain items without difficulty, e.g. radio equipment and medicine. Certain others could be supplied only at the expense of Britain's own needs, e.g. small arms ammunition, explosives, and fuel oil. The supply of still others would be facilitated if Belgium adopted the British types, e.g., aircraft and tanks. Memorandum by the Minister for Co-ordination of Defence, 2 Feb. 1938, ibid., C924/68/4.

[3] Strang to Cartier, 28 July 1938, ibid·, C7435/68/4.

come from the Germans alone? It appears that the Belgians had been interested in obtaining from Berlin a declaration like those of Eden and Delbos and that they got more than they expected.[1] Hitler's language was somewhat cryptic: 'The German Government has ... assured Belgium and Holland of their readiness to recognize and guarantee these states as untouchable and neutral regions for all time.'[2] What were the 'assurances already given', and what was meant by the word 'neutral'? The Belgians were informed that the 'assurances' were those given during the Rhineland crisis and that the word 'neutral' referred to a policy of independence and impartiality and did not imply contractual neutrality.[3] Neurath told Ambassador Davignon:

The declarations of the Chancellor are to be understood as an offer. This offer will be good both in the event that a new Western pact is concluded, as an arrangement within the framework of this Western pact, and in the event that a new Western pact is not concluded, as an arrangement in another contractual form.[4]

The Germans were thinking in terms of a multilateral guarantee of Belgium.[5] If this did not come about, they were willing to conclude a bilateral treaty with Belgium.[6]

If Hitler's offer was a surprise, it was a very timely one. The Foreign Ministry in Brussels sounded a new note of confidence. Belgium could now 'take the initiative' in ending her Locarno obligations, said Spaak.[7] The time was drawing near, said

[1] Belgian sources agree that the initiative came from Berlin, although the German Foreign Office records indicate that the Belgians were interested in getting some sort of declaration. See van Zuylen, Les Mains libres, pp. 380–1; Davignon, Berlin, 1936–1940, pp. 53–4; Davignon to Spaak, 30 Dec. 1936, DDB, IV, no. 185 and Davignon to Spaak, 25 Jan. 1937, no. 186; and Memorandum by Gaus, 23 Dec. 1936, GFMA, 1726/3315/E007623, and Memorandum by Weizäcker, 21 Jan. 1937, 717/1159/326456, and Memorandum by Neurath, 29 Jan. 1937, 326457, and Neurath to the German Embassy in Brussels, 1 Feb. 1937, 326458.

[2] Extract from speech by Hitler, 30 Jan. 1937, DIA, 1937, pp. 161–75.

[3] Memorandum by Vanlangenhove, 2 Feb. 1937, DDB, IV, no. 193. The Belgians later learned that the German concept 'of impartiality' was not identical to their own.

[4] Davignon to Spaak, 4 Feb. 1937, ibid., no. 195. See also Memorandum by Bismark, 4 Feb. 1937, GFMA, 1727/3326/E008221–3.

[5] Memorandum by Weizäcker, 3 Feb. 1937, ibid., 717/1159/326463–4. At least one German diplomat, Ribbentrop, was contemplating a procedure similar to the one recommended by van Zeeland, namely a negotiation in two stages. Davignon to Spaak, 30 Dec. 1936, DDB, IV, no. 185 and Davignon to Spaak, 8 Feb. 1937, no. 198.

[6] Davignon to Spaak, 12 Feb. 1937, ibid., no. 203.

[7] Richthofen to the Foreign Office, 3 Feb. 1937, GFMA, 717/1159/326465.

Vanlangenhove, when Belgium would simply denounce her Locarno obligations.[1] He informed Britain's Ambassador Ovey that although Belgium preferred an arrangement which included all the Western powers, she would accept Hitler's offer if the negotiations for a new Locarno broke down.[2] On 10 February the Foreign Ministry sent a note to London saying that Belgium had the right to claim the guarantee and assistance of the great powers in defending the integrity of her territory.[3]

The British were worried. A multilateral guarantee of Belgium had never appealed to them. A bilateral arrangement between Belgium and Germany would be even worse. A Foreign Office memorandum pointed out that this could lead to German predominance in Belgium and 'mark the invasion by Germany of a sphere of influence which we have made peculiarly our own'. But Britain still had an opportunity 'to stabilize a situation which threatens to slip out of control'.[4] Accordingly, Eden recommended to the French that the time had come to give the Belgians satisfaction.[5]

The Quai d'Orsay needed no persuasion. Alexis Léger, who for years had warded off the Belgians with endless and subtle arguments about their obligations to France, now executed a volte-face. France would no longer resist Belgium's desire to be rid of her Locarno obligations. It was for the Belgians to decide whether they wanted staff talks. France had never contemplated invoking article 16 to secure for her troops right of passage across Belgium without the latter's permission.[6] 'It was a complete conversion', writes Baron van Zuylen.[7]

No time was wasted. Conversations began soon in London and Paris.[8] The British and French proposed a joint declaration

[1] Memorandum by Bräuer, 4 Mar. 1937, ibid., 717/1160/326681/4.
[2] Memorandum by Strang, 8 Mar. 1937, FO, 371/20679/C1896/181/4.
[3] Spaak to Cartier, 10 Feb. 1937, *DDB*, IV, no. 202.
[4] Memorandum by Strang, 8 Mar. 1937, FO, 371/20679/C1896/181/4.
[5] Foreign Office memorandum, 6 May 1937, ibid., 432/3/C3530/1/18.
[6] Kerchove to Spaak, 6 Mar. 1937, *DDB*, IV, no. 206.
[7] Van Zuylen, *Les Mains libres*, p. 384.
[8] It should be noted that King Leopold, who happened to be visiting London anyway—evidently because his dentist resided there—was employed by the Foreign Ministry to explain the Belgian point of view to the British. His services were used probably because Spaak and van Zeeland were too preoccupied with domestic matters (a by-election campaign against Degrelle) to be bothered. Leopold conducted no formal negotiations. Eden to Ovey, 23 Mar. 1937, FO, 432/3/C2316/181/4; Capelle, *Au service du roi*, I, 68–9; and *The Times*, 22 Mar. 1937, p. 12.

releasing Belgium from her Locarno obligations in return for her promise to be faithful to the League Covenant and to defend her territory. Here the only difficulty arose. Any arrangement which was contractual in nature or which imposed conditions which were self-understood, like the obligation to defend herself, was an offence to Belgian dignity. Would it not be sufficient if the Anglo-French declaration simply 'took note' of Belgian intentions?[1] No one was disposed to argue. The declaration was published on 24 April 1937.

Here are the significant paragraphs:

[The British and French] Governments have taken note of the views which the Belgian Government has itself expressed concerning the interests of Belgium, and more particularly:

(1) the determination expressed publicly and on more than one occasion by the Belgian Government: (a) to defend the frontiers of Belgium with all its forces against any aggression or invasion, and to prevent Belgian territory from being used, for purposes of aggression against another state, as a passage or as a base of operations by land, by sea, or in the air; (b) to organize the defence of Belgium in an efficient manner for this purpose;

(2) the renewed assurances of the fidelity of Belgium to the Covenant of the League of Nations and to the obligations which it involves for members of the League.

In consequence, taking into account the determination and assurances mentioned above, . . . they consider Belgium to be released from all obligations towards them resulting from the Treaty of Locarno or the arrangements drawn up in London on the 19th March, 1936, and that they maintain in respect of Belgium the undertakings of assistance which they entered into towards her under the above mentioned instruments.

The last paragraph said that 'the release of Belgium from her obligations . . . in no way affects the existing undertakings between the United Kingdom and France'.[2]

Belgian diplomats were completely satisfied with this: 'We preserved the advantages of the old Treaty without assuming its burdens.'[3] Both Eden and Delbos paid courtesy visits to Belgium which contributed to the mood of general satisfaction.

[1] Memorandum by van Zuylen, 20 Apr. 1937, *DDB*, IV, no. 222; Spaak to Cartier, 20 Apr. 1937, no. 223; and van Zuylen, *Les Mains libres*, pp. 385–6.
[2] Joint Communication by the British and French Ambassadors in Brussels, 24 Apr. 1937, *DIA, 1937*, pp. 190–1.
[3] Van Zuylen, *Les Mains libres*, p. 388.

The compliments exchanged on these occasions suggested that relations between Belgium and her Western neighbours had never been better. 'As far as Franco-Belgian relations are concerned', said Delbos, 'if there ever existed the slightest cloud, it is now completely dissipated.'[1]

The Anglo-French declaration left two matters unsettled. One of them was staff talks. Eden had suggested to Delbos that this be left in the background.[2] The Foreign Office evidently saw the declaratory method as a good way to leave the door open for some subsequent arrangement.[3] The Belgians were frankly puzzled by Britain's ambiguous attitude about staff talks, and they said so. In March King Leopold had paid an informal visit to London. In the course of a conversation with Eden he remarked that he thought it strange that whenever in the past the Belgians had wanted staff conversations, Britain was not interested; whereas now that they were pursuing an independent policy, Britain was critical of that policy. Eden replied that there must be some misunderstanding. Britain's reluctance to have staff conversations with Belgium was based on her general reluctance to have staff conversations with anybody; it was not based on apprehensions about Belgium's close relations with France.[4] Once again Eden had missed the point that Belgium's close relations with France presupposed equally close relations with Britain. By now, of course, this was all 'water over the dam'. During his brief visit to Brussels in April, Eden asked Defence Minister Denis his opinion on the matter of staff agreements. The latter naturally replied that they were incompatible with his country's new foreign policy. Eden expressed no opposition and remarked that Britain did not have a sufficient number of troops to intervene effectively on land anyway.[5] That admission must have helped allay any Belgian qualms about the decision to end

---

[1] *L'Indépendance belge*, 22 May 1937, p. 1. See also Memorandum by Spaak, 26 Apr. 1937, *DDB*, IV, no. 229.

[2] Memorandum handed to Delbos by Eden, 24 Mar. 1937, Annex B of FO, 432/3/C3530/1/18.

[3] Ibid. and Memorandum prepared by Eden for the Cabinet, 5 Dec. 1936, 371/19851/C8745/270/4.

[4] Eden to Ovey, 23 Mar. 1937, ibid., 432/3/C2316/181/4.

[5] Memorandum by Vanlangenhove, 26 Apr. 1937, *DDB*, IV, no. 228.

formal staff agreements. In any event, Spaak told the Chamber of Deputies that the Anglo-French Declaration 'closes for us that period which one could call the era of military agreements . . .'.[1] But it was not until Delbos's visit in late May that the whole question was finally laid to rest. It was decided then that the results obtained from the talks in 1936 would remain standing and that these arrangements could be adjusted, if necessary, through the services of military attachés.[2] The available evidence suggests that nothing ever came of this, and it does not appear that there were any further staff contacts between Belgium and France until October 1939.[3]

What about article 16? The Anglo-French Declaration contained only a vague reference to the League Covenant. No effort was made to agree on a common interpretation of the disputed article, perhaps because Eden had earlier suggested to the French that an effort to do so would get nowhere and that the prudent course was to accept van Zeeland's interpretation without further conversation.[4] The upshot of the declaration's vagueness was that the French and Belgian governments could continue saying what best suited their own purposes. Here is Spaak's interpretation:

As far as the Belgian government is concerned, there are two essential conditions for the eventual application of the right of passage across our country. The first is that in no instance can the right of passage be imposed on Belgium without her consent. The second is that this consent is conceivable only if it involves the execution of a common action.[5]

Delbos's approach to article 16 was more flexible. A Polish diplomat recorded this in his diary:

[1] *Annales* (Chamber), 1936/1937, 29 Apr. 1937, p. 1287.

[2] Tournoux, *Haut commandement*, pp. 279–80. See also above, Ch. III, pp. 73–4.

[3] Tournoux, *Haut commandement*, p. 280 and General Émile Wanty, 'Les relations militaires franco-belges (de 1936 à Octobre 1939)', *Revue d'histoire de la deuxième guerre mondiale* (Paris, 1958), 8th year, no. 31, pp. 12–23. As in the case of Anglo-Belgian staff contacts the full story of Franco-Belgian contacts will remain unknown until more documentary evidence is available to scholars.

[4] Memorandum handed to Corbin by Eden, 24 Mar. 1937, FO, 432/3/C3530/1/18. Van Zeeland's interpretation was that Belgium was bound by article 16 in some circumstances, but she herself would determine when those circumstances had arisen.

[5] *Annales* (Chamber), 1936/1937, 29 Apr. 1937, pp. 1286–7. Spaak explained that a 'common action' was one in which all of Belgium's neighbours participated.

Delbos drew our attention especially to the last line of this [Anglo-French] declaration, which mentions a direct Anglo-French collaboration, and he emphasized that the matter concerning article 16 ... was handled in a rather nebulous fashion in order to open the possibility of subsequent interpretations.[1]

There were no subsequent interpretations, and Spaak's words represented the policy of the Belgian government until 1940. Delbos himself really had few illusions. In late April he admitted to an American diplomat that France's ability to aid her allies had been seriously undermined by Belgium's new policy.[2] This same diplomat reported that the effect of this policy on French strategy was causing 'acute disquiet' among France's allies. He noted that 'there is general agreement that recent developments are rapidly closing the door to French influence in Central and Eastern Europe'.[3]

The British were not as pessimistic about the significance of the Baldwin government's last major act of foreign policy. *The Times* thought that the Anglo-French Declaration could be 'the starting-point for a movement towards general economic and political appeasement'.[4] However, whatever hopes the British had that this would be the first step towards a broader settlement were soon disappointed. The French did make one last attempt in June to revive the discussions about a new Locarno. But by then no one was really interested, not even the British themselves. There was now another obstacle to a new Locarno: Prime Minister Neville Chamberlain 'had come to the conclusion that better results were likely to be obtained by a different method of approach . . .'.[5]

3. *The German Declaration*

'We will have reached a state of equilibrium only when not just the foreign ministers of England and France, but also the German Foreign Minister can come to Brussels under the

---

[1] Count Jean Szembek, *Journal, 1933–1939* (Paris, 1952), trans. by J. Rzewuska and T. Zaleski, p. 225.

[2] Bullitt to Hull, 30 Apr. 1937, *FRUS*, I, 1937, pp. 84–5.

[3] Bullitt to Hull, 22 Apr. 1937, ibid., pp. 77–80. See also Bullitt to Hull, 6 May 1937, pp. 89–92 and Bullitt to Hull, 21 May 1937, pp. 96–8.

[4] *The Times*, 29 Apr. 1937, p. 17.

[5] *Survey, 1937*, p. 363.

same circumstances.'[1] So spoke the Belgian ambassador in Berlin on the morrow of the Anglo-French Declaration. The next move, said Davignon, was in the hands of the Germans.[2] He could now speak with confidence, for in spring 1937 there were some good reasons to think that Belgium and Nazi Germany could find an arrangement acceptable to both parties.

Among them was a personal one. Adolph Hitler himself never paid much attention to the Belgian question. Joachim von Ribbentrop was interested in it, but by 1937 this meddlesome individual had been removed to London. Therefore, Ambassador Davignon could conduct business with the German Foreign Office without much outside interference. In fact, by 1937 the ambassador had established considerable rapport with the professionals in the Wilhelmstrasse.[3] Davignon later remembered that *Staatssekretär* Mackensen, who once served in the Brussels embassy, had a good understanding of Belgian resentment of Germany.[4] Foreign Minister Neurath was aware of Belgian susceptibilities, too, and thought that the normalization of German-Belgian relations should proceed slowly—in contrast to the impatient Ribbentrop.[5] The Germans, for their part, were satisfied with Count Davignon. One Foreign Office official remembered the 'credit' due to him for his work in improving relations between Berlin and Brussels.[6]

More important than the personal factor was the always sensitive question of Eupen and Malmédy. Since Ribbentrop's visit to Brussels in late 1935 it had not been acute. This did not mean, however, that Germany was going to renounce her claims to the two cantons: the Reich could not dissociate itself from the fate of people who were racial brothers, Goebbels told Davignon.[7] Moreover, tension in the cantons themselves never

[1] Memorandum by Mackensen, 13 May 1937, GFMA, 725/1143/325140–4. On 29 April Spaak told the Chamber of Deputies that the government intended to seek a formula to which Germany could subscribe, too. *Annales* (Chamber), 1936/1937, 29 Apr. 1937, p. 1286. See also Spaak, *Combats inachevés*, p. 56 and Memorandum by Vanlangenhove, 22 Apr. 1937, *DDB*, IV, no. 225.

[2] Memorandum by Bismarck, 28 Apr. 1937, GFMA, 717/1160/326707–9.

[3] A year earlier Davignon had drawn a sharp distinction between the Nazis and diplomats like Neurath and Bülow, who, he said, tried hard 'to assure the continuity of methods, aims, underlying designs of the traditional diplomacy of Germany . . .'. Davignon to van Zeeland, 22 Apr. 1936, *DDB*, IV, no. 74.

[4] Davignon, *Berlin, 1936–1940*, p. 58.   [5] Ibid., pp. 53–4.

[6] Ernst von Weizäcker, *Erinnerungen* (Munich, 1950), p. 136.

[7] Davignon, *Berlin, 1936–1940*, p. 45.

completely subsided. But this was the work of Nazi zealots who were as irritating to the German Foreign Office as to the Belgian government.[1] German diplomats wanted to leave this matter out of the limelight.[2] There was much more to be won through friendly negotiations on larger issues than through the subversion of these two relatively unimportant territories. Even a Nazi enthusiast like Herman Göring said—and he probably meant it —that it was 'laughable' to think that National Socialist statesmen would compromise German-Belgian relations over something so unimportant.[3]

For years the principal barrier to a German-Belgian agreement had been Belgium's connection with the West, and now this was ended—or almost ended. As long as the Belgians had had obligations to France and Britain, there had been no question of their taking up the various offers and suggestions made by the Germans. The Belgians were simply too concerned about preserving the Anglo-French guarantee even to contemplate an arrangement which might alienate their friends in the West.[4] After the April declaration this concern no longer existed. But there was another.

Germany still wanted Belgium's return to strict neutrality, despite Berlin's assurances to the contrary after Hitler's January 'offer' to Belgium. This became evident again when in March the Germans formally replied to the British note of 19 November: Belgium would be guaranteed by the four Locarno powers in return for her promise of neutrality in any conflict.[5] The Belgians considered this impossible on a number of grounds. An arrangement like this would violate their sense of national dignity and their desire for completely 'free hands'; it would arouse domestic hostility, especially among the Socialists; it was in conflict with even the most cautious interpretations of article 16. It was, as they told the Germans, too much like the pre-1914

[1] It is interesting to contrast the attitude of the Nazis in the Interior Ministry, who were eager to stir up trouble, with the attitude of the officials of the Foreign Office, who were not eager for trouble in Eupen and Malmédy. GFMA, 704/1250/ 338048–84 and 3973/3873/E046590–646.

[2] When Schacht went to Brussels in April 1937 to discuss economic and colonial questions, Hitler indicated that he wanted Eupen and Malmédy left out of the talks. Memorandum by Rintelen, 8 Apr. 1937, ibid., 717/1159/326473–5.

[3] Davignon to Spaak, 30 Nov. 1936, DDB, IV, no. 177. See also Davignon to Spaak, 30 Apr. 1937, no. 232.

[4] Van Zuylen, Les Mains libres, p. 383.   [5] Survey, 1937, p. 355.

arrangement.[1] It goes without saying that the French and British could not accept this German proposal, because it contradicted Belgium's obligations to the League.[2]

The Belgians therefore had to find a formula which would allay German fears of their participation in a future military operation and which would simultaneously preserve their right to participate in one. Finding such a formula was all the more difficult because in the Spring of 1937 the Belgian question was still entangled with the hopeless effort to negotiate a general settlement. But, as usual, van Zeeland had an idea, which he elaborated for Eden during the latter's April visit to Brussels. Since the efforts to negotiate a new Locarno were still getting nowhere, might not the powers seek first to negotiate a less ambitious treaty, a pact of non-aggression limited to Belgium alone? Its provisions could later be extended to include all the signatories. After the conclusion of this limited arrangement, the great powers could make unilateral declarations that they would maintain their respective guarantees of Belgian integrity.[3] Eden agreed, and the Belgians then turned to the Germans and French.

In mid-May Ambassador Davignon described the new proposal to *Staatssekretär* Mackensen, and he added that the Germans could include in their unilateral declaration a reservation about the application of article 16.[4] Mackensen was well disposed. He said that Germany preferred Belgium in a status of neutrality, but that she none the less sympathized with Belgium's desire to avoid this. Mackensen did express one reservation: since Belgium's neutrality would not be automatic, Germany's guarantee could not be automatic. In other words, the proposed non-aggression pact must include a proviso that it would be effective only so long as Belgium did not associate her-

---

[1] Memorandum by Dieckhoff, 7 Apr. 1937, GFMA, 155/141/127036-7. See also Memorandum by Bismarck, 28 Apr. 1937, 717/1160/326707-9 and Memorandum by Vanlangenhove, 18 Mar. 1937, *DDB*, IV, no. 209 and Memorandum by van Zuylen, 23 Mar. 1937, no. 217 and Memorandum by van Zuylen, 26 Mar. 1937, no. 219.

[2] Memorandum by Mackensen, 13 May 1937, GFMA, 725/1143/325140-5.

[3] Memorandum by Spaak, 26 Apr. 1937, *DDB*, IV, no. 229; Memoranda by Eden, 26 and 27 Apr. 1937, FO, 432/3/C3185/1/18; and van Zuylen, *Les Mains libres*, pp. 396-7.

[4] Memorandum by Mackensen, 13 May 1937, GFMA, 725/1143/325140-5 and Davignon to Spaak, 14 May 1937, *DDB*, IV, no. 135.

self with an attack against one of the signatories, i.e., open Belgian territory to foreign troops in accordance with article 16. Mackensen emphasized that Germany was making a real concession in not insisting on obligatory neutrality.[1]

The Germans had, in fact, gone a long way towards meeting the Belgians, and there appear to have been two reasons for their having done so. One was that Berlin now recognized that all hopes of inducing the Belgians to accept a status of strict neutrality were futile. Neurath later summed it up in a Foreign Office memorandum: it was not possible to persuade the Belgians to abandon their League obligations; it was possible only to make the German guarantee contingent on Belgian non-participation in a war against Germany and to have Belgium articulate her independence from Britain and France.[2] This leads to the second reason. The Germans distrusted the Anglo-French Declaration because therein were reaffirmed arrangements obviously directed against Germany. Belgium's proposal was well received in Berlin because its realization would nullify the April declaration.[3]

This is precisely what the French feared, and on 18 May a high official of the Quai d'Orsay informed the Belgians why France had no interest in a limited pact of non-aggression:

We cannot lose sight of the fact that the present situation, proceeding for us from the unconditional defensive alliance of England and France, is far and away the most favourable diplomatic combination which we have known in the West since 1918, and that, therefore, France is by no means disposed to exchange so precious an advantage for a contingent and hypothetical advantage.[4]

The French feared that the proposed pact would not lead towards a later, more general settlement, but would instead risk the loss of Britain's guarantee. This meant the end of Belgium's hopes for a multilateral pact of non-aggression.

---

[1] Davignon to Spaak, 21 May 1937, ibid., no. 236 and Davignon to Spaak, 26 May 1937, no. 237 and Memorandum by Mackensen, 20 May 1937, GFMA, 725/1143/325146–51.

[2] Memorandum by Neurath, 24 Sept. 1937, ibid., 1170/2175/471500–2.

[3] As Davignon explained to Mackensen, the three unilateral declarations would replace the 'provisional declaration' 24 April. Memorandum by Mackensen, 13 May 1937, ibid., 725/1143/325140–5. See also Davignon, *Berlin, 1936–1940*, p. 61 and van Zuylen, *Les Mains libres*, p. 404.

[4] Quoted ibid., pp. 398–9.

In early July Ambassador Davignon received new instructions.[1] Germany should now be asked to make a declaration corresponding to the one made in April. The German declaration should be made in spontaneous fashion without it appearing that Belgium had requested it.[2]

This time Mackensen was unenthusiastic, because the Germans still wanted to get rid of the Anglo-French Declaration. Davignon suggested that the April declaration might become definitive and that there was a danger of France's trying to make it so. In fact, said the ambassador, France was already attempting to accustom Belgian opinion to the existing situation.[3] The King and the cabinet hoped very much that this would not happen. Because Leopold's famous speech of the previous October and Hitler's speech of 30 January provided the basis for a German-Belgian agreement, only the details needed to be worked out.[4] Some days later Davignon was notified that the German government was agreeable to this course of procedure.[5]

The Germans had given in once more to the Belgians, and it is again probable that a number of factors induced them to do so. First, by July 1937 all prospects for a multilateral pact, whether it was limited to Belgium or not, were so dim that common sense suggested that a bilateral arrangement was the only remaining possibility. Secondly, van Zeeland was involved in growing difficulties at home. This caused the Germans to wonder if they might soon be dealing with a new Belgian cabinet, one which could be less committed to an 'independent' foreign policy.[6] Neurath elaborated some other factors in a memorandum. He noted that it was to Germany's advantage to

[1] The delay in the German-Belgian talks was caused by France's last effort to revive the negotiations for a new Locarno.

[2] Davignon, *Berlin, 1936–1940*, pp. 60–61 and van Zuylen, *Les Mains libres*, p. 404.

[3] Through the services of certain Walloon papers, presumably.

[4] Memorandum by Mackensen, 8 July 1937, GFMA, 1170/2175/471484–6 and Davignon, *Berlin, 1936–1940*, p. 61.

[5] Memorandum by Mackensen, 20 July 1937, GFMA, 1170/2175/471487.

[6] Ambassador Richthofen was certainly worried about this. It is interesting to note that Anthony Eden wondered what would happen when van Zeeland was gone, although his concern was that his friend's departure might mean an even more 'independent' policy. Richthofen to Foreign Office, 2 July 1937, ibid., 1727/3325/E008185–6 and Richthofen to Foreign Office, 6 Aug. 1937, 1170/2175/471488–9 and Memorandum by Eden, 5 Dec. 1936, FO, 371/19851/C 8745/270/4.

have her relations with Belgium on the same footing as Anglo-Franco-Belgian relations. While Belgium's membership in the League of Nations made this impossible, it was none the less a good idea to minimize the effects of Belgium's promise to defend her own territory and to observe her League obligations. A German-Belgian agreement would make these promises seem less directed against Germany.[1] Mackensen put it more concisely: it was to Germany's advantage that Belgium should not feel dependent on France and Britain.[2]

By late July the two governments were on the threshold of an agreement. The remaining problems were strictly technical, and Spaak proposed that the matter be turned over to the legal experts in the respective foreign ministries.[3] The Germans agreed, and it was arranged that the Belgian representative, Fernand Muuls, would go to Berlin in September to meet with Friedrich Gaus, who was the director of the legal department of the Foreign Office.[4]

Gaus and Muuls had few difficulties, and these were minor ones. For example, the Belgians wanted the German declaration to leave no doubt about their fidelity to the League, while the Germans wanted no direct allusion to the League. Here the two experts used the formula employed in the Anglo-French Declaration: Germany would simply 'take note' of the Belgian government's public declarations.[5] Ambassador Davignon wanted the German declaration to include a statement renouncing the 1914 invasion. He soon learned that this was out of the question.[6]

By 18 September Gaus and Muuls had the text of an agreement which would take the form of a note from Berlin to Brussels, to which Brussels would respond with a word of thanks.[7] Two weeks later Mackensen reported to Davignon that Hitler had given his approval.[8] After a trip to Brussels the ambassador informed the *Staatssekretär* that van Zeeland and

---

[1] Memorandum by Neurath, 24 Sept. 1937, GFMA, 1170/2175/471500–2.

[2] Circular by Mackensen, undated, ibid., 725/1143/325227–8.

[3] Richthofen to Foreign Office, 6 Aug. 1937, ibid., 1170/2175/471488–9.

[4] Memorandum by Mackensen, 25 Aug. 1936, ibid., 1170/2175/471491–2. See also Davignon, *Berlin, 1936–1940*, p. 62.

[5] Van Zuylen, *Les Mains libres*, p. 405.

[6] Davignon, *Berlin, 1936–1940*, p. 63.

[7] Memorandum by Gaus, 18 Sept. 1937, GFMA, 1170/2175/471493.

[8] Memorandum by Mackensen, 1 Oct. 1937, ibid., 1170/2175/471512–5.

Spaak had approved, too. King Leopold happened to be away from Brussels, so he was not consulted.[1] Indeed, the only hitch was the attitude of the British: Eden was furious that the Belgians had not consulted with the Foreign Office and had informed it of the wording of the declaration only when it was too late to change it.[2]

The German Declaration was published on 13 October. These are its important paragraphs:

(1) The German Government have taken official notice of the attitude to which the Belgian Government, on their own authority, have given expression—namely: (a) That they propose to follow, in full exercise of their own sovereignty, a policy of independence; and (b) That they are resolved to defend the frontiers of Belgium against every attack and every invasion, with all their forces, to prevent the Belgian territory's being used for an attack against any other country, either as a passage-way for military forces or as a base of operations by land, sea, or air, and to this end organize the defence of Belgium in effective fashion.

(2) The German Government hold that the inviolability and integrity of Belgium are common interests of the Western Powers. They confirm their decision that in no circumstances will they impair this inviolability and integrity, and that they will at all times respect Belgian territory, except, of course, in the event of Belgium's taking part in a military action directed against Germany in an armed conflict in which Germany is involved.

The German Government, like the British and French Governments, are prepared to give support to Belgium in the event of her being subjected to an attack or an invasion.[3]

There were some in Belgium who gave the German Declaration a cold reception. Certain Socialists felt that it conflicted

[1] Memorandum by Mackensen, 8 Oct. 1937, ibid., 1170/2175/471525–7.

[2] Eden disliked the wording of the declaration because it sounded as though Germany was giving Belgium a guarantee against Britain and France. Spaak had indicated earlier that the British would be kept up to date on the negotiations with Germany. Eden thus had a legitimate reason to be angry with this *fait accompli*. Spaak explained to him that the negotiations had proceeded more quickly than expected and that fear of a press leak had compelled the Belgians to accept 13 October as the date of publication. Evidently, the French suggested no revisions of the declaration because they disliked the whole thing. To propose an amendment would be to imply that they approved of the rest of the declaration. *DDB*, IV, nos. 239–43 and FO, 432/3/C6931/181/4; C7019/181/4; and C7061/181/17.

[3] Note from the German Government, 13 Oct. 1937, *DIA, 1937*, pp. 192–3. The last paragraph quoted above is the one which Eden wanted amended.

with Belgium's obligations under the League Covenant.[1] One
Walloon paper remarked that the declaration 'simply renews
the old German policy which consists of stupefying its future
victims, embracing them in order to stifle them more easily'.[2]
But this sour note was not typical, and the Belgian press gave the
declaration a generally cordial reception. The opinion in
official circles was well expressed by Baron van Zuylen, when
he wrote that 'the most elementary prudence commanded us
... to deprive the Reich of any pretext for aggression and to
induce it to undertake engagements which would render its
aggression more odious and more inexcusable, if it attacked us
again'.[3] The popular attitude was summed up by Paul Hymans,
now a figure from the remote past, when he told the Chamber of
Deputies that 'a word of peace ought to be received with
satisfaction'.[4]

4. The Fall of van Zeeland

1937 was a miserable year for Belgium, and it was a frustrating and humiliating year for her Prime Minister. Paul van
Zeeland had hoped to continue his work of social and institutional reform. Instead, he was faced with one crisis after another,
each one a little more destructive than the last. The upshot was
that his influence was progressively weakened and that his
government never regained the momentum which it had had in
June 1936, not to mention March 1935.

Belgian political life is filled with paradox, and, characteristi-
cally, the prelude to van Zeeland's downfall was his greatest
triumph. In March 1937 Léon Degrelle announced the resignation of a Rexist member of the Chamber of Deputies and his
own candidacy in the resultant by-election. Would anyone care
to accept the challenge? asked the *Chef*. Some cabinet members
wanted to prohibit the election. However, everyone remembered that Paul-Henri Spaak had used the same device in an
attempt to embarrass the government in early 1935.[5] Moreover,
only a few months earlier Spaak had 'picked up the gauntlet'

---

[1] *Annales* (Chamber), extraordinary session, 1937, 21 Oct. 1937, pp. 146–50.
Spaak had little trouble refuting these charges. See pp. 152–5, 163–5.
[2] Quoted in Miller, *Belgian Foreign Policy Between Two Wars*, p. 252.
[3] Van Zuylen, *Les Mains libres*, p. 403.
[4] *Annales* (Chamber), extraordinary session, 1937, 21 Oct. 1937, p. 159.
[5] The government of Theunis, which preceded that of Van Zeeland.

against Rexism in the name of the whole government, and therefore the cabinet now had no choice but to designate a 'champion'. It selected its most respected and popular member, namely the Prime Minister himself. The prospect of an election campaign, especially one which promised to be as raucous as this one, must have been most repugnant to van Zeeland, whose delicate health had already made it difficult for him to carry out his ordinary work. His reason for accepting personally Degrelle's challenge was that had he not done so, someone else would have. Émile Vandervelde wanted an old-line Socialist to take on Degrelle. Had that happened, conservatives would have refused their support. This might have meant the end of van Zeeland's 'government of national union'.[1] As always, the Prime Minister was the one individual in Belgian public life who could create a solid political consensus, precisely because he was not a politician.

Van Zeeland's victory in the Brussels by-election was a foregone conclusion. But the size of his victory would be an important factor in determining the future of Rexism. Actually, few realized the extent to which Degrelle's popular support had already disintegrated. His alliance with the Flemish National-ists, a growing awareness of his anti-democratic tendencies, and the ridicule heaped on his abortive 'march on Brussels' meant disaster at the polls in any event. A trip to Berlin and visit with Hitler in late 1936 caused Belgians to wonder whether he was taking orders from Berlin.[2] He made matters still worse for him-self by addressing his 'dear compatriots' in Belgium over Italian radio, thus causing Belgians to wonder if he was taking orders from Rome.[3] And, of course, there was inherent in Rexism an element of opera bouffe, which, as the months passed, made it more and more difficult for Belgians to take Degrelle and his movement seriously. For example, when the Rexists claimed that an assassin's bullet had been fired at the bullet-proof windshield of Degrelle's car and that their leader had almost been martyred, the police undermined the credi-

---

[1] Charles to Eden, 9 Apr. 1937, FO, 371/20677/C2730/145/4.

[2] There is no evidence that he was taking orders from Berlin.

[3] Ovey to Eden, 8 Jan. 1937, FO, 371/20677/C234/145/4 and Ciano, *Ciano's Hidden Diary, 1937–1938*, p. 11. There is no evidence that he was taking orders from Rome. He used Italian radio facilities because the same was forbidden him in Belgium.

bility of the incident by suggesting that the shot might have been fired from inside the car.[1] Everything was going wrong for Degrelle. But what made his situation hopeless was the biggest mistake of his entire career. Not long before the by-election Degrelle confidently said that the Catholic Primate of Belgium, Cardinal van Roey, had not, did not, and never would condemn Rexism. The enraged Cardinal, who considered Degrelle's remark an attempt by the laity to interfere with Church policy, waited until it was too late for Degrelle to make an effective reply and then announced that the *Chef* was 'a danger to the country and to the Church' and that every loyal Catholic was duty-bound to vote against him in the by-election.[2] On 11 April while the Communists paraded through the streets of Brussels chanting their new slogan—*Vive le Cardinal*—van Zeeland won seventy-six per cent of the vote. His opponent received only nineteen per cent.[3]

The Brussels by-election marked the end of Rexism as a real force in Belgian politics.[4] And, in one sense, it marked the zenith of van Zeeland's political career. The magnitude of his victory was as much a tribute to his own impressive achievements as it was a rejection of Degrelle. Van Zeeland was now 'the outstanding leader of conservative democracy against the elements which threaten to engulf it', said one foreign commentator.[5] Unfortunately, this was not the whole story. The by-election campaign, with its blaring loud-speakers and tumultuous demonstrations, was the noisiest in Belgian history. Many voters were now weary of such performances, and even van Zeeland himself lost some of the public's esteem.[6] The by-election had another unfortunate consequence. Just as a year earlier the end of the economic crisis had loosened the unity of the three major parties, so did the retreat of extremism now further loosen it. The frightened legislators who in June 1936 had voted for van Zeeland's programme were no longer so

---

[1] Charles to Eden, 17 Dec. 1936, FO, 432/2/C9079/202/4.

[2] Charles to Eden, 13 Apr. 1937, FO, 371/20677/C2815/145/4 and *The New York Times*, 12 Apr. 1937, p. 1.

[3] Höjer, *Le Régime parlementaire belge*, pp. 258–60.

[4] In the 1939 national elections the Rexists lost all but 4 of their 21 seats in the Chamber of Deputies.

[5] *The New York Times*, 9 May 1937, p. 7.

[6] Cammaerts, *The Keystone of Europe*, pp. 340–1.

frightened and were having some second thoughts.[1] Once again the Prime Minister's success had rendered him dispensable. And, at the very moment that his political support began to waver there arose one of those inflammatory issues which again set Fleming against Walloon.

In November 1936 the government had introduced a bill which would give an amnesty to all the still-imprisoned 'activists' who had collaborated with the Germans during the war. The cabinet undoubtedly hoped that this would win more Flemish support for the military reform project. In order to win Flemish votes in the Brussels by-election, van Zeeland had reaffirmed his fidelity to the amnesty bill. Walloons paid little attention at first. But once the by-election clamour had died down, the trouble began. The government was charged with 'sheltering traitors'.[2] Demonstrations broke out all over Belgium. The best the beleaguered government could do was add to its bill an amendment which provided that all amnestied prisoners would take an oath of loyalty to the Belgian state. In its amended form the amnesty bill passed through the Chamber of Deputies by a narrow margin.[3] However, ex-servicemen's associations continued to agitate against the amnesty, while the Flemish Nationalists agitated for the removal of the loyalty oath, which they considered an affront to Flemish honour.[4] The most significant feature of this episode was that the government's only solid support came from the Socialists, who were obviously more interested in preserving the van Zeeland cabinet for their own purposes than they were in granting amnesty to 'activists'. This naturally exacerbated the fears of conservatives who had always felt that van Zeeland's programme was too radical and that his increased dependence on the Socialists would make

---

[1] One historian, Höjer, thinks that van Zeeland let slip a good opportunity to realize more of his programme in the aftermath of his by-election victory. Höjer, *Le Régime parlementaire belge*, pp. 260–61. See also van Kalken, *Entre deux guerres*, pp. 92–3 and Charles to Eden, 16 Apr. 1937, FO, 432/3/C2923/145/4.

[2] Cammaerts, *The Keystone of Europe*, p. 341.

[3] Höjer, *Le Régime parlementaire belge*, pp. 261–3 and Charles to Eden, 25 May 1937, FO, 432/3/C3790/145/4.

[4] Degrelle's alliance with the Flemish Nationalists obliged him to support the amnesty bill, at least at first. However, he soon capitulated to his desire to win back some Walloon votes. The *Rex-VNV* alliance was temporarily suspended, and by the end of the year it had been eliminated altogether.

matters still worse.[1] It is no wonder that one of van Zeeland's associates should report that the Prime Minister was 'worn out by the politicians' and might retire from public life.[2]

Van Zeeland's authority was crumbling fast. The Flemish Nationalists and the Rexists, who were burning with a desire to avenge their leader's by-election defeat, found a perfect weapon with which to deliver the *coup de grâce*. They asserted that van Zeeland had received funds from the National Bank of Belgium after entering the government as a minister-without-portfolio in 1934 and that he had permitted certain irregularities while he was a vice-governor of the bank. Degrelle happened to be a shareholder of the bank, which meant, of course, that he could hurl his charges straight in the faces of the bank directors themselves.[3] Evidently, van Zeeland had received a small amount of money from the bank after entering government service. The bank did, in fact, practise certain irregularities.[4] Few serious people doubted van Zeeland's honesty; some people did question his judgement and his apparent willingness to overlook the foibles of others. In early September the Prime Minister defended himself before the Chamber of Deputies with the result that a large majority voted to 'render homage to the integrity and disinterestedness of the Prime Minister . . .'.[5]

None the less, this was the end. Worried by the disintegration of his political support, wanting his hands free to defend himself against the continuing charges of his enemies, and plagued by ill health, van Zeeland resigned. So it was that a devoted and intelligent effort to serve the higher interests of Belgium came to an end.

[1] Höjer, *Le Régime parlementaire belge*, pp. 264–5.
[2] Charles to Eden, 8 June 1937, FO, 432/3/C4146/145/4. See also Charles to Eden, 25 May and 2 July 1937, C3790/145/4 and C4855/145/4.
[3] Höjer, *Le Régime parlementaire belge*, pp. 265–7 and Cammaerts, *The Keystone of Europe*, p. 342. See also Charles to Eden, 3 Aug. 1937, FO, 371/20678/C5654/145/4; Charles to Eden, 30 Aug. 1937, C6167/145/4; Charles to Eden, 7 Sept. 1937, C6434/145/4.
[4] For example, when van Zeeland retired from his position as director of the bank, the other directors neglected to appoint a successor to him and divided van Zeeland's salary among themselves.
[5] *Annales* (Chamber), extraordinary session, 1937, 8 Sept. 1937, p. 105.

CONCLUSION

IT WAS often contended that Belgium's return to neutrality was the natural outcome of changes in the European situation. When Belgium signed the Locarno agreements, Germany was disarmed; the Rhineland was demilitarized; France enjoyed an uncontested military superiority; and the League of Nations was regarded with respect. Belgium could therefore accept heavy obligations, confident that in a conflict with Germany her own modest capabilities would be complemented by those of Britain, France, and Italy. By 1936 all this was changed. Germany was rearming fast; France and Britain were unwilling to prevent the Rhineland's re-militarization; and the League was thoroughly discredited. To make matters worse, the Italians were now in the German camp. For Belgium to have maintained her engagements in these circumstances would have been to accept burdens and risks incommensurate with her size and resources. She could only strengthen her defences and pursue the one foreign policy which offered the possibility of non-involvement in a future struggle, namely a 'policy of independence'. Had not Belgium's traditional neutrality left her in peace for nearly a century?[1]

This argument had a fundamental weakness. Europe was now too interrelated politically and ideologically for any nation—least of all Belgium—to escape the consequences of a general war. 'Pertinax' put it concisely when he wrote that 'on a continent menaced from one end to the other by totalitarian states, there is no room for "ivory towers". In the 1930s the distinction between the great and small powers is being eliminated.[2]' Critics of Belgium's neutrality policy could quote her greatest historian, Pirenne, who wrote that the pre-1914 neutrality 'had been only an expedient intended to safeguard a European equilibrium which no longer existed'. Pirenne asked:

[1] Van Zuylen, *Les Mains libres*, pp. 360–2 and *Annales* (Chamber), 1936/1937, 11 Feb. 1937, pp. 611–14.
[2] 'Pertinax', 'La déclaration allemande à la Belgique et l'Europe occidentale', *L'Europe nouvelle* (Paris, 1937), 20th year, no. 1028, p. 1029.

'... on the day when her protectors divided into two hostile camps, how could one still hope that they would remain loyal to their given word ...'?[1]

Because the grimmest predictions were borne out by events, later it was easy to lose sight of the whole story. It was very easy to overlook that Belgium's interdependence with the rest of Europe was itself one of the factors which made the change in her foreign policy necessary.

Pirenne wrote this also: 'To be Belgian is a way of being European, since Belgium herself is a microcosm of Europe.'[2] Belgium's location at the cultural and commercial heart of Western Europe is indeed her glory, but in 1936 the blessings accruing from this distinction were mixed. Two languages and a broad political spectrum rendered Belgium hyper-sensitive to outside influences, regardless of whether they were constructive ones. Facism, integral nationalism, cries for a 'popular front', all found an immediate echo in a country still suffering from the social and psychological dislocations of the Depression. Their influence in a country with its own peculiar nationality problem was an indication that the forces dividing Europe could lead to the division of Belgium herself.

The fact that *Rex* and the *VNV* were marginal phenomena, temporary disorders from which most people quickly recovered, is beside the point. Their electoral success in 1936 threw the coalition system into disarray and revealed the urgent need to re-establish confidence among the voters. Unfortunately, the very fears on which the extremists thrived were constantly exacerbated by events abroad. The Franco-Soviet Pact, the Spanish Civil War, and the birth of the Rome-Berlin Axis caused middle-class Belgians to wonder whether they might soon be involved in a losing struggle on the side of Popular Front France. Such apprehensions were bound to have an immediate effect on Belgian political life. A foreign correspondent made this interesting observation:

Railway communication in Belgium has been so speeded up that practically all deputies are able to go to their homes in the provinces every evening and return to Brussels in good time the following afternoon. The result is that on every question coming before the

---

[1] Pirenne, *Histoire de Belgique*, pp. 238–9.   [2] Ibid., pp. 281–2.

Chamber each Deputy is subjected to direct, immediate and personal pressure by different local and sectional interests, which insist
upon their own point of view, regardless of national implications.[1]

National defence was not discussed in a spirit of detachment.
Here was an issue which made vivid the very questions which
the public was already asking: was the Belgian army to be a
mere extension of the Maginot Line, a tool of French interests
in Eastern Europe? For military men it raised a related strategic
question: was Belgium to be defended at her frontiers or in
depth? For diplomats it raised still another related problem:
could Belgium afford to preserve her connection with France?
These matters had long been discussed. But so long as a Liberal-
Catholic coalition dominated the political scene, sceptics were
compelled to accept Belgium's French orientation. By 1936 this
had changed. Just as the balance of power in Europe was shifting, so too was the balance in Belgian politics. A large majority
of the electorate had now had enough of collective security, and
the prerequisite of army reform was a military and foreign
policy which was 'exclusively and wholly Belgian'.

Because Belgian statesmen tended to give their new foreign
policy a halo of sanctity by representing it in the most euphem-
istic language, it was easy to overlook or forget that this policy
was a harassed government's response to an intolerable and
dangerous situation. Belgian statesmen had no practical alternative, especially after they realized that Great Britain was neither
willing nor able to provide an effective counterweight to
Germany. The attitude of Britain was the key to Belgium's
international dilemma. If the British had fulfilled their responsibilities, Belgians could have had more confidence in collective security. The British attitude was a key to the Belgian
government's domestic dilemma, too. If Britain had undertaken
serious military arrangements with Belgium, the hand of the
Brussels government would have been greatly strengthened. It
might have convinced a sceptical Chamber of Deputies and a
frightened public that Belgium was not a satellite of France,
that her army was not an instrument of French foreign policy,
and that she was not doomed to involvement in a hopeless war
at the side of Popular Front France and the Soviet Union. Of

[1] *The Times*, 12 Nov. 1936, p. 16.

course, this is speculation. But it is clear that the government's attempt to make Britain a military ally of Belgium was also an attempt to extricate its foreign policy from the logic of domestic developments.

Historians usually judge statesmen and their policies in terms of what happened. Belgium went to war with Germany in 1940. Her neutrality policy is therefore considered a failure. But historians should judge statesmen also in terms of what did not happen. Belgian political life was not disrupted by the forces of extremism, nor was Belgian unity destroyed. Paul-Henri Spaak put it concisely when he wrote that the 'policy of independence' was 'the only one capable of keeping the country united, the only one which would allow her to survive'.[1] Perhaps he was right. Belgium did survive.

[1] Spaak, *Combats inachevés*, p. 41.

BIBLIOGRAPHY

DOCUMENTARY SOURCES

Académie royale de Belgique. Commission royale d'histoire. *Documents diplomatiques belges, 1920–1940. La Politique de sécurité extérieur.* Vol. I, 1920–1924; vol. II, 1925–1931; vol. III, 1931–1936; vol. IV, 1936–1937 (Brussels, 1964 and 1965).

Belgium. Ministry of Foreign Affairs. *The Official Account of What Happened, 1939–1940* (New York, 1940).

Belgium. Corps législatif. *Annales parlementaires de Belgique.* Senate and Chamber of Deputies, 1931–1937 (Brussels, 1931–7).

Belgium. Corps législatif. *Documents parlementaires.* Senate and Chamber of Deputies, 1935–1937 (Brussels, 1935–7).

Degrelle, Léon, *Degrelle avait raison. Recueil de textes écrits par Léon Degrelle entre 1936–1940* (Brussels, 1941).

Documents on British Foreign Policy, ed. by E. L. Woodward and Rohan Butler. Second series. Vol. VI (London, 1957).

France. *Commission d'enquête sur les évenements survenus en France de 1933 à 1945. Rapport fait au nom de la commission* and *Témoignages et documents recueillis par la Commission d'enquête parlementaire.* Vols. I–IX (Paris, 1950 (?)—).

France. Ministère des affaires étrangères. *Bulletin périodique de la presse belge.* Nos. 120–127 (Paris, 1935–7).

France. Ministère des affaires étrangères. *Documents diplomatiques français, 1932–1939.* First Series (1932–1935), vol. I, II, III. Second Series (1936–1939), vol. I, II, III, IV. (Paris, 1963–7).

Germany. Auswärtiges Amt. *Akten.* Selected German Foreign Office records microfilmed for the (Gr. Brit.) Foreign Office and the (U.S.) State Department German war documents project. U.S. National Archives. Microcopy No. T-120. Reels: 155, 704, 705, 717, 725, 1170, 1726, 1727, 3937. [Cited as GFMA.]

Germany. Oberkommando des Heeres. General Stab des Heeres. *Denkschrift über die belgische Landesbefestigung* (Berlin, 1941).

Great Britain. Foreign Office Archive. Public Record Office (London). FO, 371: 16740, 18786, 18789, 19848–54, 19896, 19908–10, 20677–81, 20683, 21561, 21565, 21653. FO, 408: 66. FO, 432: 1–3.

Great Britain. *Parliamentary Debates*, House of Commons. Fifth Series. Vol. 310 (London, 1937).

Groupement national belge. *Contribution à l'étude de la question royale.* vol. I (Brussels, 1946).

Houtman, Dr. Jur. W., *Vlaamse en Waalse Documenten over Federalisme* (Schepdaal, 1963).

League of Nations. *Official Journal.* 1936 and 1937. Vols. XVII and XVIII (Geneva, 1936 and 1937).

Muggeridge, Malcolm, ed., *Ciano's Diplomatic Papers,* trans. by Stuart Hood (London, 1948).

Rapport de la Commission d'Information instituée par S. M. le Roi Léopold III le 14 juillet 1946 (Brussels, 1947).

Royal Institute of International Affairs. *Documents on International Affairs.* 1936 and 1937. Ed. by Stephen Heald and John W. Wheeler-Bennett (London, 1937 and 1938).

United States. Department of State. *Documents on German Foreign Policy, 1918–1945.* Series C (1933–1937), vol. I, II, III, IV, V (Washington, 1957–66).

United States. Department of State. *Foreign Relations of the United States.* 1936 (vol.I) and 1937 (vol. I) (Washington, 1953–4).

MEMOIRS AND DIARIES

BLUM, LÉON, *L'oeuvre de Léon Blum,* vol. V (Paris, 1955).

CAPELLE, COMTE, *Au service du roi,* vol. I, (Brussels, 1949).

CHURCHILL, WINSTON S., *The Gathering Storm* (Cambridge, 1948).

CIANO, COUNT GALEAZZO, *Ciano's Hidden Diary, 1937–1938,* trans. by Andreas Mayor (New York, 1953).

DAVIGNON, VICOMTE JACQUES, *Berlin, 1936–1940. Souvenirs d'une mission* (Brussels, 1951).

DE GAULLE, CHARLES, *Mémoires de guerre. L'appel, 1940–1942* (Paris, 1954).

DORLODOT, BARON R. DE, *Souvenirs* (Brussels, 1947).

EDEN, ANTHONY, *The Memoirs of Anthony Eden, Earl of Avon. Facing the Dictators* (Cambridge, 1962).

FLANDIN, PIERRE-ÉTIENNE, *Politique française, 1919–1940* (Paris, 1947).

GAMELIN, GÉNÉRAL, *Servir,* vols. I and II, (Paris, 1946).

HYMANS, PAUL, *Mémoires.* Vol. II (Brussels, 1958).

The Personal Memoirs of Joffre, Field Marshal of the French Army, trans. by Colonel T. Bentley Mott, vol. I (New York, 1932).

KORDT, ERICH, *Nicht aus den Akten* (Stuttgart, 1950).

MAN, HENRI DE, *Après coup* (Brussels, 1941).

MAN, HENDRICK DE, *Gegen den Strom* (Stuttgart, 1953).

OVERSTRAETEN, GÉNÉRAL VAN, *Albert I. Léopold III. Vingt ans de politique militaire belge, 1920–1940* (Bruges, 1949).

———, *Au service de la Belgique. Dans l'étau* (Paris, 1960).

PAUL-BONCOUR, J., *Entre deux guerres. Souvenirs sur la IIIe République*, vol. III (Paris, 1946).

REYNAUD, PAUL, *In the Thick of the Fight, 1930–1945*, trans. by James D. Lambert (New York, 1955).

SPAAK, PAUL-HENRI, *Combats inachevés. De l'Indépendance à l'Alliance* (Brussels, 1969).

SZEMBEK, COUNT JEAN, *Journal, 1933–1939*, trans. by J. Rzewuska and T. Zaleski (Paris, 1952).

TEMPLEWOOD, VISCOUNT, *Nine Troubled Years* (London, 1954).

WEIZÄKER, ERNST VON, *Erinnerungen* (Munich, 1950).

SPECIAL STUDIES

***. *The Van Zeeland Experiment*, trans. by Hélène van Gelder (New York, 1943).

ARANGO, E. RAMON, *Leopold III and the Belgian Royal Question* (Baltimore, 1961).

ARONSON, THEO, *Defiant Dynasty. The Coburgs of Belgium* (Indianapolis, 1968).

BAUDHUIN, FERDINAND, *Histoire économique de la Belgique, 1914–1939*, vol. I (Brussels, 1946).

CAMMAERTS, ÉMILE, *The Keystone of Europe. History of the Belgian Dynasty, 1830–1939* (London, 1939).

———, *The Prisoner at Laeken. Legend and Fact* (London, 1941).

CARSTEN, F. L., *The Rise of Fascism* (Berkeley, 1967).

CASTELLAN, GEORGES, *Le Réarmament clandestin du Reich* (Paris, 1954).

CHLEPNER, B. S., *Cent ans d'histoire sociale en Belgique* (Brussels, 1958).

CLAEYS- VAN HAEGENDOREN, MIEKE, *25 Jaar Belgisch Socialisme. Evoluties van de Verhouding van de Belgische Werkliedenpartij tot de parlementaire democratie in België van 1914 tot 1940* (Antwerp, 1967).

COLTON, JOEL, *Léon Blum. Humanist in Politics* (New York, 1966).

COLVIN, IAN, *Vansittart in Office* (London, 1961).

COOX, ALFRED DAVID, 'French Military Doctrine, 1919–1939: Concepts of Ground and Aerial Warfare', unpublished Ph.D. dissertation, Harvard, 1951.

COT, PIERRE, *Triumph of Treason*, trans. by Sybille and Milton Crane (Chicago, 1944).

DAHL, ROBERT A., ed., *Political Oppositions in Western Democracies* (New Haven, 1966).

DAYE, PIERRE, *Léon Degrelle et le Rexisme* (Paris, 1937).

DE GAULLE, CHARLES, *Vers l'armée de métier* (Paris, 1944).

DODGE, PETER, *Beyond Marxism: the Faith and Works of Hendrik de Man* (The Hague, 1966).

DRAPER, THEODORE, *The Six Weeks War. France, May 10-June 25, 1940* (New York, 1944).

DUCHESNE, JEAN, *1934–1940. Un tournant dans l'histoire de la Belgique* (Brussels, 1967).

DUMONT, G.-H., *Léopold III. Roi des Belges* (Saverne, 1946).

ÉTIENNE, JEAN-MICHEL, *Le Mouvement rexiste jusqu'en 1940* (Paris, 1968).

FABRE-LUCE, ALFRED, *Une Tragédie Royale* (Paris, 1948).

FEILING, KEITH, *The Life of Neville Chamberlain* (London, 1946).

FENAUX, ROBERT, *Paul Hymans, Un homme, un temps* (Brussels, 1946).

FURNIA, ARTHUR H., *The Diplomacy of Appeasement: Anglo-French Relations and the Prelude to World War II, 1931–1938* (Washington, 1960).

GALET, LIEUTENANT-GÉNÉRAL, *Albert. King of the Belgians in the Great War*, trans. by Major-General Sir Ernest Swinton (London, 1931).

GILBERT, COLONEL B. E. M. ÉMILE, *L'armée dans la nation. L'entre-deux-guerres en Belgique* (Brussels, 1941).

GORIS, JAN-ALBERT, ed., *Belgium* (Berkeley, 1946).

HÖJER, CARL-HENRIK, *Le régime parlementaire belge de 1918 à 1940* (Uppsala, 1946).

HOUTTE, J. A. VAN, *et al.*, *Algemene Geschiedenis der Nederlanden*, vol. XXI (Gouda, 1958).

HUIZINGA, J. H., *Mr. Europe: A Political Biography of Paul Henri Spaak* (London, 1961).

JONG, LOUIS DE, *The German Fifth Column in the Second World War*, trans. by C. M. Geyl (Chicago, 1956).

KALKEN, FRANS VAN, *Entre deux guerres. Esquisse de la vie politique en Belgique de 1918 à 1940* (Brussels, 1945).

KIRKPATRICK, IVONE, *Mussolini. A Study in Power* (New York, 1964).

LISKA, GEORGE, *International Equilibrium* (Cambridge, 1957).

LUYKX, THEO, *Politieke Geschiedenis van België van 1789 tot heden* (Brussels, 1964).

MILLER, JANE K., *Belgian Foreign Policy between Two Wars, 1919–1940* (New York, 1951).

MILLMAN, RICHARD, *British Foreign Policy and the Coming of the Franco-Prussian War* (Oxford, 1965).

MOYERSOEN, LUDOVIC, *Prosper Poullet en de Politiek van zijn tijd, 1868–1937* (Bruges, 1946).

NARVAEZ, LOUISE, *Degrelle m'a dit . . .* (Paris, 1961).

NOLTE, ERNST, *Three Faces of Fascism* (New York, 1966).

NOVILLE, JEAN ALBERT, *Paul van Zeeland au service de son temps* (Brussels, 1954).

ÖRVIK, NILS, *The Decline of Neutrality, 1914–1941* (Oslo, 1953).

OVERSTRAETEN, CAPITAINE-COMMANDANT R. VAN, *Des principes de le querre à travers les ages*, vols. I and II (Brussels, 1921).

PIRENNE, HENRI, *Histoire de Belgique des origines à nos jours*, vol. IV (Brussels, 1952).

PRIBRAM, ALFRED, *England and the International Policy of the European Great Powers, 1817–1914* (London, 1966).

RAEMAEKER, O. DE, *België's Internationaal Beleid, 1919–1939* (Brussels, 1945).

RAPPARD, WILLIAM E., *The Quest for Peace* (Cambridge, 1940).

RICHEMONT, JEAN DE, *L'Europe devant l'indépendance belge* (Paris, 1939).

ROGGER, HANS, AND WEBER, EUGEN, eds., *The European Right. A Historical Profile* (Berkeley, 1965).

ROLIN, HENRI-A., *La Belgique neutre?* (Brussels, 1937).

ROOSBROECK, R. VAN, et al., *Geschiedenis van Vlaanderen*, vol. VI (Brussels, 1949).

SCHÖFFER, IVO, *Het nationaal-socialistische Beeld van de Geschiedenis der Nederlanden. Een historische en bibliographische Studie* (Arnhem, 1956).

SCOTT, WILLIAM EVANS, *Alliance Against Hitler. The Origins of the Franco-Soviet Pact* (Durham, 1962).

SHEPHERD, HENRY L., *The Monetary Experience of Belgium, 1914–1936* (Princeton, 1936).

SIMON, CHANOINE A., *Le Parti catholique belge* (Brussels, 1958).

SMET, ROGER DE, and EVALENKO, RENÉ, and FRAES, WILLIAM, *Atlas des élections belges, 1919–1954* (Brussels, 1958).

TARDIEU, ANDRÉ, *La Note de semaine, 1936* (Paris, 1937).

THOMAS, HUGH, *The Spanish Civil War* (New York, 1963).

TOURNOUX, GÉNÉRAL PAUL ÉMILE, *Haut commandement. Gouvernment et défense des frontières du nord et de l'est, 1919–1939* (Paris, 1960).

TOYNBEE, ARNOLD J., *Survey of International Affairs, 1935–1937* (London 1936–8).

WALTERS, F. P., *A History of the League of Nations* (London, 1965).

WEBER, EUGEN, *Varieties of Fascism* (Princeton, 1936).

WILLEMSEN, ARIE WOLTER, *Het Vlaamse-Nationalisme, 1914–1940* (Groningen, 1958).

WOLFERS, ARNOLD, *Britain and France between Two Wars. Conflicting Strategies of Peace since Versailles* (New York, 1940).

WULLUS-RUDIGER, J. A., *En marge de la politique belge, 1914–1956* (Paris, 1957).

———, *La Belgique et la crise européene*, vol. I (Villeneuve-sur-Lot, 1944).

———, *La Défense de la Belgique en 1940* (Villeneuve-sur-Lot, 1940).

———, *Les Origines internationales du drame belge de 1940* (Brussels, 1950).

ZUYLEN, BARON PIERRE VAN, *Les Mains libres. Politique extérieure de la Belgique, 1914–1940* (Brussels, 1950).

NEWSPAPERS

L'Indépendance belge, Brussels, October 1935–October 1937.

The New York Times, March 1936–October 1937.

Le Pays réel, Brussels, August 1936–October 1937.

Le Peuple, Brussels, October 1935–October 1937.

The Times, London, January 1936–October 1937.

ARTICLES

***, 'La déclaration allemande et la politique extérieur de la Belgique', *La Revue générale*, CXXXVIII (November 1937), 525–539.

***, 'Le discours du roi', *La Revue générale*, CXXXVI (November 1936), 532–9.

***, 'Les élections du mai 24', *La Revue générale*, CXXXV (June 1936), 716–22.

BINION, RUDOLPH, 'Repeat Performance: a Psycho-historical Study of Leopold III and Belgian Neutrality', *History and Theory*, VIII, no. 2 (1969), 213–59.

BROQUEVILLE, COMTE DE, 'Pourquoi j'ai parlé en mars 1934', *La Revue générale*, CXLII (March 1939), 289–98.

BRUYNE, EDGARD DE, 'Le mouvement flamand et les tendances fédéralistes', *La Revue générale*, CXXXVII (April 1937), 451–72.

BUTTGENBACH, ANDRÉ, 'Le mouvement rexiste et la situation politique de la Belgique', *Revue des sciences politiques*, LIX (October–December 1936), 511–54.

CALLENDER, HAROLD, 'Fascism in Belgium', *Foreign Affairs*, XV (April 1937), 554–63.

CHARLYVEL, G., 'La nouvelle orientation de la politique étrangère belge: l'aspect militaire du problème', *L'Europe nouvelle*, XIX (October 1936), 1056–8.

DE GAULLE, CHARLES DE, 'Le Problème belge', *Revue des questions de défense nationale*, New Series, I (1945), 1–5.

DE JOUVENEL, BERTRAND DE, 'La nouvelle orientation de la politique étrangère belge: les raisons intérieurs', *L'Europe nouvelle*, XIX (October 1936), 1061–2.

FRANQUEVILLE, BERNARD DE, 'La position internationale de la Belgique', *Revue de droit international*, XXIII, no. 1 (January–February–March 1939), 21–73, and no. 2 (April–May–June 1939), 435–82.

HELMREICH, JONATHAN, 'The Negotiations of the Franco-Belgian Military Accord of 1920', *French Historical Studies*, III, no. 3 (1964), 360–78.

HYMANS, PAUL, 'Belgium's Position in Europe', *Foreign Affairs*, IX (October 1930), 54–64.

LEURQUIN, ROBERT, 'La nouvelle orientation de la politique étrangère belge: les consequences pour la défense nationale de la Belgique', *L'Europe nouvelle*, XIX (October 1936), 1059–61.

LICHTERVELDE, LOUIS DE, 'La Belgique et la S.D.N.', *La Revue générale*, CXXXVIII (October 1937), 385–91.

——, 'Les cantons de L'est', *La Revue générale*, CXXXVIII (August 1937), 129–47.

——, 'Réflexions sur le fédéralisme', *La Revue générale*, CXXXV (March 1936), 294–312.

MELOT, AUGUSTE, 'Des conversations Barnardiston à l'accord militaire franco-belge', *Le Flambeau*, XIX (March 1936), 257–71.

NOTHOMB, PIERRE, 'Le second cabinet van Zeeland', *La Revue générale*, CXXXVI (July 1936), 26–42.

PARKER, R. A. C., 'The First Capitulation: France and the Rhineland Crisis', *World Politics*, VIII (April 1956), 355–73.

'PERTINAX', 'La déclaration allemande à la Belgique et l'Europe occidentale', *L'Europe nouvelle*, XX (October 1937), 1027–9.

——, 'La nouvelle orientation de la politique étrangère belge: les répercussions diplomatique', *L'Europe nouvelle*, XIX (October 1936), 1055–6.

PIERARD, LOUIS, 'Notre politique extérieur', *Le Flambeau*, XX (May 1937), 571–86.

REQUETTE, LT.-COLONEL C., 'Serions nous prêts?', *La Revue belge*, XIII (April 1936), 22–33.

'TAEDA', 'L'astrolabe', *Le Flambeau*, XIX (November 1936), 616–640.

TASHIN, H., 'Le statut international de la Belgique', *Revue de droit international*, XX (July-August-September 1937), 114–26.

VANDERVELDE, ÉMILE. 'Belgian Foreign Policy and the Nationalities Question', *Foreign Affairs*, XI (July 1933), 657–70.

WHITTIER, RICHARD, 'Belgium Emphasizes Security', *Contemporary Review*, CLI (January 1937), 26–37.

WANTY, GÉNÉRAL ÉMILE. 'Les relations militaires franco-belge, 1936–octobre 1939', *Revue d'histoire de la deuxième guerre mondiale*, VIII (July 1958), 12–23.

WILLIQUET, JACQUES, 'Regards sur la politique belge d'indépendance', *Revue d'histoire de la deuxieme guerre mondiale*, VIII (July 1958), 3–11.

ZEELAND, PAUL VAN, 'La position internationale de la Belgique', *La Revue générale*, CXLI (May 1939), 589–605.

INDEX

200

Maglinse, General, 41, 43, 48
Malmédy *see* Eupen and Malmédy
Man, Henri de:
  ideas and influences of, 34; joins van Zeeland's governments, 38, 100; and national defence, 48 n., 52 n., 104; and foreign policy, 104
Massigli, René, 118–19
Maurin, General, 9
Maurras, Charles, 33, 89
Mixed Commission of Inquiry, 48, 128–30
Munitions:
  Belgium's need for British aid, 72, 75, 76, 164–6
Mussolini, Benito, 28, 80, 91
Muuls, Fernand, 178

The Netherlands:
  and the Utrecht forgery, 5; and Flemish nationalism, 36; Hitler's January 1937 offer to, 166–7
New Locarno *see* Western Pact
Neurath, Constantin Freiherr von, 142, 167, 173, 176, 177–8
Nuyten, General, 10, 43 and n., 161

Overstraeten, R. van, 41–2, 75, 133, 134, 136, 160, 161 n.
Ovey, Ambassador, 23, 139

Paul-Boncour, Joseph, 60
Le Pays réel, 111
Pertinax, 185
Pétain, Marshal, 5, 8, 12, 17
Le Peuple, 46, 111–12, 145
Pirenne, Henri, 185–6
Piux XI, Pope, 33
Plan du Travail, 34
Poincaré, Raymond, 12
Poland, 5, 7, 9, 12, 14 n., 17, 54 n., 120
Popular Front:
  its impact in Belgium, 83, 90, 119, 124
Poullet, Prosper, 14
Proposals of 19 March 1936:
  drafted by van Zeeland, 65–6; German response to, 67–8; Belgium's obligations under, 107, 150, 157–8

Rexism:
  programme and appeal of, 89–92; and foreign policy, 91–2, 111, 146; and domestic politics, 96, 124, 125–6, 127, 181; significance of, 127–8, 186; decline of, 181–2; and attack on van Zeeland, 184; mentioned, 101, 143
Reynaud, Paul, 7
Rhineland:
— Franco-Belgian occupation of: 5, 6
— Remilitarization of:
  Belgian and allied reaction to, 57–67; aftermath of, 67–82; effect of, 82–4
Ribbentrop, Joachim von, 27, 116, 173
Richthofen, Herbert Freiherr von, 142 n.
Roey, Cardinal van, 182
Rolin, Henri, 111, 159 n.
Rome-Berlin Axis, 156, 186

Sanctions (against Italy) 28–9, 78–9
Sargent, Orme, 115, 165–6
Schacht, Hjalmar, 174 n.
Scheldt River:
  as defensive position, 42, 75, 118
Schrijver, August de, 52 n.
Schweisguth, General, 74
Seeckt, General von, 26
Severen, Joris van, 92–3
Simon, Sir John, 20, 21, 22–3, 26–7
Socialist party:
  and Franco-Belgian Military Agreement, 5, 19; and Ethiopian War, 28; ideological tendencies within, 33–4; and national defence, 40–1, 43, 45–6, 48, 129–30, 131, 147; and recognition of USSR, 50; and 1936 election, 97; and foreign policy, 111, 131, 145–6, 179–80; and amnesty question, 183
Spaak, Paul-Henri:
  early career of, 34; joins first van Zeeland government, 38; becomes Foreign Minister, 100, 103–5; and national defence, 103–4, 129–30, 148, 160, 161 n., 171; and foreign policy, 104–5, 109–11, 145–7, 171, 188; and the Germans, 116, 178–9; and the French, 117–18, 119–20, 143, 153; and the Rexists, 126, 180–1; and Leopold III, 132, 135–136, 139; and the British, 162 n., 164